CORK 365

Seán Beecher was a well-known local historian and broadcaster. He regularly contributed to television and radio programmes, including the popular *Sunday Miscellany* on RTE radio. His previous publications included *The Story of Cork, A Dictionary of Cork Slang, An Gaeilge in Cork City, The Fastnet File* and *The Blues*, a history of St Finbarr's GAA club.

A
RELATION OF THE

M oft lamentable Burning of the Cittie,
of Corke, in the weft of Ireland, in the Province
of MONSTER, by Thunder and Lightning
With other moft dolefull and miferable accidents
which fell out the laft of May 1622 after the
prodigious battell of the birds called Stares
which fought ftrangely over and neare
that Cittie the 12 & 14 of May 1622
As it hath beene Reported to
divers Right Honourable
PERSONS

Printed this 20 of June 1623
LONDON
Printed by I.D. for Nicholas Bourne, and Thomas Archer, 1622.

CORK 365

A DAY-BY-DAY MISCELLANY OF CORK HISTORY

SEÁN BEECHER

The Collins Press

Published as *Day by Day: A Miscellany of Cork History* in 1992 by
The Collins Press,
West Link Park,
Doughcloyne,
Wilton,
Cork

Reissued as *Cork 365: A Day-by-Day Miscellany of Cork History* 2005

British Library Cataloguing in Publication Data

Beecher, Seán
    Cork 365 : a day-by-day miscellany of Cork history
    1. Cork (Ireland) - History - Anecdotes 2. Cork (Ireland) -
    History - Chronology
    I. Title
    941.9'5

    ISBN 1903464927

Typesetting: The Collins Press

Printed in Germany by Bercker

Front and back cover image: 'View of Cork City' by
Thomas Sautell Roberts,
courtesy Crawford Municipal Art Gallery Collection

1 January

CORK GAS COMPANY

The need for effective public lighting had been obvious to the citizens of Cork for many years. Its absence constituted a major danger in a city where there were more streams than streets. It was not uncommon for both citizens and visitors to fall into them and drown. In the 1830s a London firm had provided a supply of gas, but by the late 1850s their scale of charges had risen to an exorbitant level. It was this very factor that convinced a group of local businessmen that an alternative supply could be provided at a reasonable cost. Thus the Cork Gas Consumers' Company came into being.

The London company was not content to take this challenge lying down, and announced that they were prepared to reduce their charges from seven shillings and six pence to two shillings and six pence per thousand feet of gas. They were aware that the projected price of the Cork company's gas was four shillings and six pence. The *Cork Examiner*, which came to the defence of the Cork Gas Consumers' Company, pointed out that this was a mere stratagem and that the offer was no more than a desperate bribe. If it were accepted, and if the new Cork company failed, then the day would not be far distant when the London company would once again increase the price.

The newspaper's view prevailed and the Cork Gas Consumers' Company switched on its 1,100 public lights in Cork on 1 January 1858.

1858

A CHARTER FOR CORK

In the year 1242 Henry III of England consented to grant a fresh charter to the city of Cork in return for an annual payment of £80. This charter greatly expanded the range of powers and privileges of the citizens. In general it provided for a substantial degree of local autonomy as well as being conducive to the development of trade.

The principal municipal benefit accruing from the grant of charter was the right of the city corporate to collect taxes and appoint officers, a degree of autonomy enjoyed by only a few other cities.

The charter conferred both civil and criminal rights on the citizens. With regard to criminal matters, no citizen could be tried for murder outside the jurisdiction of the city. Should a citizen be indicted for murder he could no longer purge himself by challenging his accuser to battle; he was obliged to submit to trial by a jury of twenty-four fellow citizens.

The civil provisions were numerous. The citizens were given a monopoly on trade, foreign merchants not being permitted to purchase corn, leather or wood within the city, except from citizens. Likewise, merchants were not permitted to keep a wine tavern except on board ship. A citizen, his widow, sons and daughters were free to marry without seeking the permission of the local Lord. The citizens were given extensive protection in the matter of debts. They were allowed to form guilds, and were free to take possession of land and to erect buildings within the city. They and their heirs were permitted to levy a tax on imported wines.

The Charter of Henry III was granted to the city of Cork on 2 January 1242.

1242

EMIGRATION

'They fly the land as if a pesthouse, and quit the soil of their youth and manhood, as if the demon of plague was running riot in the fields.' The editor of the *Cork Examiner* was expressing the thoughts of many who, in 1849, contemplated the flight of countless thousands from the country. John Francis Maguire (who was editor), denied that it was a natural migratory pattern or that it was a case of people deserting unproductive land to seek fairer pastures, or that the people were uncivilised. Rather, the reason was that land division and land ownership were such that the great bulk of the people were denied all tenure of the soil they cultivated, and were thus reduced to being degraded recipients of public charity. The alternative was emigration – 'An Imirce'.

The people fled in their hundreds of thousands. They sailed across the Atlantic, sometimes in seaworthy craft, but as often as not in leaking tubs, known as 'coffin ships'. A correspondent, identifying himself simply as 'An Exile', described a voyage in one of these vessels. *The Surinam* left Dublin with 120 passengers for New York. No sooner had they put to sea than the ship began to leak, and soon their belongings and clothing were saturated. They could not cook their meals. On 12 November 1848, they rounded Cape Clear and immediately sailed into a head wind which continued to blow until 12 December.

The captain reluctantly turned back for Cork Harbour. All the passengers had to man the pumps. They eventually reached Cork on 28 December without possessions, without food and without money for another passage.

That incident provoked John Francis Maguire into an attack on the evils of emigration in the *Cork Examiner* of 3 January 1849.

1849

4 January

NEW IRISH CURRENCY

An Act of the British Parliament was passed in 1825 in order to 'Assimilate the Currencies and Monies of Account throughout the United Kingdom'. The purpose of the Act was to do away with the old Irish copper coinage and replace it with the new imperial currency. The new coins were to be worth twelve pennies to the British silver shilling. The old Irish copper coins, as long as they remained current, were to pass at the existent rate, thirteen to the British silver shilling.

An announcement was made that a British ship, the *Pheasant*, had left London for Cork with a consignment of the new coins and would arrive in the city before the day decreed for the change over, 5 January 1826. This news caused great excitement as it was thought that it could lead to a run on the banks.

The change in the rate of exchange would affect the value of goods in the shops as well as the wages of the workers. It meant that labourers' wages, static at eight shillings per week for some time, would be reduced in value to seven shillings and four pence halfpenny. However, in a letter to the newspaper, a shopkeeper pointed out that, while the wages might be reduced, the cost of the goods would remain the same. The labourer would, accordingly, suffer. The problem was resolved when landowners and manufacturers agreed, at a meeting in the Commercial Buildings, to continue to pay the rate of eight shillings per week to the labourers.

The *Pheasant* and the new coinage, arrived in Cork on 4 January 1826.

1826

RICHARD BARTER

Richard Barter was born in Macroom in 1824. Showing an aptitude for art, he went to Dublin around 1844 to study. He was by all accounts a most sociable person, and became friendly with Daniel O'Connell. He then went to London to continue his studies, where he met and was befriended by the Cork sculptor, John Henry Foley.

Some time later, however, he returned to Ireland and accepted an invitation from his namesake, Dr Richard Barter of St Anne's Hydropathic Baths, Blarney, to settle in Blarney, where he constructed a studio in the gardens. He was most versatile, and was able to repair watches and dentures as well as design and construct a musical instrument combining the characteristics of violin and piano. He was a good musician, consummate on the flageolet.

A competent artist, his best known work is the bust of Fr Prout, which is in the Crawford College of Art. His residence in Blarney isolated him from the national and international art scenes, but he executed a fine bust of Charles Stewart Parnell from a photograph, and friends of the 'Uncrowned King' were very much taken by the work. Barter also executed a bust of Cardinal Newman. A sculpture of his, The Warrior, was shown at the Cork Exhibition of 1883 and it demonstrated a power which he did not always permit, unfortunately, to show in his work. His range of subjects was quite wide and included religious and romantic works in addition to the contemporary.

Richard Barter died at St Anne's, Blarney on 5 January 1896.

1896

6 January

YOUNG MEN'S SOCIETY

The 38th Annual General Meeting of the Cork Young Men's Society was held in the Society's premises in Castle Street. There was a capacity attendance, which included Members of Parliament, Members of the Corporation, Justices of the Peace, as well as prominent business people, when Bishop O'Callaghan took the chair. Some members were unable to gain admission.

The President, Canon Sheehan, then gave his address, and listed the activities which the Society had arranged during the year: a trip to Dublin; four excursions to France to visit the Paris Exhibition; evening classes and a series of lectures with a diverse range of subjects, all of which had been well attended.

Dr O'Callaghan was received with loud applause. He pointed out that the members of the Society were in the vanguard of lay Catholicism in the city and diocese, and that they were the young men who proclaimed their religion publicly. The Society was invaluable in that it offered a friendly and Catholic environment to those young men who came to work and live in the city. He stated that the teaching of the Catholic Church on secret societies was clear and unequivocal. Members of such societies were excluded from the Church. The 'Supreme Council' of one such society – a clear reference to the Irish Republican Brotherhood – had the power of life and death over its members, and no Catholic could involve himself in such an organisation and remain a Catholic.

The Bishop of Cork's declaration against the Irish Republican Brotherhood appeared in the *Cork Examiner* of 6 January 1890.

1890

SCHOOL OF DESIGN

The incentive to establish a Society of Fine Arts in Cork followed the presentation of the famous Canova casts by George IV in 1819. These casts had originally been a gift of Pope Pius VII, and the King had, in turn, given them to Cork.

In 1830, a building in Emmet Place known as the Custom House had been presented to the Royal Cork Institution, and the casts were transferred to that new location. This is the section of the Crawford College of Art nearest to the Opera House. A committee was set up in 1849, under the chairmanship of James Roche, and it included among its members Fr O'Shea of Ss Peter and Paul's, Horace Townshend, Sir William Lyons, Alderman Dowden, W.C. Logan and F.M. Jennings. In September 1849, William Willes, a Corkman, was appointed the first headmaster of the new School of Design.

'A large concourse of the rank and respectability of the city', as the *Cork Examiner* put it, assembled for the formal inauguration of the Cork School of Design. The headmaster gave a long dissertation on the desirability of having a Design School in the city, and on the benefits which would accrue to Cork as a consequence. He pointed out how design had long been appreciated on the continent of Europe, and a school of design had been operating in Paris for nearly 200 years. He revealed that the Corporation and Government had grant aided the School.

The Cork School of Design was inaugurated on 7 January 1850.

1850

LIFE IN GLANMIRE

The village of Glanmire, although a mere three miles distant from the city, could only be reached by means of the Upper Road through the 'new town' of Barrackton (now Dillon's Cross), or the Strand (now Lower Road). The village itself was described by James Alexander in 1814 as being 'of inordinate beauty fit to rival Sweet Auburn'. He had come to live in Glanmire in 1806, on taking up a position as excise officer with responsibility for the several paper factories then functioning in the village.

In his book, *Amusing Summer Companion to Glanmire*, Alexander provides a fascinating glimpse of a rural community in the early nineteenth century. He regrets that he had never heard so much swearing and cursing as he had in Glanmire, and identifies the culprits as the workers in the flour mills. Much of the cursing and swearing was reserved for Sundays and fair days in the summer, excessive drinking being the cause.

Alexander mentions the names of several shopkeepers and publicans. The Glanmire Yeomanry was the first pub one met on entering the village, the proprietor, David Draddy, being described as a 'pleasant type'. Denis Regan owned the Sign of the Freemasons Arms, and he was 'a shrewd, sensible young man well capable of dealing with his drunken and obstreperous customers'. David Kenneally was another publican; Patrick Hayes a grocer; Thomas Cotter, a butcher and grocer; Honest Cronin, the smith, and so on.

James Alexander wrote of life in Glanmire on 8 January 1814.

1814

A STRANGE TRIAL

The Rev Robert Bury, a Protestant clergyman in Glanmire, had some horsehair stolen by one or other of his tenants. He summoned his steward, Matthew Barry, who could not name the culprit. The Rev Bury then requested Barry to undertake a most unusual task.

It appears that a farmer in Lisgoold possessed a famous stone which had a cross carved on it. The stone was known as *Ceann Eoin Baiste* (Head of John the Baptist). Bury prevailed on Barry to steal the stone and bring it to Glanmire. He intended to have those tenants whom he suspected of stealing the horsehair swear an oath on the stone attesting to their innocence. Those who refused to do so would be the guilty ones.

Fourteen of the tenants swore on the stone and four refused. One of them was immediately evicted from his land. The threat of eviction was held over the other three. Barry was then brought before the magistrates and charged. He was advised that if he were to plead not guilty he could be found guilty and sentenced to transportation for life. The courtroom was crowded for this bizarre affair and the magistrates advised those present that swearing on the stone was not only absurd but criminal. The chairman of the magistrates wanted the police to search for and destroy the stone, but another magistrate insisted that the matter would be more appropriately dealt with by the clergy.

The Rev Bury's horsehair, which gave rise to this extraordinary affair, was stolen on 9 January 1845.

1845

THE 'BREAD MARCHES'

In January 1880, there was widespread unemployment and poverty in Cork. On this occasion, however, the victims were not prepared to suffer in silence, but determined to bring their case to the public and the municipal authorities.

They marched through the streets bearing black flags as a sign of their distress, with loaves of bread spiked on top of the flagpoles – hence the name 'bread marches.' There was no violence. When the marchers arrived at the Mayor's office, three of their number interrupted a meeting of the Corporation and requested permission to state their case. A spokesman said that they and their families were starving, and that they were without fire, light and food. They complained that the Corporation was giving preference in the filling of jobs to men coming in from the countryside. If they could not get work they would join a union.

The Corporation, denying this allegation, said that the cause of the trouble was that the high wages being paid by the Corporation were attracting people into the city.

On 17 January four men, all from Philip's Lane, off North Main Street – Timothy Buckley, James Brien, George Holmes and John Walsh – were charged with offences relating to the marches and sentenced to a month's hard labour.

One such bread march took place through the streets of Cork on 10 January 1880.

1880

DAN CASEY, BARD

Daniel Casey was one of that rare breed who looks with a critical but humorous eye on the passing scene and puts his observations down on paper. Like the bards of old, he appreciated that his commentaries, when put to music, would more likely stand the test of time and, accordingly, most of his observations appeared in ballad form.

A collection of his work was published as *Cork Lyrics or Scraps from the Beautiful City* in 1857 and re-issued in *Gems of the Cork Poets* in 1885. A recitation of some of his titles captures the flavour of his balladry: 'Kattie Kief, the Maiden of Baghdad', 'Bill Fogarty's Freedom', 'De Corporation Wake', 'The Clock of Shandon', The Queen's visit to Cork' etc. Casey was a devoted supporter of Daniel O'Connell, and on the Liberator's election in County Clare in 1829, he composed a song commemorating the occasion.

Dan Casey loved his bit of fun and on one occasion, using the pseudonym 'Phelim O'Neill', wrote to the *Southern Reporter* newspaper, insisting that the great Swedish singer, Jenny Lind, was an impostor. Her origins lay not in Sweden but in Cork, and more precisely in Blackpool! He claimed that Jenny and her brother, the celebrated Chinese Mr Lin, left Ireland in protest at the Act of Union and forsook their real name of Looney. Casey wrote a ballad in praise of Jenny.

Daniel Casey, bard, died on 11 January 1881

1881

12 January

JOHN FITZGERALD

John Fitzgerald was a teacher of mathematics and lived in Drawbridge Street. He taught for some time in St Stephen's Blue Coat Hospital, off Barrack Street, but was later employed as a private tutor in the homes of wealthy merchants.

John Fitzgerald is best known, however, for one work, *Fitzgerald's Remembrancer or A Chronological Account of all the Remarkable Occurrences that have happened since the Creation to the Present Year, 1783, more especially for the City of Cork.*

The *Remembrancer* is remarkable for the accounts it contains of practically all criminal executions that took place in the city, a factor that prompted Crofton Croker to suggest that the book could more accurately have been called the 'Cork Criminal Recorder'. The book also gives detailed descriptions of Fitzgerald's numerous drinking bouts with his friends and especially with his son!

Batt Murphy's was a favourite watering hole, and he records that he could stay there drinking porter and punch all night at a cost of one shilling and one penny (six new pence). He was critical of some publicans and, when charged thirteen pence for two pints of mulled porter, he told the proprietor, John Cotter, that he would not again drink in the establishment.

John Fitzgerald embarked on one of his celebrated drinking sessions on 12 January 1793.

1793

13 January

TROOPS LEAVE FOR S. AFRICA

After the French Revolution Irishmen who had, in previous generations, enlisted in the continental armies, began to join the British Army in ever increasing numbers.

They joined for many reasons, some personal, some idealistic, some for adventure, but the majority joined simply for the pay. With no prospect of employment in Ireland, a life in the army with a regular, if small, income was better than slow starvation at home. In 1899, hundreds of Corkmen enlisted with the 9th Battalion, King's Royal Rifles, and volunteered for foreign service. On the morning of 12 January 1900, at their passing out parade, they were informed that their posting was not to Gibraltar or Malta (as they had been led to believe), but to South Africa and the Boer War. Popular sentiment was in favour of the Boers.

They marched from the barracks to the railway station in sullen silence. The news of their posting was soon known in Cork and thousands of relatives – wives, mothers, children, brothers and sisters – set out for Cobh to see them off. Some were so poor they could not afford the train fare, and walked to Cobh from Cork city.

The families were denied access to the soldiers and, when they attempted to scale the barriers, were beaten back by British Militia. There were dreadful scenes of lamentation in Cobh when the King's Royal Rifles sailed for the Boer War on 13 January 1900.

1900

BISHOP GEORGE BERKELEY

George Berkeley was born on 12 March 1685, in County Kilkenny. Educated at Kilkenny School, he later attended Trinity College where he graduated in 1700. He became a scholar in 1702 and a fellow in 1707.

Stimulated by the teaching of Locke, he showed an interest in philosophy, and in 1709, he published a treatise *Concerning the Principles of Human Knowledge*. In 1713 he published *Dialogue between Hylas and Philonous*. On Dean Swift's recommendation Berkeley was appointed secretary to Lord Peterborough. Later, Swift's Vanessa bequeathed Berkeley half her property. As her executor, Berkeley suppressed for some time her correspondence with Swift.

In 1734, Berkeley first published his celebrated *Querist*. He was appointed to the Bishopric of Cloyne where he remained for eighteen years. He had earlier married Anne Forster, who brought with her a dowry of £1,500 and a questioning mind.

Berkeley, although born in Ireland, always considered himself an Englishman. He considered the Irish as a people of no consequence, and yet displayed great humanity during the extraordinarily severe winter of 1739, when he distributed £20.00 to the poor every Monday morning. Later, when he went to live permanently in England, he left the rents of his lands to the poor of the district.

George Berkeley, Bishop of Cloyne and renowned philosopher, died on 14 January 1753.

1753

15 January

O'CONNELL PROTEST

There was little surprise, and no great anxiety, when Daniel O'Connell and others were charged and arraigned before the courts in 1844. The Repeal Movement was at its height, and it was expected that the British authorities would do everything possible to thwart the demand for Home Rule.

However, a fury was let loose when the authorities, in a desperate effort to convict, conspired to have all Catholics debarred from the juries. The Catholic Establishment, clerical and lay, aided by the more liberal and fair-minded Protestants, perceived this manoeuvre not only as an underhand way of obtaining a conviction but as a negation of the Act of Emancipation. A campaign to have this wrong rectified was immediately promoted, and a series of mass meetings was organised. In Cork the Mayor was requested to arrange one such meeting. The venue chosen was the South Chapel, where the great Emancipation meetings of the 1820s had been held.

A capacity audience was present when the Mayor opened the meeting. Not only Catholics but Protestants, conformist and non-conformist, including F.B. Beamish, Richard Dowden, G. Crawford, Messrs Carmichael and Nicholson, were in attendance. The meeting adopted motions, among others, pledging loyalty to the Queen and requesting Her Majesty to intercede.

This historic meeting in support of O'Connell and freedom for Catholics was held in the South Chapel on 15 January 1844.

1844

CORK TECHNICAL INSTITUTE

One of the most productive of voluntary efforts organised in the city in the latter part of the nineteenth century was the introduction of scientific and technical classes. These courses were conducted in the School of Art in Emmet Place, but they became so popular that some classes had to be accommodated in the Model School in Anglesea Street and in other premises on Union Quay. Such arrangements were clearly unsuitable.

It was not until 1907, when the headmaster, Mr E.A.O'Keeffe, devised an ingenious scheme whereby the funds might be raised – the capitalisation of the annual state grant – that Cork Corporation could proceed with the provision of a new purpose-built premises. The project was made more feasible through the generosity of Mr A.F. Sharman Crawford, who presented the site, formerly the location of Sir John Arnott's Brewery in St Marie's of the Isle, now known as Sharman Crawford Street.

Mr A. Hill was appointed architect and Mr Samuel Hill was given the contract for building the new school. The architect found it possible to incorporate some of the old brewery structures into his plans and the remainder provided some excellent building materials, which helped reduce the cost of construction. Sandstone and limestone, quarried locally, are the principal materials used in the building. Many types of Irish marble are used in the decoration of the premises. In the main entrance hall, there are two or three varieties of Cork red marble, and black and white marble from Mitchelstown. The grey-veined stone on either side of the large window is from the Beaumont Quarry, and the green marble in the hall is, of course, from Connemara. The black flagstones are from Kilkenny, and the columns which separate the main staircase from the entrance hall are of Galway granite.

The Lord Mayor, Alderman Simcox, presided at the opening ceremonies of the Cork Technical Institute on 16 January 1912.

1912

A CORK CHARACTER

Bernard Sheehan was a pawnbroker who lived in Adelaide Street in the middle years of the nineteenth century. He was also one of the most popular individuals in the city, and was returned on many occasions as a town councillor. It is said that he spoke on practically all matters of Corporation business, but his contributions were noted more for their humour and oddity than for their relevancy. However eccentric he may have been, he rarely missed an opportunity to promote himself, and the visit of Messrs Fowler and Wells to Cork in 1862 presented him with a golden opportunity.

The visitors were giving a series of lectures in the Athenaeum on the science of phrenology, that is, the study of the skull. It was their practice to invite members of the audience to appear on stage and have their heads examined. Bernard Sheehan attended one of their performances and, when volunteers were called for, he was first on stage. He was greeted with roars of delight and shouts of 'Bravo Barney!' from the audience.

Mr Fowler's initial diagnosis after examining Barney's head was that 'he could go through with those hardships which would kill three or four other individuals'. This brought the audience to their feet, and they again cheered when he told them that if they wanted to kill Barney, they would have to shoot him through the heart otherwise he would live. Through this and subsequent revelations Barney sat smiling and imperturbable. When Fowler had concluded, Barney faced the audience and informed them that, as a fair and moderate man himself, he believed Mr Fowler's comments to be generally accurate.

Bernard (Barney) Sheehan had his head examined in the Athenaeum on 17 January 1862.

1862

18 January

PUBLIC HEALTH IN CORK

The frequent recurrence of outbreaks of typhoid fever in Cork in the 1870s compelled the government of the day to authorise an investigation under three broad headings: the extent of the outbreaks, their probable causes, and whether pollution of the River Lee above the waterworks was a contributory factor. A Dr McCabe, an inspector of the Local Government Board, was appointed to conduct the enquiry.

Dr Robert Cummins, in his book *Unusual Medical Cases*, wrote that 'siege and warfare, starvation and unemployment, overcrowding and misery, were the soils on which this terrifying ally of human suffering battened'.

Dr McCabe's report showed that while there were incidences of the disease in each of the ten years prior to 1878, the number of people affected – varying between 28 and 114 – did not constitute epidemic status. He also concluded that while the effluent discharged into the river at Macroom and Ballincollig did contaminate the river, it was not the cause of the incidence of typhoid in the city. The water from the waterworks was clean.

A population of 78,000 people lived in 10,000 houses in the city. Only one half had water closets; one quarter had no toilet facilities. There were 1,733 houses let in tenements and there were 2,282 cases of whole families living in single-room accommodation. Unemployment was chronic. Many people took their water from private wells, and there was a poor appreciation of hygienic practices. All the preconditions for the spread of typhoid, as enunciated by Dr Cummins, were present.

Dr McCabe's Report on the incidence of typhoid in Cork was presented to the public on 18 January 1878.

1878

ROBERT GIBBINGS

Robert Gibbings was the son of the rector of Carrigrohane and grandson of Robert Day, the Cork antiquarian.

He attended Cork Grammar School and later went to Queen's College, now University College, Cork. He was not the most dedicated of medical students and appears to have spent most of his time in the pursuit of art. He was intensely interested in the art of woodcuts, and presented to the college authorities an engraved bookplate featuring the college crest.

Having moved to London he studied at the Slade school and soon demonstrated his skill in woodcuts becoming, eventually, the premier artist in this medium in the world. At the outbreak of the First World War, Gibbings joined the Munster Fusiliers and fought at Gallipoli and the retreat through Serbia, suffering a severe neck wound. He returned to Ireland to complete his convalescence.

He travelled extensively for a period, and while in the South Sea Islands did some underwater swimming amongst coral reefs. This resulted in some beautiful woodcuts featuring corals and tropical fish. Back in England, with Eric Gill, he founded the Golden Cockerel Press and greatly influenced the business of publishing and design in England. Later still, when he published his own works, among them *Sweet Cork of Thee* and *Lovely is the Lee*, he illustrated them with his own remarkable woodcuts. He had not bothered to take a degree while a student but University College, Cork, presented him with an honorary degree as Master of Arts.

Robert Gibbings made his home in Footbridge Cottage, Long Wittenham, on the borders of Berkshire and Oxfordshire. He died there on 19 January 1958.

1958

JONATHAN SWIFT

Jonathan Swift was born in Dublin on 30 November 1667. He was the son and grandson of Church of Ireland ministers, and was sent to Kilkenny College, the foremost school in Ireland, for his early education. He then transferred to Trinity College, but was at best an indifferent scholar and graduated *Speciali Gratia* (by special grace).

He went to England in 1689 and entered the service of Sir William Temple. It was while in Temple's employment that he met Esther Johnson, the future Stella. Swift was writing at this time and it would seem that his preference was for verse, but when his interest turned to prose he began to excel, and he became the most brilliant satirist in the English language.

In 1704, *A Tale of a Tub* was published, and this was followed by such famous works as *Gulliver's Travels*, *Drapier's Letters* and *A Modest Proposal*. In *Drapier's Letters* Swift attacks the English Government for its plans to supply Ireland with copper halfpence and farthings. His 'Modest Proposal' was that the conditions in Ireland could be improved if children were used for food! Swift was a fierce defender of Ireland and urged that Irish people support native industries by using only native products. He advised his readers to 'burn everything English but their coal!'

When Swift was holidaying in the county, Cork Corporation, probably in acknowledgement of his efforts to defend native industries, decided to nominate him a freeman of the city.

Jonathan Swift was presented with the freedom of Cork on 20 January 1736.

1736

PARNELL IN CORK

A huge crowd, which included all the nationalist dignitaries of the city, and four bands, (Barrack Street, Butter Exchange, Blackpool and the Tailors) were present at Cork railway station to greet Charles Stewart Parnell. When he took his seat in the Mayor's coach for the drive to Mr John J. Horgan's house in the Mardyke, the people unhitched the horses and dragged the coach through the crowded streets.

Mr Parnell dined with Alderman Dwyer, and then proceeded to the theatre where he was scheduled to give a major speech. Admission to the gallery was free, and within minutes of the doors being opened, it was full. There was a charge of sixpence for the pit seats. The stage was specially decorated to greet the Member of Parliament for Cork. A neatly executed, gas-lit decoration, surmounted by his initials and surrounded by shamrocks, was at the rear. The proceedings began with the crowd singing 'God Save Ireland'.

The Mayor introduced Mr F.W. Mahony, who read the resolutions to be put before the meeting. The first was:

That we, the people of Cork, in meeting assembled, hereby declare our unanimous confidence in our representatives, Messrs C.S. Parnell and C. Deasy. We also desire to endorse the political conduct of the political chief of the Irish Parliamentary Party, and to express our admiration for the patriotic action and of the gallant band he leads in an alien House of Commons.

The second resolution called for support for the Irish National League, and called upon the citizens of the city to give practical help by joining the ranks. The speaker was greeted with great rounds of applause.

Thus was the scene set as Charles Stewart Parnell rose to address the citizens of Cork on 21 January 1885.

1885

A SAFE HARBOUR

The United States Mail Steamer, *Atlantic*, had set out from Liverpool on 28 December 1850, with mail and passengers bound for New York. The initial part of the voyage was uneventful, but after the ship had weathered a severe storm off the south-west coast of Ireland, the main shaft of the engine broke and the *Atlantic* was disabled.

The captain rigged up a jury-mast and there was great relief and rejoicing among the passengers when the *Atlantic*, twenty-four days out of Liverpool, came within sight of Ireland. When the ship entered Cork Harbour the passengers assembled and passed a series of votes of thanks to Captain West, Mr Rogers, the engineer, and the owners of the *Atlantic* who had built so fine and strong a vessel. The ship being in need of urgent repair, Mr Lecky, of Lecky and Beale's shipyard on Penrose Quay, was asked to undertake the work.

The *Atlantic* was not the only ship in difficulties at that time. The De Witt Clinton, with 350 emigrants on board, was forced into Cork after being at sea for forty days and the schooner, *Harriet*, bound from New York to St Johns, Newfoundland, was compelled to sail east across the Atlantic Ocean and find refuge in Cork Harbour.

The location of Cork Harbour on the fringe of Europe and the existence of local shipbuilding yards, like Lecky and Beale, were some of the salient reasons why Cork enjoyed a well-earned reputation as a safe haven for ships, and lived up to its motto, *Statio Bene Fida Carinis*.

The US Mail Steamer, *Atlantic*, limped into Cork Harbour on 22 January 1851.

1851

FR EDMUND HOGAN

Edmund Hogan, the son of William Hogan of Great Island and Mary Morris from Killeagh, was born at Belvelly, Cobh, in 1831. He showed an interest in the Church and, under the guidance of a Franciscan cousin, he entered the Jesuit Order in France on 29 November 1847. It is said that while still a student, Hogan was taunted by a fellow cleric for his limited command of Irish. He determined to master the language.

He completed two years of study on the Continent before being sent to Wales, and was eventually ordained at St Bueno's College, Flintshire, on 23 September 1855. In 1859 he was teaching German in Clongowes Wood College, and a year later he taught French, German, Logic and Music in what is now Crescent College, Limerick. He was in Rome for a period and while there devoted much time to research in the Roman Archives, particularly into items of Irish interest. On his return to Ireland he taught Moral Theology in University College, Dublin. Fr Hogan was a member of the Royal Irish Academy and Todd Professor of the Celtic Languages.

His first book was published in 1866, and from then until his death he produced a steady stream of scholarly and popular works. However, it was not until 1900, prompted by Robert Armstrong of the Royal Irish Academy, that he undertook the work for which he is famous, *Onomasticon Goedelicum*. It is a huge volume, consisting of some 700 double pages, each page containing up to fifty entries, on the meanings of words of Irish origin. Fr Edmund Hogan devoted ten years to this work and, when he had finished it, lived in semi-retirement until his death on 26 November 1917.

Dr Douglas Hyde described him as a gentle, unassuming individual who delighted in relating stories of people he had met. Fr Edmond Hogan, Gaelic scholar, was born at Belvelly, Cobh, on 23 January 1831.

1831

24 January

THE HIDDEN IRELAND

Daniel Corkery was born on 14 February 1878 at Number 1 Gardiner's Hill. He was the son of William Corkery and Mary Barron. He was educated at the Presentation Brothers' School in Douglas Street where he subsequently taught as a monitor. He later studied in St Patrick's College in Dublin, and returned to Cork to teach in St Patrick's School.

Corkery was intensely interested in the Irish language and wrote plays for the Cork Dramatic Society, which he helped establish. In 1919 his first significant work, *A Munster Twilight*, was published, followed, a year later, by *The Threshold of Quiet*. His play, *The Labour Leader*, was performed by the Abbey Theatre in 1919.

He was appointed to the position of Irish Language Organiser with the Vocational Education Committee. In 1929, he received his Master of Arts degree from University College, Cork. In 1931 he was appointed Professor of English there, a position he held until his retirement in 1947. In 1948 he was honoured with a Doctorate in Literature from the National University of Ireland.

Daniel Corkery is best remembered for his book, *The Hidden Ireland*, a study of eighteenth-century Ireland from 'the viewpoint of the underdog', as Seán Ó Faoláin summarised it. It is a most controversial book, dismissed by some as fantasy, lauded by others. However, it would appear that Corkery's purpose was to direct attention to an aspect of Irish life that had been ignored by professional historians, such as Lecky.

The book is romantic in its portrayal of what might have been, but for all that it stands as a landmark in Irish scholarship.

The Hidden Ireland was published on 24 January 1925.

1925

PRESENTATION ORDER

In 1774, Nano Nagle was fifty-six years of age and had already accomplished much. She had spent twenty years caring for the poor of Cork, especially the children. She had established schools in the slums of the city and had been instrumental in introducing the Ursuline Teaching Order.

She had, however, been unhappy for some time with the direction the Ursulines were taking, and particularly with the fact that their constitution restricted them to an enclosed lifestyle. Nano Nagle believed that conditions in Cork made it essential for the nuns to live and work among the people. She also found it difficult to accept that the Ursulines were catering for the rich as well as the poor.

Fr Moylan, parish priest of St Finbarr's South, who had helped her down the years, was not surprised at her misgivings. But when he discovered that Nano Nagle had taken a lease on property in Cove Lane within a short distance of the Ursulines' School, both he and the Ursulines were very upset. The Ursulines perceived that Miss Nagle's involvement with the new school would entail the withdrawal of her financial support from their order, and Fr Moylan was apprehensive that the establishment of yet another Catholic school would greatly upset the political establishment. He went so far as to order her to remove her school to some other location in the city but she replied that, if forced to leave Cove Lane, she would leave the city altogether. Fr Moylan relented, and so the first steps towards the establishment of the Presentation Order were taken.

Nano Nagle and two assistants, the Misses Mary Fuohy and Elizabeth Burke, took possession of their home in Cove Street on 25 January 1775.

1775

RICHARD CAULFIELD

Richard Caulfield was born into a cultured Cork family on 23 April 1823. His grandfather, Henry Gosnell, had been physician to the Lying-in Hospital for Women and also the first resident surgeon of the North Infirmary Hospital. His father was a merchant with premises in the North Main Street.

He was educated locally, then in Bandon Endowed School and later entered Trinity College, Dublin. It was intended that he study for the church, but while in Trinity, he displayed an interest in history and took a BA Degree and later an LLB In 1866 he was awarded an LLD.

He became involved with the Royal Cork Institution, and in time he became Secretary, Librarian and Custodian. He was a member of the Cuvierian Society also and lectured to both organisations on many occasions. Caulfield became the first librarian to Queen's College (now University College) Cork. Having developed an intense interest in manuscripts and seals, he acquired a comprehensive and important collection. He edited manuscripts also, his first effort being the *Journal of the Very Reverend Rowland Davies*, for the Camden Society. With Robert Day he edited Smith's *The Ancient and Present State of the County and City of Cork*, an amended edition of which was published in the *Journal of the Cork Historical and Archaeological Society*.

His range of interests was immense and embraced almost every aspect of history. He was an annual summer visitor to the great libraries of England, researching manuscripts pertaining to Cork.

Richard Caulfield amassed the largest private collection of historical material relevant to Cork, and the great pity is that the Caulfield collection was broken up on his death. The sale of Richard Caulfield's library took place on 26 January 1888.

1888

MINISTER'S MONEY

The Act of Parliament of 1665 (17/18, Charles II), provided for the imposition of a property tax on houses in eight named towns in Ireland. In Cork, the rate of tax was twelve pence for every pound of the yearly valuation of the property. The proceeds of the tax were distributed among clergymen of the Established Church.

The Church Warden was authorised to oversee the annual valuation of property, collect the money and distribute it among the clergymen. Houses could be entered on default of payment and property seized.

The tax, which became known as 'Ministers' Money', was fiercely resented by Catholics, who objected to being compelled to contribute to the upkeep of ministers of religion of a church to which they did not belong. Many efforts had been made over the intervening years to have this pernicious piece of legislation repealed and, in 1846, the propertied citizens of Cork gathered in the City Courthouse to again express their outrage.

The Lord Mayor, Alderman F. Roche, was in the chair, and among the prominent citizens present were Fr Matt Horgan, Denny Lane, Bernard Sheehan and many members of the Corporation. The proposer of the first motion described the legislation as an unjust tax, levied on the Catholic population of 8,000,000 to support the clergy of the minority population of 700,000. Denny Lane said it was such an obvious injustice it was difficult to enunciate a coherent argument against the provisions of the Act.

This public meeting in protest at the payment of 'Ministers' Money' was held on 27 January 1846.

1846

28 January

LAST CATHOLIC BISHOP

Henry VIII came to the throne of England in 1509. Such was his standing with the Pope that he was conferred with the title, *Fidei Defensor*, (Defender of the Faith). One of his prerogatives was the nomination of bishops.

A vacancy arose in the diocese of Cork due to the death of Bishop John Fitzedmund Fitzgerald some time before 27 August 1520. Cardinal Wolsey was informed of the vacancy and the Earl of Surrey recommended the appointment of an Englishman in the interests of security. He recommended that the 'Bysshop of Leyghlyn might do good service here'. Later again Surrey proposed Walter Wellesley, whom he described as 'a famous clerk, noted for the best in the land, a man of gravity and virtuous conversation and a singular mind'. Wellesley declined the offer.

The situation was resolved when a priest of the diocese of Cloyne, John Benet, was appointed Bishop of the dioceses of Cork and Cloyne. Benet occupies a unique position in the history of the Catholic Church in Cork in that he was the last Catholic Bishop to rule the united sees of Cork and Cloyne before the introduction of the Reformation.

John Benet was appointed as Bishop of Cork and Cloyne on 28 January 1523.

1523

CHORAL FESTIVAL

This being the First Festival held in Ireland on the principle of the English Festivals, the Public are now called upon to come forward and assist the originators of this great undertaking, their object being solely to cultivate and reform Music in the City and large County .... The City and County Cork Choral Society propose, if supported and assisted by the Public, to establish a Fund for the Poor and to give their Festivals for that object and that object alone.

Thus the City and County of Cork Choral and Festival Society advertised the festival held in the Athenaeum (now the Opera House), in January 1862.

The artists contracted to perform included Madame Rubersdorf; Miss Julia Elton, Contralto; Miss Cruise, Soprano; Mr Topham; Mr J.F. Horton (Tenor, Cork Cathedral); Mr Dunne, Counter-Tenor and Mr Wood, the Celebrated Basso. The programme consisted of three performances: *Judas Macabaeus* (its first performance in Cork) on the opening night; *Der Freischutz* and a Grand Miscellaneous Selection on the second night; and Handel's *Messiah* on the third and final night.

The orchestra and chorus numbered about 300 performers and included members of Bandon, Youghal, Limerick, Belfast, Armagh and Dublin Choral Societies. The organist was Mr Handel Rogers and Mr J.C. Marks was the conductor.

The audience must have numbered at least 2,000 persons, while many hundreds had to leave the doors disappointed,' The *Cork Examiner* reported on the performance of *Der Freischutz* on 29 January 1862.

1862

LANCASTERIAN SCHOOL

Joseph Lancaster, the English educator, was born in 1778. He developed a system of monitorial tuition whereby older boys taught the younger pupils the basic subjects. Joseph Lancaster visited Ireland in December 1811, and was invited to lecture in Cork in January 1812.

There was a great need at the time to provide for the education of the destitute boys of the city, as Nano Nagle and the Presentation Order were already doing for the girls. The Catholic Bishop, acting through the Cork Charitable Society, had already arranged for the introduction of the fledgling Christian Brothers Order, who were to establish a school in the north side of the city.

However, inspired by the ideas of Joseph Lancaster, a group of philanthropic gentlemen arranged for the establishment of a 'Lancasterian' school. A site was procured from the Cork Charitable Society on Hammond's Marsh in the western suburbs and plans were drawn up to build a school to cater for 1,000 pupils. The foundation stone was laid on 4 May 1812, and construction continued until October when the walls and roof had been erected. Work was then suspended for two years.

The delay was due to an issue of religion, in this particular case, the absence of religious teaching. The promoters of the project visualised it as a non-sectarian school, a concept which led to opposition from the churches. Eventually the administration of the Lancasterian School was taken over by the Cork Charitable Society.

Joseph Lancaster enunciated the principles of the Lancasterian system of education in the Assembly Rooms, South Mall, on 30 January 1812.

1812

31 January

THE LOUGH

The Lough is situated in the south suburbs of Cork. It was formerly known as *Loch na bhFearnóg* (the lake of the alder trees), and in all probability formed part of the lands attached to the ancient monastery of St Finbarr, which extended from the site of the monastery itself, near the present Gillabbey, southwards to The Lough, and were known as the 'faiche', or green. At the time of the Reformation, when the monastic property was confiscated, The Lough and the surrounding lands came into the possession of Cork Corporation.

In his book, *Researches in the South of Ireland*, Crofton Croker recounts the 'Legend of the Lake', a mythical tale as to how the lake was formed. Recent investigation has shown that The Lough is fed by no less than eight underground streams; in the 1920s an attempt to drain it proved unsuccessful.

Marlborough bivouaced his troops on its shore during the siege of Cork in 1691. From 1773 onwards Cork Corporation was entitled to hold two fairs each year near The Lough, and imposed a charge of one penny per head on 'all black cattle that stand in the Lough, or on the ground about the Lough, in order to cool for slaughtering'. The fee for each pig or sheep was one halfpenny.

The Corporation was often called upon to defend its rights against people who attempted to remove earth from the lake shore or to fish with nets in the waters. Cork Corporation regularly leased the Lough and the surrounding land to private individuals, but the leases were often revoked due to infringement of the terms.

On 31 January 1725, the Corporation of Cork compelled William Masters to surrender his lease of The Lough.

1725

1 February

CORK TAKEN BY HIGH KING

In the early years of the twelfth century there was great turmoil in the country. Even though Turlough O'Connor of Connacht was High King of Ireland, his authority was being challenged in Munster. Both the O'Briens of Dal Cais and the MacCarthys of Eoghanacht, while paying lip service to the supremacy of the king of Connacht, harboured aspirations for autonomy, and even coveted the High Kingship.

In 1123, Tadhg MacCarthy submitted to O'Connor and gave hostages. He was deposed from his kingship of Eoghanacht and his brother, Cormac Mór, was elected in his place. Cormac Mór was one of the outstanding figures of his time, a patron of the arts, and probably the greatest of the MacCarthy kings. He transferred his capital from Cashel to Shandon, which overlooked and threatened the Viking city of Cork.

Meanwhile the High King, anxious to assert his authority, attacked Kerry, captured Limerick and devastated the Decies. Cormac Mór MacCarthy retaliated by organising a conspiracy against him. He attempted to invade Connacht, but was repulsed at Athlone. The High King executed the hostages given by Tadhg, including Cormac's son, Maolsheachlann. Cormac Mór MacCarthy took up arms against the High King but his troops were defeated and Cormac Mór himself deposed. He retired to Lismore and became a monk.

Turlough O'Connor consolidated his position and invaded the Kingdom of Desmond. Accompanied by Conchubhair and Turlough O'Brien, the king of Connacht launched an attack upon the town of Cork by land and sea. The Norsemen resisted, but after a brief struggle capitulated.

The king of Connacht put Cork to the flames on 1 February 1127.

1127

MICHAEL DAVITT

In 1887 Michael Davitt was at the height of his fame. He had concluded an agreement with Charles Stewart Parnell which brought him within the accepted political fold.

In 1886 Davitt, recently married, had gone on a lecture tour of America which was an unqualified success. He was hailed as the man who had achieved freedom for the farming community. The three Fs: Fixity of Tenure, Fair Price and Freedom of Sale, had been accomplished. On his return to Ireland early in 1887, he was fêted in Cork, a dinner being arranged in his honour in the Chamber of Commerce Building. Mrs Wilson of the Victoria Hotel was in charge of the catering.

The Mayor, Alderman John O'Brien, presided as tributes were paid to Davitt. Davitt, in reply, expressed his pleasure at the number of Protestants then active in the National cause. He put the blame for emigration at the door of the landlords and landlordism. After the meal some songs were rendered.

The dinner itself was of gargantuan proportions, commencing with a choice of soups between hare and julienne. The fish course was a choice of salmon with a fennel sauce, or turbot with a lobster sauce. The entrées consisted of oyster pâtes, mutton cutlets, asparagus and grenadines of veal spinach. The main course had a choice of boiled turkey with celery sauce, braised hams, sirloin of beef, haunch of mutton, olio of chicken and tongue. The second course consisted of plum pudding and Venetian pudding. For entremets there was a choice of eleven dishes which included five types of jelly, and the dessert offered a choice of twelve kinds of fruit.

The dinner in honour of Michael Davitt was held on 2 February 1887.

1887

ST PETER'S

St Peter's Church is situated on the western side of the North Main Street almost opposite the junction with Kyle Street. It is set back a little from the roadway and is in a dilapidated condition at present. Churches have been on this site since the thirteenth century. A charter of Henry III of England, dated 20 May 1270, confirmed the Bishop of Cork in 'the patronage and right of presentation of St Peter's'.

In 1382 the Irish Parliament was in session in St Peter's. The most important decision taken was the appointment of Dean Cotton as Lord Justice. The original church was apparently a substantial edifice and contained several small chapels. A belfry stood on the west end of the graveyard adjacent to the city walls in what is now Grattan Street. This belfry was taken down in 1683.

In 1782 the existing church was demolished and, shortly afterwards, the present building was erected. It has been described as 'mean in the exterior, but elegant in the interior'.

The construction of the present St Peter's Church began on 3 February 1783.

1783

CORK & MUSKERRY RAIL

The Tramways and Public Companies Act, passed on 29 August 1883, provided for the establishment of light railways which would act as feeder lines to the major railways. In October of the same year a group of interested parties – farmers, landowners and ratepayers – met to consider the possibility of promoting a railway to serve the Muskerry district of County Cork. A Mr S.G. Fraser was commissioned to investigate and report on the most advantageous route.

Fraser recommended a southern route beginning on the Western Road, and progressing through Carrigrohane, Leemount, Cloghroe and Dripsey to Coachford. His plan also provided for branch lines to Blarney and Donoughmore. This route was accepted, and the Cork and Muskerry Light Railway Company was incorporated on 12 December 1883.

The railway was to become part of local folklore and was known under various names, 'The Muskerry Tram', The Blarney Tram' and, most familiarly of all, 'The Hook and Eye Express'. The terminus was on Bishop's Island, the present location of Jury's Hotel. Country people used to have their purchases, made earlier in the day, delivered to the terminus in the afternoon. The messenger boys, in an effort to attract the attention of their employers' customers, would call out the names of the shops, 'Lipton', 'Home and Colonial', 'London and Newcastle' (adding an imperial flavour) to 'Cash's', 'Sutton's' and 'Woodford Bourne's'.

'The Hook and Eye Express' provided an invaluable service to the Muskerry district until escalating costs, and competition from road transport, forced its amalgamation with Córas Iompair Éireann and ultimately the closure of the line on 29 December 1934.

Work began on the construction of the 'Muskerry Tram' on 4 February 1887.

1887

See below

5 February

CORK CITY BYE-LAWS

At the beginning of the eighteenth century the finances of Cork Corporation were in a deplorable state. A small organised group had succeeded in gaining control and were manipulating the authority's affairs for their personal benefit.

The abuse of authority was rampant. The Mayor was not in receipt of a fixed salary, but the clique had conferred privileges on him in regard to commission on the collection of certain taxes – to the Mayor's advantage. When the Corporation was obliged to raise loans, the agreed procedures were ignored and the business given to members of the clique. Freemen were being appointed illegally, on receipt of cash and payments of other kinds.

A putsch brought a new administration to power, and it was decided to introduce bye-laws to regulate the authority's financial affairs. Invoking their rights under the various charters, the members insisted that no payments be made without the express authority of the Corporation sitting in the Court of D'oyer Hundred. They required that an annual budget be prepared, that it be sanctioned in advance and that no works be commenced without prior costing and permission. The rules controlling the making of freemen were clarified.

The Corporation of Cork accepted a new set of bye-laws on 5 February 1721.

1721

MASS FOR FRENCH KING

Francis Moylan was born into a prosperous Cork merchant family on 17 September 1735. He was sent to Paris to be educated but had no inclination to enter the world of business. He wanted to join the Carthusian Order. The family objected, however, and he was influenced by a Jesuit uncle to enrol at the Jesuit College in Toulouse. One of his fellow students at the college was Henry Essex Edgeworth, better known as Abbé Edgeworth, friend and confessor of Louis XVI. The pair became lifelong friends.

After his ordination in 1761, Francis Moylan decided to remain working in France, and while there developed an intense dislike for the teachings of Voltaire and Rousseau. He was to become a bitter opponent of the French Revolution and the ideals of *Liberté, Égalité, Fraternité*.

On returning to Ireland, he took up duty in the South Parish, Cork. He was made parish priest and in 1775, was appointed Bishop of Ardfert and Aghadoe. Almost immediately his loyalist or establishment tendencies involved him in a serious dispute, which led to a reprimand by the Congregation of the Propagation of the Faith. Fr Arthur O'Leary had argued that it was lawful for Catholics to pledge their loyalty to the king of England. Dr Moylan supported this viewpoint, but the Congregation disagreed.

Dr Moylan was appointed Bishop of Cork, where he continued to proclaim his royalist beliefs. His confidant, Abbé Edgeworth, was present at the execution of Louis XVI.

Dr Moylan offered a mass for the king, in Ss Peter and Paul's Church, on 6 February 1793.

1793

JOHN BOLSTER'S MAGAZINE

In the early years of the nineteenth century Cork had an enviable reputation in the arts. Writers like Fr Prout, William Maginn and William Thompson were dazzling London society, and artists like Daniel Maclise, John Hogan and James Barry enjoyed high reputations and patronage. Cork was known as the 'Irish Athens'.

One of the most prominent literary figures in the city was John Bolster. He was a bookseller whose shop was in Patrick's Street, at the junction of the street leading to Ss Peter and Paul's Church. His shop was the hub of intellectual life in the city; when Sir Walter Scott visited Cork he made a point of calling to Bolster's. Daniel Maclise sketched the writer's portrait in the shop.

Bolster decided to publish a magazine and named it *Bolster's Quarterly*. He solicited articles from many of the local writers, among whom were John Windele, the antiquarian (who was also editor), Jeremiah J. Callanan the poet, John Augustus O'Shea and the Rev Horatio Townsend. The publication had the grandiloquent subtitle, *The Magazine of Ireland*.

John Bolster had the reputation of being careful with money, and slow to pay contributors. On one occasion he solicited an article from a visiting literary figure who, when informed that a fee would not be forthcoming, suggested that Bolster rename his magazine 'The Cork-Screw'.

Bolster's Quarterly survived from 1826 to 1830. It then succumbed to the old problem – irregularity of issue – brought about by the difficulty in obtaining sufficient regular copy for the magazine.

The first edition of *Bolster's Quarterly* appeared on 7 February 1826.

8 February

SMALLPOX IN CORK

Smallpox is one of the world's most dreaded plagues. It is a contagious disease and is passed directly from one person to another. People may be carriers of the virus, though immune themselves. It is a particularly abhorrent illness which leaves lesions, or scabs, on the skin, especially the face, thus clearly identifying a person who has been infected.

The early history of the disease is unclear, although there is evidence of an epidemic in Syria in the year AD 302, but it was not until AD 900 that smallpox was identified as a malady distinct from measles. Gilbert of England first referred to smallpox as a contagious disease about the year 1200.

The first authenticated case of smallpox in Cork occurred in 1708, and there were epidemics in 1719, 1720, 1721 and 1731. In 1721, vaccination was introduced into Cork and the procedure was tested on criminals in the public jails! In 1773, the doctors in the South Infirmary volunteered to vaccinate all the poor of the city. A further epidemic in the years 1855 and 1856 was curbed by the policy of vaccination. The public vaccinator treated 1,076 children in nine days; in all 2,474 persons were treated over a period of six weeks.

Cork, being a port city, was particularly vulnerable. In the years 1871 and 1872, 4,000 people were infected, of whom 1,000 died of the disease. The source of the infection was traced to a sailor who shared lodgings in Evergreen Street.

Francis H. Tuckey, in his book, *The County and City of Cork Remembrancer*, records that 'the small-pox was very prevalent in this city', on 8 February 1818.

1818

9 February

ST LUKE'S CHURCH

Initially opposed by vested interests, the construction of St Patrick's Bridge was eventually undertaken. This was a significant event in the growth of the city, as it opened up for development the north-eastern area, which soon became one of the more exclusive residential districts.

As the population grew, the need became apparent for a chapel of ease to accommodate the considerable number of Protestants then attending services in Shandon. In 1837, Bishop Kyle dedicated a small church, St Luke's, designed by the Pain brothers in the Gothic style. In 1872, a new parish was created and it was decided to erect a larger church, which was dedicated on 14 January 1875.

This new church was built to the plans of W.H. Hill in the Romanesque style, and had the distinction of being the first church erected after the passing of the Irish Church Disestablishment Act of 1869. It was embellished with red marble pillars and a carved stone pulpit. There were valuable stained-glass windows. The organ, by Forster and Andrews of Hull, cost £700.

In February 1887, St Luke's was destroyed by fire. The conflagration began in the boiler house and swept through the building, destroying everything except the vestry room. Fortunately the church plate, registers and parochial records were in this section. A restricted supply of water hindered the Corporation fire brigade, aided by military units, in their efforts to save the building.

The Mayor and other dignitaries came to view the scene, on the morning of the disaster, 9 February 1887.

1887

10 February

PROTESTANT PROTEST

A reporter from the *Cork Examiner* took the precaution of adopting a disguise when he attended a meeting of about 100 of 'the very dregs and canaille of petty Protestantism', as he put it, in the Cumberland Rooms, Faulkner's Lane. The purpose of the meeting was to object to the grant of financial aid to Maynooth College.

The meeting was chaired by the Rev Dr Neligan, described by the reporter with, one suspects, tongue in cheek, as 'that tolerant, exemplary, and truly Christian Pastor'. The Chairman reminded the attendance of the real threat that 'an infidel college was rearing its walls within the land'. A Mr Shea then took the floor and proceeded to attack 'holy water, national school education and Catholicism in general'. He regretted that the interdenominational school system provided an opportunity for Catholics and Protestants to intermix, as it allowed 'Rome to raise her idolatrous temples within the "Protestant Jerusalem".'

Dr Neligan described a visit to the Sunday's Well National School and his horror at finding 'Butler's Penny Cathecism, Scapulars, and prayers to the angels in use'. The children were sent to the mass house for purification and the 'word of God' – meaning, presumably, a knowledge of the Bible – had been kept from them.

Mr Sampson Kemp then addressed the gathering. He explained that the rationale behind Mr Pitt's decision to aid Maynooth was to ensure that Catholic clergy would be educated at home, thus, 'preventing their minds from being imbued with revolutionary and democratic principles'.

This meeting of Protestant zealots was reported in the *Cork Examiner* of 10 February 1843.

1843

JAMES ÓG DESMOND EXECUTED

In the latter half of the sixteenth century the Catholic dynasty of Desmond was goaded into open rebellion against the English. James Óg, the brother of the Earl of Desmond, set out for Muskerry to attack Teigue MacCarthy, Lord of Muskerry, who had sworn allegiance to the English.

Teigue MacCarthy's son, Cormac, in a surprise attack, defeated the Desmond forces, capturing James Óg. The prisoner was sent to Cork where he was detained for nearly a month. He spent the time, we are told, 'preparing himself for death, doing penance for his sins, and asking forgiveness for his misdeeds'. A writ was dispatched to Sir Warham St Leger ordering the execution of James Óg. He was hanged and his body quartered.

The writ of martial law, which provided for the execution of James Óg of Desmond, was issued on 11 February 1580.

1580

12 February

ABRAHAM ABELL

Abraham Abell was born on 11 April 1783, into a Quaker family that had lived in Cork for 200 years. He was a successful businessman and regarded as one of the most distinguished philanthropists of his day. For many years he was treasurer of the Cork Dispensary and Humane Society.

His interests were many. He was a founder member of both the Literary and Scientific Society and the Cuvierian Society. He was treasurer of the Cork Library, manager of the Cork Institution, managing director of the Cork Savings Bank, and a member of the Royal Irish Academy, Irish Archaeological Society, Camden Society, London Society and the South Munster Antiquarian Society.

Abell was intensely interested in archaeology and conducted a study of Irish round towers. He was responsible for the first collection of Ogham inscriptions ever made in Ireland, which he deposited in the Cork Institution. This collection is now in University College, Cork.

Abraham Abell was somewhat eccentric. On his birthdays he liked to walk a mile for every year of his life, his last effort being from Cork to Youghal and back on his fifty-eighth birthday. For a period of a couple of weeks he slept between two skeletons to overcome a fear of the supernatural instilled during his childhood. He read late into the night, and to help him remain awake, always stood at his desk, sometimes on one foot.

He was subject to bouts of depression and, during one attack, consigned his collection of books and music to the flames. He regretted the decision and immediately set about establishing another collection.

Abraham Abell died on 12 February 1851.

1851

13 February

BRIAN DILLON

The Fenian, Brian Dillon, was arrested in 1865. He was tried and sentenced to ten years penal servitude, five years of which he spent in various British prisons. Although offered a conditional amnesty, he refused to accept the terms. In 1871 he was granted a pardon and sailed for Ireland. He landed in Dublin, en route to his home city of Cork.

There were crowds at all the intervening railway stations to pay tribute to the returning Fenian. A huge throng of tens of thousands was assembled in and around the Cork terminus when the train arrived at ten past eight in the evening. Many city bands, rendering patriotic airs like 'Let Erin Remember' and 'God save Ireland', were at the station to greet him. Tar barrels blazed in King Street (now MacCurtain Street), and along Summerhill.

There was another huge throng at Dillon's Cross where, in response to demand, Brian Dillon addressed them from a window of his house, thanking them for their support. There was a minor fracas between the police and a section of the crowd, but Dillon pleaded with the people to disperse peacefully and not provoke a police attack.

Brian Dillon was dead within two years of his release from prison. He was accorded a public funeral to Rathcooney cemetery on 25 August 1872. A Celtic cross was erected over his grave and, in 1909, a commemorative plaque was inserted in the wall of his house.

Brian Dillon returned to Cork from imprisonment in Britain on 13 February 1871.

1871

14 February

FORD COMES TO CORK

Henry Ford of Detroit, keen to extend his interests into the European market, approached the British Government requesting permission to open a plant in Southampton. He proposed to manufacture tractors on an extensive scale. However, Britain was engaged in the First World War and the cabinet was concerned that the venture would attract workers employed in the munitions factories. It was suggested to Ford that he consider Ireland as a location.

Ford, however, seems to have already considered that option, and had approached Cork Corporation for the purchase of land which comprised the Cork Racecourse The Cork Corporation and Cork Harbour Commissioners agreed to sell the land subject to certain conditions.

The cost of the site was agreed at £10,000. Ford would take ownership of the existing roadway that adjoined the river and would, in return, construct a new road (now known as Centre Park Road). A minimum of 2,000 male workers, earning one shilling per hour, were to be employed. Ford undertook to expend the sum of not less than £200,000 on 'commercial shipping and manufacturing premises and out offices or dwellings for industrial workers and in providing plant and equipment and in fitting out the same'.

Ford also agreed to pay £500 for the race course tenancy and £1,000 for land in the possession of Shandon Boat Club and the Gaelic Athletic Association. These conditions were to be fulfilled within a period of five years. In return, the Corporation undertook to expedite, through Parliament, whatever legislation was necessary.

Henry Ford presented his plan for the erection of a factory in Cork to the British Cabinet on 14 February 1917.

1917

15 February

'THE POPE' O'MAHONY

Eoin O'Mahony BL, KM, was one of Cork's last great 'characters'. He was born in Cork in 1905, the son of Daniel J. O'Mahony, the city analyst. He was educated locally and in Clongowes Wood College before enrolling in University College, Cork, where he was auditor of the Philosophical Society and won that society's gold medal.

He then went to Trinity College, Dublin, and had an outstanding academic career. He was auditor and triple gold medallist of the Historical Society, and double gold medallist in the Literary and Scientific Society. He was also a member of the College's Cumann Gaeltacht. O'Mahony then read for the Bar, to which he was called in 1930. Three years later he was called to the English Bar. He practised on the Munster Circuit and was eventually appointed State Counsel for Cork City and County.

Eoin O'Mahony's interests ranged far beyond legal affairs. He was Vice-President of the Cork Catholic Young Men's Society and Life Governor of the Aged Poor Society. His involvement in Catholic organisations led to his being nicknamed 'The Pope'. He was a council member of The Cork Historical and Archaeological Society and of The Irish Genealogical Society. His interest in history and particularly in genealogy led to a career in radio, and he won distinction for his presentation of the programme 'Meet the Clans'. He was an acclaimed raconteur and travelled the country visiting his many friends, entertaining them in their homes.

'The Pope' aspired to a career in politics. He contested the East Cork constituency in the 1933 General Election, but was defeated. He did, however, succeed in being elected to both Cork Corporation and Cork County Council. In 1966 he tried, but failed, to get a nomination for the Presidency of the country.

Eoin 'The Pope' O'Mahony died on 15 February 1970.

1970

SIR ROBERT KANE

Robert Kane was recognised as one of the foremost scientists of the nineteenth century. A Dubliner, born on 24 September 1809, he studied chemistry at Trinity College, Dublin. Later he studied medical and practical science in Dublin and Paris. In 1831, he was appointed Professor of Chemistry to the Apothecaries Hall and in that year published Elements of Practical Pharmacy, and established the *Dublin Journal of Practical Pharmacy*. Kane became a licentiate of the King and Queen's College of Physicians in 1832 and a fellow in 1841.

He became editor of the *Philosophical Magazine* and, in 1841, parts one and two of his *Elements of Chemistry* appeared. In 1843, he delivered a series of lectures on the development of industries in Ireland, and the following year published them in book form, under the title *Industrial Resources in Ireland*. The book, in which Kane alerted the public to the country's various natural resources, was an outstanding success, and went into several editions. He was appointed director of the Museum of Irish Industry, established by the government in 1846.

In 1844, in his book *The Large and Small Farm Question Considered*, Robert Kane urged the formation of small farms in Ireland, and in the following year, he was appointed a member of the commission to enquire into the potato blight and the relief of Irish distress. In 1845, Kane was named first President of the new university, Queen's College, Cork. The College was opened in 1849 and he played a significant role in its development. He was later appointed a commissioner of National Education in Ireland. In 1877, he was elected President of the Royal Irish Academy.

Robert Kane was knighted on 16 February 1846.

1846

FR MATHEW

In 1838, Fr Mathew consented to become leader of the Cork Total Abstinence Association, two years after it had been established. His involvement led to the enrolment of countless thousands of members and the establishment of branches, not only in Ireland, but throughout the English-speaking world. Fr Mathew became an international celebrity and toured extensively, administering the pledge and establishing branches of the movement.

In 1843, Mr Peter Purcell proposed that Fr Mathew be honoured with a National Testimony. A great soirée was organised in the hall of the Corn Market, attended by Fr Mathew and thousands of the respectable citizens of Cork. Congratulations were offered to 'The Temperance men of Cork', the clergy, members in England and Scotland, the ladies, the press and the trustees of the Corn Market. After tea and biscuits a series of toasts was proposed, beginning with one to the Queen of England, the proposer expressing the 'best feelings of his heart, and all the enthusiasm that human nature was capable of'. This was greeted with acclaim and a spirited rendition of 'God save the Queen'.

The second toast was to 'His Royal Highness, Prince Albert', and that was followed by the playing of 'Prince Albert's March'. There followed toasts to the Prince of Wales, Princess Royal and the rest of the royal family. The final toast was to 'Ireland and Universal Temperance'.

Messrs Ford and O'Sullivan sang a duet, and then the attendance joined in singing Mr William Hackett's song, 'Hail to our Glorious Apostle'.

The Cork Testimony to Fr.Mathew was held in the Corn Market Hall on 17 February 1843.

1843

BROTHERS PUBLISH

The Christian Brothers were invited to Cork during the first decade of the nineteenth century to provide an education for the poor boys of the city. Later, the introduction of the National School System brought about the expansion of educational opportunities. Most of the pupils, however, were destitute, and could not afford essential educational aids. Slates and chalk, and sand scattered on flat surfaces, were used instead of paper to teach 'the three Rs': reading, writing and arithmetic.

There was a great need for text books and, since the Brothers felt that those then available were unsatisfactory, they decided to provide their own. The *Cork Examiner* greeted the first edition of the new books with great enthusiasm, stating that they would 'diffuse that spirit of Catholic teaching so happily inculcated by these publications'.

There were five sets of Reading Lessons, a set of Tables, three Geography Books, two School Expositor, A School Grammar of the English Language, two books of Commercial Arithmetic, and Arithmetical Tables. The price of the books varied from three pence to two shillings and six pence each. The *Cork Examiner* selected the Grammar of the English Language for special mention: 'this admirable little book is at once a grammar and a text book of our language. It contains a very interesting historical account of the rise and progress of the language and of the writers who distinguished themselves both in its prose and poetry.'

The text books, published by the Christian Brothers, went on sale in Cork for the first time on 18 February 1850.

1850

DEFENCE OF CORK

Whenever England was involved in wars, a recurring anxiety was that Ireland might be attacked and used as a base for an invasion of Britain. In 1740, England was at war with Spain, and the spectre of an invasion once again concentrated the mind of the British monarch on Ireland's defences.

In a letter to the Duke of Devonshire, the King warned of a possible attack, as it was known that a Spanish force had been assembled in Galicia in north-west Spain. Devonshire advised that the Irish defences be strengthened, and recommended that a supply of 20,000 firearms be made available. He informed the king that payment for the first 10,000 pieces would be made immediately on delivery, and the balance remitted within one month. The Irish House of Commons voted the sum of £35,000 to pay for the armaments, with the interesting proviso that 6,000 pieces be manufactured in Ireland.

General Jean Louis Legonier, commandant of Kinsale and Charles Fort, prepared the defence of Cork. He proposed to recruit 500 young men in Cork and to draft a further 500 recruits into the city from Bandon. He would station 500 soldiers, provisioned with biscuits, water and beef for ten days, and with ten pieces of cannon, in Elizabeth Fort off Barrack Street. He intended to maintain communications by barricading the streets between the Fort and the South Gate, and placing an officer and 30 men with two pieces of cannon on each barricade. Fifty men were to be positioned in the South Gate and 180 grenadiers would be stationed in the North and South Main Streets as reinforcements.

The directive from the king of England to the Duke of Devonshire, to provide for the defence of Cork, was dispatched on 19 February 1740.

1740

TYPHOID CONTROLLED

The symptoms of typhoid fever were described in medical journals at the time of Hippocrates in the fifth century BC. However, it was not until the first half of the nineteenth century that typhoid fever was clearly distinguished from other such diseases. Typhoid is contagious and the bacteria, *Salmonella typhosa*, may be found in contaminated food or water – especially water polluted by sewage – and is transmitted through the mouth. Typhoid was practically endemic in armies, a factor which contributed to the spread of the disease here, Cork being a garrison city.

In 1800, there was a virulent outbreak of typhoid in Cork and not less than 4,000 persons were treated. The disease affected all classes but especially the poor, who lived in extremely unhygienic and insanitary conditions. Unemployment and poverty were major contributory factors.

In 1802, John Milner Barry established the first fever hospital in the city. The response to his appeal to the citizens for financial help was immediate and generous. At the first meeting of the Fever Hospital Committee, the Church of Ireland Bishop, Thomas Stopford, presided. The following were Vice-Presidents: Dr Moylan, Catholic Bishop; John Longfleld MD; John Callanan MD; William Beamish; Richard Lane, and Cooper Penrose. From then on the Fever Hospital served the citizens well through many outbreaks of typhoid.

In 1890, the chief medical officer was able to report to the annual general meeting of the committee that there had been only 143 patients with the disease during the previous year. The last reported case in Cork appears to have been in 1937.

That meeting of the Cork Fever Hospital was convened in the Crawford Institute of Science and Arts on 20 February 1890.

1890

OPERATIC COMPOSER

Paul MacSwiney was born in Cork in 1856. He was an accomplished musician but, unfortunately, died at the early age of 34 in 1890.

He is best known for a composition which was performed in 1881, an opera entitled *Amergen*. The unusual, if not unique, setting is the palace of the High King of Ireland. The opera consists of a prologue and two acts. The title, *Amergen,* is of particular interest to Cork people. Amergen was a silversmith from Connacht who came to County Cork, married a slave and was the father of St Finbarr.

Amergen was performed in the Opera House with an entirely local cast, but for one exception. Mr R.D. Howard conducted the orchestra, the leader being Herr Kleinstuber. The principal parts were played by Messrs W. McCormack, J.D. Fitzgerald, F. O. Keeffe, J. Maskill, and the Misses Craig, Cahalan and Henderson. The band and chorus numbered 80. The performance was well received and Mr D'Oyly Carte sought an introduction to the composer.

'The unanimous verdict', the *Cork Examiner* critic stated, 'is one of unqualified success.' The opera was also performed in Limerick, but plans to take it to America were abandoned on the death of the composer. Paul MacSwiney composed several other works, the most successful being a cantata, *The Bard and the Knight*, which was produced in the Irish language at the Steinway Hall, New York. He wrote many songs, including The Green Hills of old Ireland' and 'Brian, a tragedy'.

The first performance of Paul MacSwiney's opera, *Amergen*, was given on 21 February 1881.

1881

GERALD GRIFFIN

Gerald Griffin was born into a wealthy Limerick family on 12 December 1803. His parents emigrated to America in 1820 but he remained in Ireland, living with his brother in Adare, County Limerick.

He pursued a literary career, writing four tragedies, among which was *Gisippus, or the Forgotten Friend* and many fine lyrics. In 1823, he went to London to further his career and contributed to the *Literary Gazette*.

Griffin turned his attention to short stories: 'Holland Tide' and three others were well received. He returned to Ireland in 1827 and completed three volumes of *Tales of the Munster Festivals*. In 1829 he published, anonymously, *The Collegians*, which attained wide popularity at the time, and is regarded as Griffin's masterpiece. Thomas Davis considered *The Collegians* and *Súil Dhow* as 'two of the most perfect prose fictions in the world', and he compared Griffin to Sir Walter Scott. Gerald Griffin's output was impressive, and included *The Rivals*, a second series of *Tales of the Munster Festivals*, *The Invasion*, *Tales of my Neighbourhood*, *Duke of Monmouth* and *Talis Qualis, or Tales from the Jury-room*. His play *Gisippus* was finally produced at Drury Lane, London, in 1842.

In 1838, he returned to Ireland and entered the new religious order, the Christian Brothers. He died on 12 June 1840, and is buried in the graveyard attached to the North Monastery School, Cork.

The first edition of the collected works of Gerald Griffin was issued on 22 February 1842.

1842

ST MARY'S

The Dominican Order of Friars has been in Cork for over 700 years, the original foundation being in St Marie's of the Isle. Following the Reformation the property was attained, and the Dominicans moved to the north side of the city. They remained in a house off Shandon Street until 1721, when they moved to a location where the Butter Market now stands.

In 1832, the foundation stone of St Mary's Church on Pope's Quay was laid. The architect was Kearns Deane, and the church was consecrated in 1838. In 1848, the priory was constructed and a year later, on 10 May 1849, James Willard of Pope's Quay was commissioned to erect a high altar of Italian marble. This altar was subsequently replaced and removed to the church of St Finbarr's West.

In September 1861, substantial alterations were carried out and the centre aisle and nave were formed. Later in the year, the statue of the Virgin was installed on top of the portico. The statue was executed by Mr Cahill, a pupil of Hogan, and is a copy of the statue in the Piazza di Spagna, in Rome. Then, on 27 October 1872, there was the solemn opening of the apse and chancel, and the unveiling of the baldachino (which was made by John Fitzgerald of Cork). Later the two side altars were designed by the architect, Mr Hynes, and executed by Messrs Daly and Son of Cook Street, Cork.

In 1896, it became obvious that essential repairs had to be undertaken to the magnificent plaster ceiling (executed by local workmen), and the public were asked to contribute.

The meeting soliciting funds for the refurbishment of St Mary's, Pope's Quay, was held in the church on 23 February 1896.

1896

GILL ABBEY ROCK

The members of Cork Corporation, in the 1870s, appear to have given little consideration to the historical significance of Gill Abbey Rock, when they discussed a proposal to demolish it to facilitate the construction of a roadway. Not one member mentioned that this was, in all probability, the site, endowed by Cormac MacCarthaigh in 1134, of the Abbey of the Cave. No one adverted to the tradition that St Finbarr frequently withdrew to a cave in the rock for periods of contemplation.

The Jennings brothers had proposed the construction of a new roadway from Gill Abbey to the Western Road. They were prepared to build a bridge over the south channel of the river and erect 50 or 60 houses for the labouring classes. They sought permission to demolish Water Lane, Love Lane and Gillabbey Lane. If the work were not completed within a period of twelve years the land would be ceded to the Corporation. The promoters argued that the proposal would open up 60 acres for development which would be of benefit to the city revenues.

As usual the Corporation was divided. Some councillors, including the ebullient 'Barney' Sheehan, complained that objectors to the proposal were motivated by self interest, in that the new road would take from the business of Barrack Street traders – an allegation that almost led to blows in the Chamber! Councillor O'Sullivan considered Gill Abbey Rock no more than 'an unsightly rock that ought to be removed'.

The promoters informed the Corporation, on 24 February 1873, of their decision to withdraw the proposal.

1873

25 February

WILLIAM O'BRIEN

William O'Brien was born in Mallow on 2 October 1852, the second son of James O'Brien, a law clerk, and Kate Nagle. Although his parents were Catholic, he was educated at the Cloyne Protestant Diocesan College and later attended Queen's College (now University College), Cork.

He became a reporter in the *Cork Daily Herald* and, in 1881, Parnell appointed him editor of the *United Ireland* newspaper. The paper was suppressed and O'Brien was committed to Kilmainham Prison. At the request of Parnell, who was also imprisoned, O'Brien wrote the famous 'No Rent' manifesto. When this document was read at a meeting, the Government proclaimed The Land League an illegal organisation.

In 1883, he was elected a nationalist Member of Parliament for Mallow and held that seat until 1892, when he was elected for the City of Cork constituency. However, in 1886 O'Brien and John Dillon published, without Parnell's consent, the 'Plan of Campaign'. The plan was declared illegal and O'Brien was convicted and sent to Tullamore Jail. He refused to wear prison uniform and lay naked in bed until a warder smuggled in a suit of Blarney tweed!

After Parnell's downfall, William O'Brien established the 'All for Ireland League'. At the 1918 election O'Brien and his League followers stood down to give a clear field for the contest between Sinn Féin and the Irish Party, which resulted in the extinction of the latter.

William O'Brien was the author of two novels: *When we were Boys* and *A Queen of Men*. He wrote several other works including *Recollections*, *Evening Memories* and *The Irish Revolution*.

William O'Brien died on 25 February 1928.

1928

26 February

DAVY DAN CURTAYNE

The *Cork Sentinel* newspaper was published in the city during the 1830s. Mainly concerned with local affairs and gossip, it reflected perfectly the opinions and attitudes of its eccentric editor, Davy Dan Curtayne. Curtayne derived much amusement and entertainment from the courts of law, bringing before the magistrates outrageous and unsubstantiated charges.

On one occasion Davy Dan rushed into a crowded courtroom in a very agitated state. Having brushed his hair and composed himself, he delivered an address to the Chief Magistrate, Mr Besnard, in the course of which he described those who congregated in courts as 'low, mean, dirty blackguards who make it their constant study daily to mock the sufferings of the poor wretches who resort here for justice and are unable to follow me in the line of argumentative reasoning I have now adduced'. He accused Mr Besnard of 'rude impertinence' when the magistrate declined to offer an opinion on a verdict given previously by the Recorder.

On being reprimanded by the magistrate, Curtayne proceeded to inform all and sundry that, when a difference of interpretation of the law arose, he always had recourse to 'Blackstone or some other authority, although his own judgement was superior to their "balderdash"'. He described the court as 'a miserable den' and the magistrates as 'numbskulls'. When Curtayne was eventually prevailed upon to state his complaint, he accused a fishwoman of assaulting him with a 'minion' as she placed the fish in his basket!

Having heard the lady give her version of the affair the magistrate dismissed the case, and Curtayne departed from the court – well satisfied that he had again involved Mr Besnard in one of his little charades.

Davy Dan Curtayne enjoyed his day in court on 26 February 1836.

1836

CHOLERA IN CORK

Cholera was endemic in the Ganges River valley from ancient times. As early as the fifth century BC Thucydides described an incidence of the disease in Athens, but it was not until the fifteenth century that the most serious form of the illness, *Vibrio Cholerae*, was described.

The first of the great pandemics started in India in 1817; the second, in 1826, spread to Europe. It was in Moscow in 1830, and in Edinburgh in 1832. Cholera struck Belfast on 22 March of that year, followed by Dublin some two weeks later. In Cork, the first recorded case of cholera occurred on 17 April 1832.

The contaminating agent, in polluted water or food, enters the body via the mouth. Conditions in Cork city in the 1830s were conducive to the spread of the disease, unemployment and concomitant poverty being rampant. In the parish of St Nicholas, for instance, with a population of 17,642, only 4,684 were in employment; the rest were paupers living in filthy, overcrowded tenements.

The British Government reacted to the crisis by passing legislation (8, George III), providing for the establishment of Boards of Health. Concerned Cork citizens requested the Mayor to summon a meeting to consider the establishment of a Board of Health. In the absence of the Mayor, Bishop Murphy took the chair. Others present included Messrs Daly, Crawford, Hayes, Callaghan, Whateley, O'Leary, Reynolds, Lane, Fitzgibbons, Fagan, Parker and McCarthy.

The meeting was held in the City Courthouse, on 27 February 1832.

1832

DEATH OF A BANKER

The Pike family of Cork is descended from a Cromwellian soldier named Richard Pike, of Berkshire, who came to Ireland as a corporal in 1648. He was given possession of Sarsfleld's Court but, on becoming a Quaker, forfeited the property. He then moved to Kilcrea for a period before settling in Cork, where he opened a shop.

The Pikes were related by marriage to the Hoare family, who were wealthy bankers. Towards the end of the seventeenth century a Joseph Pike became a partner in Hoare's Bank. In 1770, two of Richard Pike's descendants opened a bank in Hoare's Lane, now Liberty Street, in premises formerly occupied by the Hoares.

Practically all the Cork private bankers at that time were Quakers. Their banking hours were from 10 am to 2 pm and they invariably affected the austere Quaker mode of dress – antique coat, plain shoes and hose. However, many of these private banks failed to survive periodic difficulties, and competition from the new joint stock banking companies.

In 1816, Joseph Pike supported one faction in a stormy election campaign, and his partiality provoked a run on his bank. The bank, however, survived due to the support of political friends. In the financial crisis of 1820, other banks were not so fortunate: Roche's Bank failed and business at Leslie's was suspended for a period. Joseph Pike had prepared for such eventualities and had sufficient liquid reserves to enable him to continue to trade.

By 1826 he had arranged for his assets to be converted into gold, and the Bank of Ireland paid all of Joseph Pike's creditors in full after his death, which occurred on 28 February 1826.

1826

FR MAT HOGAN DIES

Fr Mat Horgan was born in the townland of Ballinraha in 1774. He was ordained and eventually appointed parish priest of the parishes of Blarney and Waterloo, where he ministered for 34 years.

He was, by all accounts, extraordinarily popular, with a wide circle of friends and acquaintances, rich and poor, simple and talented. He had a diverse range of interests and committed his ideas, theories and opinions to paper, mainly in the form of letters to the newspapers under the pen-name 'Victor'.

Fr Horgan had a very good command of the Irish language. He transcribed many of the old manuscripts and translated Moore's *Melodies* and Horace into Irish. He also had a deep love of Irish music, particularly pipe music, and in the early days of the nineteenth century he patronised the Pipers' Congress, held in Bruree and Raheen. His dearest wish was to collect a corpus of Irish music, but the death of his collaborators – William Forde of Cork and William Elliot Hudson of Dublin – put an end to that project. He held open house for wandering musicians and storytellers, one of whom, named Sullivan, he maintained permanently in his home.

He spent much time studying the origins of the Ogham script, and is rightly credited with being responsible for discovering the clue to these ancient inscriptions in the keyword, Maqui, several years before Bishop Graves.

Fr Mat Horgan published a poem entitled, 'Gortroe, or Lamentation of the Widows for their Sons', an elegy, or *caoineadh*, for the victims of those killed and wounded at Gortroe on 18 December 1834, during the tithe war.

Fr Mat Horgan died at his residence at Clogheenmilcon on 1 March 1849.

1849

2 March

CHRISTY RING DIES

As a general rule it is unwise and unfair to compare athletes of one era with those of another. Athletes should only be judged within the context of their own time, their achievements measured against those of their contemporaries.

Despite these reservations, there are some athletes of such exceptional talent that there is an almost irresistible temptation to pit them, in the imagination, against the greatest of earlier and later times.

Christy Ring is widely recognised as the greatest hurler of his era, and probably the finest exponent ever of the game of hurling. He had all the attributes of a master: skill, speed, courage, scoring ability and an indomitable will to win. His playing career spanned almost three decades, during which he dominated the game. He perfected the skill of solo-running and introduced the modern technique of penalty taking.

Born in Cloyne, he was first selected to represent Cork, as a substitute, on the minor team of 1937. He was on the minor team a year later, joined the Glen Rovers Club, and made his debut on the Cork senior team in a league match against Kilkenny on 23 October 1939.

Christy Ring captained Cork to three All-Ireland Championships, in 1946, 1953 and 1954. In the latter year he became the first hurler to win eight All-Ireland medals. In the Railway Cup Competition he made 44 appearances, winning an unequalled eighteen medals and scoring 42 goals and 105 points. With his club, Glen Rovers, he won thirteen County championships.

Christy Ring died on 2 March 1979.

1979

3 March

BLACKROCK CASTLE

It is impossible to state precisely when the original fort was constructed on the site of the present Blackrock Castle. However, a document published in the Calendar of State Papers, dating from before 1585, is a petition to the Queen of England, in which it is stated that Cork has 'a fort called Blackrock' maintained by the citizens 'with artillery to resist pirates and other invasion'. Another document in the Calendar, dated 13 January 1600, indicates that the first fortification was constructed by the citizens *circa* 1582.

Lord Deputy Mountjoy took possession of the site in 1604 and either reconstructed the old fort or erected a new one. In 1608, the Charter of James I returned the castle to Corporation ownership. The building had a beacon, lit by turf, to guide shipping. It was destroyed by fire in 1722 and a new castle, a circular tower, was constructed by the citizens at a cost of £296. Later an octagonal-shaped room with a cupola was added to the top of the tower.

As the danger of attack by foreign forces or pirates receded the castle was, on occasions, rented to individuals. The building was, however, used principally as an Admiralty Court. Every third year, on 1 August, the members of the Corporation set out from the castle down river to the mouth of the harbour for the function of 'Throwing the Dart', the Mayor entertaining his guests in a lavish manner on their return from the ceremony.

That building was also destroyed by fire in 1827, and the Corporation built the present structure at a cost of £1,000. The architects were James and G.R. Pain.

The Corporation took possession of the new Blackrock Castle on 3 March 1829.

1829

'REPEAL' AGITATION

In the early decades of the nineteenth century the country was in a ferment. Catholic Emancipation having been achieved in 1829, the people turned their attention to the repeal of the hated Act of Union. The British Government, concerned at the level of agitation, reacted by introducing the Irish Disturbances Bill in the House of Commons.

The emerging middle classes responded with fury. Protest meetings were held. The Cork Trades' Association discussed the situation at a meeting, the secretary reporting that petitions from the various parishes had been sent to the government. One of the City Members of Parliament, Mr Beamish, who received a standing ovation on entering the meeting room, confirmed that the 'Irish popular members (of parliament) were resolved to oppose it (the Bill)'. His contribution was received with acclamation.

Many of those at the meeting condemned the measures proposed in the Bill as 'unparalleled despotism' and insisted that the 'honour of the country was at stake'. There was an obligation on the Trades' Association to give a lead to the people as to how they should act in the event of 'the arbitrary measures of Lord Grey's Government being passed into laws'.

The Cork Trades' Association decided, on 4 March 1833, to call a meeting of all the Trades of the City, to protest at the legislation proposed by Lord Grey's Whig administration.

5 March

THE FENIAN RISING IN CORK

Several dozen employees of Murphy's Brewery, as well as compositors from the *Southern Reporter* newspaper and other workers throughout the city, had arranged for leave of absence from work in early March 1867. They were members of the Fenian Brotherhood and were about to launch the Fenian Rising.

There were either three or four Fenian Circles in Cork. Their drilling rendezvous were the Fair Field and the 'Tawnies' on the northside, and the Black Ash and Rochestown Road on the southside. Meetings were conducted in Hegarty's Forge, near the South Gate Bridge, and the Coopers' Society rooms in Dominick Street. The leaders of the Fenian movement in the city included Brian Dillon, Charles Underwood O'Connell, James O'Connor, John Lynch, J.J. Geary and John Kenealy.

The plan for the uprising called for the assembly of the members at Prayer Hill, in Shanakiel. The northern contingent first met in the Fair Field, and the southside people gathered in Bishop Street. Upwards of 2,000 members had been alerted, and about 1,000 assembled at Prayer Hill. The leaders were William Francis Lomasney, better known as Captain Mackay, and James Francis Xavier O'Brien. Only about 200 of those present had weapons. Having been marshalled into military formation they set out for Mallow. It appears that the plan of campaign envisaged that the Cork and Kerry contingents would join forces at Mallow and then proceed to Limerick Junction, the rallying place for the new 'Army of the Irish Republic'.

The weather had deteriorated, and there was a blinding blizzard as the Cork City Fenians assembled on the evening of 5 March 1867.

1867

6 March

A NUNNERY IN CORK

In 1291, King Edward I of England directed his Irish judiciary to investigate the legality of the Barry family's intention to grant land on the Great Island, where the town of Cobh is now situated, for the establishment of a nunnery. The Barrys proposed to endow Agnes de Hareford, described as 'a recluse in Cork', with a church and land.

The enquiry was held in Cork on 29 June 1297, before fifteen jurors, four of whom were knights. The report of the enquiry, while conceding that the grant of land would affect the King's rights and those of other landowners, was sympathetic to the proposal. It argued that 'it would be much to the convenience and utility of the country if the house should be founded for nuns, for there is no other house of nuns where knights and other free men in those parts may have their daughters brought up or maintained, nor in the counties adjoining'.

Edward did not permit the grant of land. But Agnes de Hareford, aided by her benefactors, appealed, and a second enquiry was held in Cork on 23 August 1301. On this occasion the report unequivocally favoured the grant of the Cobh land, provided that the nunnery itself be located in the House of St John the Baptist outside the Cork city walls, where John Street is now.

Agnes de Hareford appears to have been an anchorite, a follower of the rule of St Anthony. Anchorites chose to live an ascetic life in remote areas. In 1306, there were at least four such anchorites, three females and one male, in Cork. In the course of time the anchorites were prevailed upon to attach themselves to monasteries, where their desire for solitude was respected.

The enquiry that led to the establishment of a nunnery in Cork was ordered by King Edward I on 6 March 1291.

1291

THE BOTANIC GARDENS

The establishment of the Royal Cork Institution was inspired by the Rev Thomas Dix Hincks, who organised a series of lectures in 1803 and persuaded a group of influential citizens to set up an institution where scientific research could be conducted.

In 1806, a parliamentary grant of £2,000 per annum was obtained by the Institution, and it was decided to establish a botanic garden and library. A lease was obtained on land where St Joseph's Cemetery is now situated, at an annual rent of £47.75. James Drummond, a Scotsman, was appointed curator, and he proceeded to lay out the gardens. Specimens of plants, local and foreign, were cultivated and made available to the lecturers in botany at the Institution. Specimens were also sold to farmers in the immediate environs of the city.

James Drummond was a most conscientious employee and worthy of his annual salary of £180.00. He planted many trees and hedges at his own expense. When, however, the annual grant from the government was progressively reduced, and finally withdrawn in 1830, the Cork Institution decided to close the Botanic Gardens. The curator proposed to assume personal responsibility for the operation of the garden, but his offer was rejected.

James Drummond, for twenty years curator of the Botanic Gardens of the Royal Cork Institution, left Ireland for a new life 'as a settler to the Colony to be formed at Swan River on the West Coast of New Holland' on 7 March 1829.

1829

FACTION FIGHTING

It is impossible, at this remove, to identify the causes of the communal violence that raged in Cork city during the latter years of the eighteenth century. Blood sports such as bull-baiting, bull-running, dog fighting and cock fighting were very popular. However, in the 1770s an even more brutal 'sport' was in vogue – faction fighting. There was an especially fierce rivalry between the citizens of Fair Lane and Blackpool.

Francis Tuckey in his book, *The County and City of Cork Remembrancer*, chronicles the progress of faction fighting in that era. It was the practice for the crowds to gather in certain establishments known as 'rendezvous houses' prior to doing battle. The Corporation, in an effort to quell the violence, closed down these establishments on 7 March 1771, but the effort failed. By the end of the year, the rivalry had become so intense that warring factions met every Sunday and holiday to do battle. During one such encounter two men were killed. Another battle took place on the day of their interment; a Blackpool man was taken prisoner by the Fair Lane mob, and only the arrival of the army saved him from being hanged.

Tuckey provides a graphic description of one battle between 'the warlike sons and daughters of Fair Lane and Blackpool, who met in a long field near Fair Hill and fought with one another till night came on. The females were armed plentifully with stones, and the male combatants according to the Chewkee custom, with tomahawks of a new construction, which were about four feet long, and so dexterously contrived (having a hook and spear at the end) that any who missed grappling were sure to stab with the sharp point'.

That encounter between the combatants of Fair Lane and Blackpool took place on 8 March 1772.

1772

9 March

STEAMSHIPS ON THE LEE

The first steam-powered boat built in Ireland (by Mr Hennessy of Passage West) was launched on 10 June 1815. It was commissioned by Mr Michael John O'Brien of Tuckey Street and named the *City of Cork*. It had a large saloon cabin and good promenade deck and provided the first steam-powered regular ferry service to Cobh. The return fare was ten pence for a cabin and five pence steerage, the journey to Cobh from Cork taking about two hours.

In 1816 another steamer, the *Waterloo*, owned by Messrs Barrett and Denny of the Marsh, was introduced on the river. The intense rivalry that developed between the two companies was celebrated in a ballad:

Oh, 'tis here you'd see the steamboats sporting
Upon Lough Mahon, so fair to view;
Bold Captain O'Brien, and his colours flying,
And he a-vieing with the *Waterloo*.

Competition on the river increased with the advent of two more ferries; the *Princess Charlotte* in 1821 and the *Lee* in 1825. The next significant development was the establishment of the River Steamer Company in 1844 who acquired four steamers (*Queen, Maid of Erin, Prince* and *Royal Alice*) and provided an excellent service. In 1851 the newly-formed Cork, Blackrock and Passage Railway Company started its own ferry service with the *Queenstown*. All this competition for custom led to a reduction in the return fare to four pence (cabin) and two pence (steerage).

The Citizens' River Steamers Company was established in 1859 and continued in operation until 1890 when it was forced into liquidation. The auction of the company's four boats, *City of Cork, Citizen, Lee* and *Erin* took place on 9 March 1890.

1890

BLACK EAGLE

John James Murphy was born at Ringmahon Castle, Blackrock, on 3 December 1796, into a wealthy Cork family. He was educated in England, but returned to Cork in 1810 and signed up as a midshipman on the *Charles Grant* of the British East India Company. Having spent some time in China, he returned to Cork in 1814 and then went to Canada to join the Hudson Bay Company.

The next twenty years of John Murphy's life are shrouded in mystery. It is known that he worked as a clerk for the Hudson Bay Company for several years; he was in London in 1828, but returned, it appears, to Canada.

He left his employment with the Hudson Bay Company and lived for many years with a Red Indian tribe, by whom he was given the name, *Keesh na Geesha*, which has been translated as 'Black Eagle of the North'. He never elaborated on his experiences with the Indians, whether he married, or had a family. There is a tradition that he met a Franciscan friar in the forest and supplied him with flour to make the Eucharist. Shortly afterwards he abandoned his life with the Indians and returned to Cork.

He visited Rome and while there decided to become a priest. He was ordained at the age of 42 years. His first parish was in Liverpool, but he was summoned back to Cork in 1848 to care for the poor of the city during the worst years of the Famine. He was appointed parish priest, first of Ss Peter and Paul's Church, then a ramshackle building in Carey's Lane. John Murphy commissioned the younger Pugin to design the present church, which was opened for worship on 29 June 1866.

Fr John Murphy, sometimes known as 'Black Eagle of the North', died on 10 March 1883.

1883

CONFISCATION OF PROPERTY

The inhabitants of Cork claimed, in a memorandum to King Charles II, that they had been loyal both to his father and to himself during the rebellion of 1641-1653. During his father's reign they had admitted Sir William St Leger and his army to the city, had provided billet and forage, and advanced the sum of £30,000 – which had never been repaid.

Despite their loyalty they had been expelled from the city in 1644 and their property, to the value of £60,000, in the city and suburbs, had been confiscated. In January 1649, their property had been restored to them, but at the end of the year they had again been banished and compelled to settle in Macroom.

They petitioned the King and, on 12 August 1660, he made an order restoring their rights. Their property had, however, in the meantime, come into the possession of Roger Boyle, son of that Lord Boyle who was one of the most avaricious Englishmen ever to settle in Ireland. Roger Boyle procrastinated in complying with the order, and the citizens again petitioned the king.

Charles II consulted with the Lord Justices of Ireland, Charles Coote, Maurice Eustace and Roger Boyle on 11 March 1661, whereupon he altered his previous decision and refused to restore their property to the 'ancient inhabitants' of Cork.

1661

12 March

THE FOUNDLING HOSPITAL

The history of the care of abandoned children in Western Europe makes for depressing study. In 1757, of the 14,934 children admitted to the London Foundling Hospital, 10,389 died. Between 1784 and 1838, 146,900 out of 183,955 inmates died in the Vienna Foundling Hospital. In Dublin, 41,524 died out of the intake of 52,152 between the years 1796 and 1826.

In 1735, an Act of the Irish Parliament provided for the establishment of a Workhouse to care for the foundling children of Cork. A committee or 'Perpetual Corporation', which consisted of the Lord Bishop of Cork, the Recorder, Aldermen, Sheriffs, Common Speaker of the City and 26 other persons, was established to manage the proposed hospice. Finance was provided by the imposition of a special tax on coals coming into Cork Harbour, and other specified duties. The governers were empowered to receive all the exposed and foundling children, who were to be nursed, clad, taught to read and write, and thoroughly instructed in the principles of the Protestant religion.

A site was acquired on the Watercourse Road, near the present Murphy's Brewery. There were four schools in the institution as well as an infirmary for the sick, which was attended daily by a physician. The reformer, John Howard, commented in 1788: 'The hospital has been greatly improved since my visit in 1787 and the children are more healthy. As a stream (the Kiln River) runs close to the house, a convenient bath might be easily procured.'

The hospital had 1,765 inmates in 1833. In 1838, the governors decided not to take in any more children, in accordance with the terms of the Irish Poor Relief Act. The Foundling Hospital was closed in 1854, the children being transferred to the Workhouse.

The Cork Foundling Hospital was opened on 12 March 1747.

1747

13 March

CORK COURTHOUSE

On Good Friday 1891, the Courthouse on Washington Street was gutted in what was described as the greatest conflagration ever experienced in Cork. The identity of the architect of that building is a matter of contention: it has been accredited both to Kearns Deane and to the Pain brothers. It impressed Lord Macauley, however, who considered it 'worthy of Palladio'. It was decided to rebuild on the same site, and a request to Parliament for help resulted in the Cork (City and County) Courthouse Act of 1891.

On 10 July 1891, the Grand Juries of Cork City and County invited architects to submit plans for the design of a new Courthouse. The brief was detailed, stipulating a maximum reconstruction cost, and a proviso that the façade and portico of the old building be retained. Thirteen entries were received, and an independent assessor selected that submitted by William Henry Hill. On 10 March 1892, tenders were invited from builders, as a result of which Samuel Hill was awarded the contract.

Construction commenced in May 1893, but progress was slow because of inclement weather and a series of strikes by stonecutters, carpenters and labourers. A major change from the original building was the inclusion of a cupola supported by massive marble pillars, surmounting the grand hall. The marbles used in the building are native: Black Kilkenny, Green Connemara, Cork Red and dove-coloured Meath. The Corinthian columns of the portico are 30 feet high, projecting twenty feet from the façade. The portico is 72 feet in length and 66 feet in height.

The Grand Jury of County Cork took possession of the new Courthouse on 13 March 1895.

1895

JAMES II IN CORK

James II, the last of the Stuart Kings, landed at Kinsale on 12 March 1689. He was accompanied by a fleet of 22 ships, which included twelve great men-of-war with French colours, three fire ships and eight merchantmen, all the property of King Louis XIV of France.

Two days later James entered Cork and was received by the Irish 'after their rude and barbarous manner, by bagpipes, dancing and throwing their mantles under his horse's feet, making a garland of a stump of cabbage, and such expressions of joy'. The dance was the *Rinnce Fada*, performed by six people, three facing three, holding handkerchiefs. The performance delighted James.

The historian, Charles Smith, tells us that the king 'on the next Sunday heard mass in a new chapel, lately erected near the Franciscan Friary. Through the streets he was supported by two friars of that order, and attended by many others in their habits'.

There is doubt as to where James lodged while in Cork. A contemporary account, by citizens who had fled the city at his approach, maintains that he stayed at the old Dominican Friary, then in St Marie's of the Isle. According to another report he lodged in Shandon Castle, near the present St Anne's, Shandon. However, the balance of evidence supports the view that he resided in the home of Major General MacCarthy in the South Main Street. That house remained standing until about 1829 when it was demolished to make way for the construction of an Arcade.

King James II, of England, Scotland, Wales and Ireland, Defender of the Faith, arrived in Cork on 14 March 1689.

1689

15 March

FOUNDRY STRIKE

The strike by the workers in Perrott's Iron Foundry in 1890 was bitter and prolonged. It began with a demand for parity of pay with workers in other foundries in the city. The rate of pay for a smith in Perrott's was thirteen shillings a week, whereas in McKenzie's Foundry the rate was sixteen shillings.

There were conflicting accounts of the strike – the employers claiming that the men were not on strike as they had given a week's notice; the men countering that notice was mandatory, as it was illegal for workers to walk off the job without notice. They claimed to be 'adopting a new style of fighting because they were fighting a legal and square battle, and because they did not give Messrs Perrott an opportunity of putting them in prison'. The workers quoted from Perrott's own letter to the Workhouse Engineer, admitting that a contract could not be fulfilled as the men were on strike. When Perrott's rejected the offer of a local priest, Canon Sheehan, to mediate in the dispute, the men claimed that the firm's refusal amounted to an insult to the Canon.

A pamphlet was distributed by the workers informing the public of the issues involved in the strike and countering allegations made by the employer. The men claimed that Perrott's were losing substantial sums as a result of the strike, £1,000 approximately having been lost since the beginning of the action.

At a meeting of the South of Ireland Labour Union, held in their offices in the North Main Street, a motion was unanimously carried, pledging support for the ironworkers on strike.

That meeting of the Labour Union took place on 15 March 1890.

1890

DON JUAN DE AQUILA

On 23 September 1601, a Spanish expedition, under the command of Don Juan De Aquila, landed in Kinsale and captured the town. The Spaniards had come to help O'Neill and O'Donnell in their revolt against the British Crown.

O'Neill and O'Donnell marched from the north of Ireland to link up with the Spaniards, now themselves besieged by English troops. The Irish forces encircled the English and settled in to starve them into submission. However, the impetuous O'Donnell and Don Juan De Aquila persuaded the more cautious and astute O'Neill to attack the English. The result was a disastrous defeat for the Irish and Spaniards. O'Neill and O'Donnell retreated to the north, subsequently going into exile in Spain, along with other Irish chiefs, in what became known as the 'Flight of the Earls'.

On 12 January 1602, Lord Deputy Mountjoy and Don Juan De Aquila signed articles of composition. Don Juan agreed to surrender Kinsale and other ports, and undertook not to bear arms against the British, even in the event of additional troops arriving in Ireland from Spain. Mountjoy agreed to provide the Spaniards with sufficient shipping and victuals (which the Spaniards paid for!) to enable them to return to Spain.

Don Juan De Aquila was removed to Cork on 19 January and lived in the street now called Portney's Lane, but which may have been known as Faulkner's Lane in 1602. He was deceived by Mountjoy, a most disingenuous individual, who intercepted and withheld dispatches from the King of Spain advising Don Juan of the imminent arrival of further help from Spain, and exhorting him to continue the war against the English. The Spaniard left Cork for Kinsale on 8 March. He eventually reached Spain, was ostracised by the Court and died shortly afterwards.

Don Juan De Aquila embarked for Spain on 16 March 1602.

1602

MONUMENT UNVEILED

In 1898, the centenary of the United Irishmen's rebellion, it was decided to erect a monument to the memory of those who had died fighting in the cause of Ireland's freedom. Originally the project foundered through apathy, the foundation stone lying for several years on the site in the Grand Parade.

The Cork Young Ireland Society eventually assumed responsibility for the design, construction, and funding of the memorial. Collections were organised at church doors and in the streets. The satellite towns contributed. Exiles in America forwarded over £600.

Architects were requested to submit designs, and the plans of Mr D.J. Coakley were deemed the most suitable. The construction contract was awarded to Mr Ellis. A feature of the monument is the group of figures, representing Wolfe Tone, Michael Dwyer, Thomas Davis, O'Neill-Crowley and Erin, sculpted in local stone by Mr Davis of College Road. The *Cork Examiner* was effusive in its praise of the work, especially the statue of Erin, which the paper considered a 'creditable work of art'.

The date chosen for the official unveiling of the monument was, appropriately, St Patrick's Day. There was a procession prior to the ceremony in which representatives of city and county bodies took part, including the Young Ireland Society, trades' unions, temperance societies, Irish dancing groups, the Gaelic League and city bands. Thousands of people thronged the footpaths along the procession route and a great concourse filled the Grand Parade and South Mall.

O'Donovan Rossa addressed those present at the unveiling of the National Monument on 17 March 1906.

1906

FR THOMAS ENGLAND

Thomas England, who for 23 years was parish priest of Passage West, was the brother of the more well-known Fr John England, first Catholic Bishop of Charlestown, USA.

His duties included the care of the convicts held on Spike Island prior to their transportation to Australia. In this capacity he distinguished himself for his humanitarianism and concern. Bishop Ullithorne, a pioneer missionary in the Southern Hemisphere, recorded his appreciation of Thomas England's work: 'He heard every man's confession, gave books to all who could read and letters to all who deserved particular attention.'

Thomas England published *Letters from the Abbé Edgeworth* to his friends, with a memoir of Bishop Moylan of Cork. He also contributed papers on local history, but his most important work was his *Life of the Rev Arthur O'Leary*, published in 1822.

His sister was the superior of the first Presentation Convent School founded in Cork by Nano Nagle.

The Rev Thomas England died on 18 March 1847.

1847

WILLIAM M. BRADY

William Maziere Brady was born in Dublin on 8 January 1825. His father, a Lord Mayor of Dublin, was knighted; his uncle, Nicholas, was the author of a metrical version of the psalms. William Brady went to Trinity College in 1842, took a BA in 1848 and was ordained a minister of the Church of Ireland. In 1851 he became rector in Farrahy, County Cork.

He was a supporter of the Disestablishment of the Church of Ireland, and contributed many papers to *Fraser's* and *The Contemporary* magazines. He caused a sensation when preaching a sermon in the Chapel Royal, Dublin, attacking the Established Church, and published many books and pamphlets including, 'The Alleged Conversion of the Irish Bishops to the Reformed Religion at the Accession of Queen Elizabeth and the Assumed Descent of the Present Established Hierarchy from the Ancient Irish Church Disproved', 'Some Remarks on the Irish Church Bill' and *Essays on the English State Church in Ireland*. He was the author of the invaluable book, *Clerical and Parochial Records of Cork, Cloyne and Ross*. His only work on a nonecclesiastical subject was *The McGillicuddy Papers; a Selection from the Family Archives of The McGillicuddy of the Reeks, with an Introductory Memoir*.

After the passing of the Church Disestablishment Act in 1869 he went to Rome and, in 1873, was received into the Roman Catholic religion. He studied in the Vatican archives, extracting ecclesiastical material relative to Ireland, England and Scotland. He was made a Cavalier of the Order of Pius IX and was private chamberlain to both Pius IX and Leo XIII.

William Maziere Brady died in Rome on 19 March 1894.

1894

20 March

NEW CORPORATION

On assuming power the first Cumann na nGaedheal Government abolished many local authorities. Cork Borough Council, the republican Corporation elected in the famous Sinn Féin local elections of 1920, was dissolved on 30 October 1924. Mr Philip Monaghan was appointed Commissioner by the government to perform the functions of the authority.

In 1929, the government introduced the Cork City Management Act, instituting the managerial system of local administration and naming Mr Monaghan as first City Manager. The government also arranged for local authority elections.

Sixty-eight candidates contested the 21 seats for Cork Corporation. The seven receiving the highest number of votes would hold office for three years, the next seven for two years and the remaining seven for one year. The two with the highest number of votes were declared Aldermen.

The three main parties, Cumann na nGaedheal, Fianna Fáil and Labour, were opposed by the Business Party, Town Tenants and numerous Independents. The counting of votes, by the Proportional Representation System, was conducted in the Technical School in Sharman Crawford Street under the supervision of the Returning Officer, Mr C. Harrington.

The result was a victory for the Independents, who took seven seats, and the Business Party who took six. Both Cumann na nGaedheal and Fianna Fáil won three each and the Labour Party took two seats.

The elections to Cork Corporation were held on 20 March 1929.

1929

ST NICHOLAS

The area immediately south of the South Gate Bridge is of great antiquity and ecclesiastical importance. In addition to the Parish of St Finbarr there were other small parishes in the vicinity: St Nicholas, St Bridget, St John of Jerusalem, St Stephen, St Mary (de Narde) and St Dominick. Each of these parishes possessed its own church but, in the course of time, the parishes lost their identity and the churches fell into disuse.

In 1702, St Nicholas Church stood in the street leading to the Red Abbey. On 19 January 1720, work was begun on the construction of a new church.

In 1752, an Act of Parliament (25, George II), provided for the amalgamation of all these parishes: 'that St Nicholas parish in Cork is so small that there is no provision for a minister ... that there is no church at all for these other parishes ... the said united parish shall be the corps of the Chancellorship of St Finnbarry's.'

The church is notable for the Tracton monument, the work of John Bacon RA who was responsible also for the monument to Pitt in Westminster Abbey as well as those to Dr Johnson and Howard in St Paul's Cathedral. It has a carillon of eight bells cast in 1869 by J. Murphy, Dublin.

The present Church of St Nicholas was consecrated on 21 March 1850.

22 March

WILLIAM A. O'CONOR

William Anderson O'Conor (he adopted the O'Conor form of the name after the O'Conor head of the clan) was born in Cork in 1820. Ill-health interrupted his education so that he did not enter Trinity College until 1847. There he studied for the Anglican Ministry, completed his studies in England, and was eventually appointed rector in Manchester.

O'Conor contributed papers on a regular basis to *Proceedings of the Manchester Statistical Society* and Manchester Literary Club, and was involved with the Dramatic Reform Association and the Art Museum Committee. In 1885 he went to Rome to recover his health and, while there, performed as chaplain to the Anglican Church.

He published works of a religious nature, including, *The Truth and the Church, A Commentary on the Epistle to the Romans* and *A Commentary on the Gospel of St John*. His magnum opus was, undoubtedly, *A History of the Irish People*, a refutation of the work of Carlisle, Macaulay and Froude, all of whom were extremely critical of the Irish.

William Anderson O'Conor died in Torquay on 22 March 1887.

1887

DR PATRICK BLAIR

Patrick Blair was born in Scotland in 1712. He graduated in medicine at Edinburgh University in 1738 and continued his studies in Leyden. He arrived in Cork about the year 1745, opened a shop in Millerd Street, and later built Blair's Castle on a five-acre site in Sunday's Well.

Three years later he was embroiled in a controversy with four Cork doctors. Pamphlets were produced on both sides and the upshot was that Blair was catapulted into popularity. Blair was a free-thinker in religious matters having, it appears, been influenced by the thoughts of Voltaire while on the Continent.

In 1775, he published a pamphlet entitled 'Thoughts on Nature and Religion. Or an Apology for the right of Private Judgement, maintained'. The pamphlet was signed 'Michael Servetus' (a physician and theologian who, 200 years before, had been condemned as a heretic and burned at the stake). Once again Blair was involved in controversy.

The pamphlet was widely circulated and was attacked, in turn, by a member of the Established Church, a Dissenter and a Quaker. Finally the Capuchin, Fr Arthur O'Leary, was prevailed upon to take issue with Blair and, in a series of four letters, confounded his arguments. In the words of Fr England, 'seldom did a writer obtain an easier or a bigger triumph'.

Dr Patrick Blair was made a freeman of Cork in September 1778, but died three years later, on 23 March 1781.

1781

INTERNATIONAL RUGBY

In 1913, Cork was chosen as the venue for an international rugby game – Ireland in opposition to France in the last game of the 'Home' Internationals. Both teams had failed to register a win in that year's championship, and the final game was to determine who should be left holding the unwanted 'wooden spoon'.

The rugby game was timed to commence at half past noon, to avoid a clash of fixtures with the horse racing in Cork Park. The venue for the game, the Cork Football Ground in the Mardyke, was the subject of some concern, ownership having changed in the very recent past to a new proprietor, University College, Cork. However, arrangements on the day were entirely satisfactory.

'Glorious sunshine played on the huge crowd that was thronging by steady degrees every position from which a view of the pitch could be had,' the *Cork Examiner* reported, and the No 1 Barrack Street Brass and Reed Prize Band played a classical selection before the arrival of the teams.

Unfortunately, there were no Cork representatives on the Irish team when R.A. Lloyd, Dublin University, kicked off – the ball was supplied by Robert Day and Sons Ltd., Sports Warehouse, Cork. Ireland enjoyed an eight points to nil lead at the interval. In the second half Ireland continued to dominate, scoring three goals and three tries to achieve a handsome 24 points to nil win.

The game was played in the Mardyke Grounds on 24 March 1913.

1913

NORTH CHAPEL TOWER

About the year 1635, a 'baptismal church' was erected near the site now occupied by St Mary's Pro-Cathedral, or, as it is more commonly called, the 'North Chapel'. Described in contemporary accounts as a mass house, it was replaced about 1700. Bishop McCarthy Rabagh built a third church in 1730, on the actual site of the present chapel, which was built in 1808, by Bishop Moylan.

The style of the church is pointed Gothic, but the identity of the architect is not known. A fire damaged the property in 1820 and George Pain was commissioned to undertake the reconstruction and renovation of the building.

In 1850, it was decided to erect a bell tower. Money was, however, very scarce and after the initial flurry, the work was suspended. In 1862, Fr Dan Foley was administrator of the Cathedral and he undertook the task of building the tower. Money was so scarce that Fr Foley is said to have assumed the responsibility of acting clerk-of-works on the site, and to have contributed a fair share of the labouring tasks. When the tower was eventually completed a scribe penned the following lines;

> Southward on us fondly gazing
> Through its Gothic-windowed eyes
> Is the massive tower, raising
> Its new structure to the skies;
> Lofty monument, revealing
> Persevering strength of will
> In the priest, whose loud appealing
> Placed it standing on the hill.

A huge congregation assembled when the Bishop, Dr Delaney, laid the foundation stone of the bell tower of the North Chapel on 25 March 1850.

1850

18th-CENTURY VOLUNTEERS

Because of the British Government's involvement in the American War of Independence in the 1770s, all available regular army units were engaged in that theatre of war. Ireland was left practically devoid of military forces, and the government, to compensate for this, encouraged the raising of volunteer corps.

Although the first volunteer corps in Ireland, the True Blue of Cork, was founded by the Earl of Shannon in 1745, the majority of the corps were not established until the 1770s. In April 1778, John Wesley recorded seeing 'independent companies, raised by private persons, without any expense to the Government. If they answer no other end at least keep the Papists in order, who were exceedingly alert ever since the army was removed to America'.

There was a proliferation of volunteer corps in Cork: Blackpool Association of Militia, Blackpool Horse Cavalry, Aughrim Society of Volunteers, Culloden Volunteers, Union Society, Boyne Society, Blarney and Inniskillen Societies. Their commanding officers designed and provided the colourful uniforms, and the Corporation provided weapons. The corps drilled and paraded regularly.

The Cork Union Corps of Volunteers was raised by Commandant Henry Hickman on 26 March 1777.

JOHN HOGAN

John Hogan was born in October 1800, at Tallow, County Waterford. The family moved to Cork in 1813 and lived in Cove Street. Hogan was articled to a solicitor, Mr Michael Foote, but showed no aptitude for the work. His skill as a draughtsman was noticed by Sir Thomas Deane, who took him into his employment and presented Hogan with his first set of chisels.

To familiarise himself with the human form, Hogan attended demonstrations in anatomy in Dr Woodroffe's College in Parnell Place, at which time he carved a complete skeleton from timber. Other early examples of Hogan's work are Minerva, carved from pine timber, casts for a Drunken Faun and a Dead Christ, all now in the Crawford Gallery of Art.

John Hogan, aided by local people anxious that he should develop his talent, went to Rome and became one of the foremost sculptors of his time, being elected to the Society of the Virtuosi of the Pantheon. He returned to Ireland in 1829 and enjoyed a successful exhibition in the rooms of the Royal Irish Institution.

During the remainder of his life commissions were never as plentiful as Hogan's talents deserved, but he did execute some outstanding works, of which there are some fine examples in Cork. His statue of William Crawford, originally in the Cork Savings Bank, is now in the Crawford Art Gallery; the Dead Christ lies under the main altar in St Finbarr's (South Parish) Church; a Fr Matthew statue cast in concrete is at the Mathew Memorial Tower; the Beamish Memorial is in St Michael's Church, Church Road, Blackrock; there is a statue of Bishop Brinkley in Cloyne, and the figure of an angel crowns a sarcophagus in St Joseph's Cemetery.

John Hogan died in Dublin on 27 March 1858.

1858

SIR JOHN ARNOTT

John Arnott was born in Auchtermuchty, Scotland, in 1814. He arrived in Cork in 1837, and worked in Grant's of Patrick Street before opening a small shop which did not prosper. He went to Belfast and, in partnership with his brother-in-law, opened a shop that flourished and led to the establishment of a chain of businesses.

He returned to Cork and opened a large drapery store in Patrick Street. His success was phenomenal and he opened shops in Limerick, Dublin, Glasgow, Newcastle-on-Tyne and other cities. He acquired both *The Irish Times* and the *Northern Whig* newspapers, although he disposed of the *Northern Whig* when it attacked Catholics, and especially the Christian Brothers.

John Arnott was the proprietor of St Fin Barre's Brewery in St Marie's of the Isle (on the site where the Crawford College of Art now stands). He owned river steamers, railways and race horses. He acquired a flour mill, opened a string of bakery shops and sold bread to the poor at a price 25 per cent cheaper than the other bakeries. He opened a number of 'People's Refreshment Rooms' throughout the city where substantial meals were provided, at a nominal charge, for the poor. When the Cork shipbuilding trade slumped, Arnott commissioned a ship, the *Woodlands*, to be built in the city in order to alleviate unemployment.

John Arnott was one of the wealthiest and most respected of business people in Cork. He was Mayor on three occasions, and was knighted in 1861 on the occasion of the official opening of St Patrick's Bridge.

Sir John Arnott left a fortune of over a million pounds on his death, which occurred on 28 March 1898.

1898

EMIGRATION IN 1842

The band played 'See the Conquering Hero Comes' when Fr Mathew entered the sumptuously decorated Church Street Hall to be greeted by Mr Besnard and over 250 quests.

The room was illuminated by over 50 arc lights, some suspended from the ceiling in three elegantly cut chandeliers. Thirteen transparencies and paintings, including one of the Apostle in the Act of Administering the Pledge to an Eager Multitude (the work of Mr Drummond), decorated one wall. A large painting of Mr Besnard, flanked by two smaller paintings, one showing the emigrant ship, the *Clyde*, leaving Cork Harbour; the other of the vessel reaching it destination, St John's, New Brunswick, hung on the opposite wall.

Two pictures hung on the end wall, one 'fearfully descriptive of the horrors of a drunkard's life, the other of the joys and delights of strict sobriety'. Tables were arranged around the room 'all groaning under pyramids of good and substantial fare. That in the centre was literally covered with every delicacy that the most fastidious could desire'.

Toasts were proposed to Her Most Gracious Majesty the Queen, Prince Albert, The Prince of Wales and Prosperity to Ireland. The toasts were followed by the band playing 'God Save the Queen', 'Rule Brittania', and Patrick's Day.'

Mr Besnard, Fr Mathew, Captain Pentreath of the *Clyde*, Councillor Welsh, Mr Dowden and others gave stirring addresses on the night of 29 March 1842, to 250 emigrants on the eve of their departure for the shores of New Brunswick.

1842

30 March

UNIONS AMALGAMATE

Mr Michael Egan, President of the United Trades and Labour Council, presided at a special general meeting called in 1913 to legitimise the amalgamation of several groups to form the National Union of Railway Workers. Mr Egan reminded the packed meeting of the benefits that a strong union could give to the workers, especially protection against victimisation.

A motion was proposed and seconded by Joseph Geany and John Dineen:

That this mass meeting of railway workers, representing all grades in the service, welcomes the fusion that has brought us together. Whilst we regret there is still one organisation outside, we hereby extend to them a further welcome to join us and thereby consolidate the whole of the railway men of the United Kingdom into one organisation. We would urge all non-unionists to immediately join the National Union of Railwaymen, and to enable us to meet the huge amalgamation of the railway companies as one body, thus hastening the time when we can press for a further reduction of hours, increased wages and deal effectively with the question of victimisation.

Alderman Kelleher PC, who received a tumultuous welcome, congratulated the men on their achievement, 'As far as railway management was concerned,' he observed, '... they always promised the workers a great deal and gave them very little.' Mr Rimmer, National Organiser, detailed the struggles and achievements of the Union over the past 40 years and reminded the men that their strength depended on their unity.

The meeting was held in the Mechanics' Hall, Grattan Street on 30 March 1913.

1913

31 March

ALL-FOR-IRELAND LEAGUE

There could be no doubting the antagonism of the *Cork Examiner* to the establishment of the 'All-for-Ireland League' in 1910. It was the second effort, the *Examiner* told its readers, that William O'Brien had made to organise a meeting and, considering the composition of the promoters, it might be taken for 'a poor relation of the Primrose League'.

Notwithstanding such comments, there was a good crowd at the City Hall when Mr McDonald, Chairman, County Council, was moved to the chair at the inaugural meeting of the All-for-Ireland League. The platform party included Members of Parliament, City and County Councillors, members of religious denominations and prominent members of the community, including a good sprinkling of ladies.

William O'Brien proposed the motion to establish the League, 'whose primary object shall be the union and active co-operation in every department of our national life of all Irish men and women who believe in the principle of self-government for Ireland'. Mr O'Brien questioned the pedigree of their opponents who, in the 'days of real sacrifice and danger', had failed to stand by his side. He reminded the attendance how he had led them in the past 'into the midst of the bayonet charges and the bullets and the jails and the eviction campaigns', while his opponents 'so far from endangering their own skins in the lists, the only penalty that they expect to overtake them is a fat Crown Prosecutorship, or a university professorship, or some unconsidered trifles of that kind from the Exchequer of the hated Saxon'.

William O'Brien established the All-for-Ireland League on 31 March 1910.

1910

1 April

BISHOP JOHN MURPHY

John Murphy was born in 1772 into one of the wealthiest families in Ireland. At a very early age he was encouraged by Bishop Moylan to enter the priesthood, and in 1787 he began his studies at the Irish College in Lisbon. In 1797 John Murphy returned to Cork, where he served as curate in the church of Ss Peter and Paul. Later he became parish priest and, in 1815, was named Bishop of Cork.

He was a leading opponent of the veto sought by the British Government over the appointment of Irish bishops. He was a patron of the artist John Hogan, and he commissioned scribes to copy old Irish manuscripts. On his appointment as Bishop he decided to learn Irish, and persuaded his clergy to do likewise so they could minister to the Gaelic-speaking members of their communities.

Bishop Murphy collected probably the most extensive private library in the country, an estimated 70,000 volumes. John Windele admired the collection, describing it as 'particularly valuable for its collection of Irish literature'. The German traveller, Kohl, described the bishop's house in Chapel Street as being 'turned into a library – everywhere books are piled up even to the garrets'. On his death, this great collection was unfortunately broken up and sold by weight in Sotheby's Auction Rooms in London. He had, however, already left his collection of Irish manuscripts to Maynooth College, where they are still preserved.

Bishop John Murphy died on 1 April 1847.

1847

RIVER STEAMERS CO.

Mr John Francis Maguire MP presided at a special general meeting of the Citizens' River Steamers' Company, held in the Imperial Hotel in 1861, to consider an important motion. The directors of the company had lately negotiated the purchase of the stock and trade of a rival concern, the River Steamers' Company, operating from Merchants' Quay. The transaction included the acquisition of three vessels, *The Prince of Wales*, *Arthur* and *Alice*, as well as offices, equipment and plant and, in Mr Maguire's estimation, a most valuable asset, a private pier at Queenstown (Cobh).

Mr Maguire pointed out that the company had been formed to serve the citizens of Cork 'who live on the banks of this beautiful and lovely river ... to keep it in our own hands, for our own enjoyment, for the purpose of business, of convenience, or of pleasure'. Despite opposition from the River Steamers' Company and the Queenstown branch of the Cork/Youghal Railway Line, the Citizens' River Steamers' Company had also contracted for the construction of two vessels at a Clyde shipyard. The addition of these vessels to the fleet would enable the company to retain the contract for the transport of troops on the river.

The Chairman, in assuring the shareholders that the primary function of the company was to serve the citizens, formally proposed that the shareholders sanction the directors' decision to purchase the River Steamers' Company.

The motion was unanimously adopted on 2 April 1861.

WILLIAM COOKE

William Cooke, a native of Cork, left for London in 1766. He became a member of the Middle Temple but resigned after a short time, on acquiring an interest in a number of journals.

He achieved some success with the publication of his first poem, 'The Art of Living in London' and wrote an essay, 'Elements of Dramatic Criticism'. He wrote biographies of Macklin, the Irish actor, and of Samuel Foote, a celebrated wit. A long didactic poem, 'Conversation', which went into four editions, contained references to such famous personalities as Goldsmith, Johnson, Burke, Reynolds, Garrick and Boswell, with many of whom Cooke was friendly.

William Cooke, writer, died in Halfmoon Street, Piccadilly, on 3 April 1824.

1824

4 April

THE *SIRIUS* SAILS

The steamship *Sirius* was built for the Saint George Steamship Company of Cork by Robert Menzies and Son, Leith, her machinery being supplied by J. Wingate and Co., Glasgow. The ship arrived in Cork for the first time on 9 August 1837.

In 1836, a Dr Lardner, at a meeting of the British Association, had declared that it was impossible for a steamship to make the crossing from Europe to America. Mr James Beale, President of the Cork School of Art and Science, and a partner in Lecky and Beale, shipbuilders, Cork, announced his intention of making an attempt. He chartered the *Sirius* and employed Captain Roberts of Ardmore, Passage West, as skipper for the historic voyage. A rival consortium arranged for another vessel, the *Great Western,* to vie with the Sirius for the honour.

The *Great Western* started from London on 31 March, intending to call at Bristol; the *Sirius*, with 40 passengers aboard, sailed from London on 2 April, calling at Cork Harbour.

Thousands of people lined the shores of the harbour when Captain Roberts of the *Sirius* fired a gun to signal his departure. The battery at Rock Lodge, Monkstown, fired a salute as the *Sirius* steamed out at ten o'clock on the morning of 4 April 1838, to become the first vessel to complete a steam-powered crossing of the Atlantic Ocean.

1838

5 *April*

In 1870, the House of Commons at Westminster was debating a piece of legislation, entitled 'The Peace Preservation Bill'. In Ireland it was perceived as yet another Coercion Act.

The Bill provided for a dramatic extension to the government's power. The police were entitled to search houses at any time, day or night, and to do so as often as was deemed necessary. Constables were empowered to arrest strangers or other persons found in public before six o'clock in the morning, and justices of the Peace were entitled to imprison such persons without trial. The government was empowered to confiscate the property and plant of any newspaper, to condemn the proprietors unheard, and convict them without evidence or trial.

The Mayor presided at a public meeting called to protest against the Bill. Many of the local councillors, in addition to a large group of citizens, were present. However, the absence of the Members of Parliament for the city was commented upon, several of the speakers noting that the Members had not spoken against the Bill in its passage through the House of Commons.

Mr J.P. Ronayne stated that the Constitution of England was a grand institution for the protection of the English people, but

> when it comes to Ireland it displays itself the embodiment of English prejudice, founded on English ignorance, instigated by English pride and avarice and crammed down our throats by English bayonets ... These clauses as enunciated here cost Charles I his crown and justified the Commonwealth; cost James II his throne and justified the Revolution. And if they brought that round, should we the people of Ireland not look to ourselves ...?

The remainder of Mr Ronayne's words were lost in applause at the public meeting, details of which were reported in the *Cork Examiner* of 5 April 1870.

1870

THE WORKHOUSE

In 1859, Sir John Arnott wrote some trenchant comments in the visitors' book at the Cork Workhouse which, when published, caused a sensation.

I have been shocked – I may say appalled – from my observation of the state of the children; and the results of my enquiries have led me to the deliberate conclusion that it would be a mercy to close the gates of the Union House against them, and let them attain the mercy of death rather than be reared deformed, maimed and diseased objects, through the system of feeding them, to which, I have reason to believe, their terrible state is attributable. For want of proper nutriment, and change of diet, scrofula has so infected those young creatures that there was scarcely one of them whom I examined that did not bear plain and frightful tokens that their blood had been wasted to that degree, that the current, which should have borne vigour and health to their frames, was only a medium to disseminate debility and disease.

There is no separate register of the deaths of children kept in the house, but I have been told, and can well believe it from what I have witnessed and detailed, that four out of every five die before they are adults, and that the survivor is, in the majority of instances, destroyed in constitution.

Such were the observations of Sir John Arnott when he visited the Cork Workhouse on 6 April 1859.

1859

WESLEYAN CHURCH

In 1752, at the suggestion of John Wesley, the Methodist congregation of Cork erected a preaching house in the vicinity of Henry Street. The construction of St Patrick's Bridge in 1788, opening up the new suburbs of Montenotte and Tivoli, made the acquisition of a new premises desirable, the preaching house in Henry Street being then considered unsuitably located.

The Methodists were permitted to conduct services in the Huguenot Church in French Church Street, but this building was too small to cater for the size of the congregation. At a meeting in Hammond's Marsh (Henry Street) in 1804, it was decided to build a new preaching house, and a site was acquired in Patrick's Street.

To celebrate the jubilee year many necessary repairs were effected to the church. The porch was covered with a glass roof; ornamental panels were installed as well as new lighting and a ventilation system. In 1872, further renovations were carried out; a heating system was installed and the old pulpit and reading desk replaced.

In 1921, a new entrance porch – a memorial to those who had served in the First World War – was added to the Wesleyan Church in Patrick Street, where services had been conducted for the first time on 7 April 1805.

1805

SAMUEL FORD

Samuel Ford was the son of an impoverished artisan who fled to America leaving a young family in Cork. Samuel displayed exceptional skill as an artist, Thomas Davis considering him the greatest artistic genius Ireland had ever produced. Daniel Maclise, a fellow student, declared that Ford's drawings were as vigorous and correct as Michelangelo's.

Ford's notebooks indicate a great talent – Davis much admired the pen drawings. His major works included 'The Veiled Prophet of Khorassan', 'Tragic Muse', and 'Genius of Tragedy'. 'Fall of the Angels', commenced in 1827, is regarded as his masterpiece. A self-portrait shows all the signs of a man suffering from consumption.

William Crawford established a fund to finance Ford while he prepared for an exhibition in London. Unfortunately Samuel Ford died of tuberculosis on 28 July 1828. He is buried in an unmarked grave in St Finbarr's Cemetery.

Samuel Ford's works were exhibited at the Great Cork Exhibition of 1852. John Francis Maguire, in his comments on the Fall of the Angels, contrasted Ford's work to that of James Barry: 'How different were Ford and Barry, the latter austere, daring, full of a grandeur stern and rugged; the former all tenderness and gentleness and love, who if he rose aloft soared on the pinions of an angel. Barry might well be termed the Michelangelo of modern art, whilst Ford was styled by his associates "The Young Raphael".'

Samuel Ford was born in Cork on 8 April 1805.

1805

CORK RACECOURSE

Inclement weather and travel restrictions did not deter a huge crowd from attending the last race meeting at Cork Park Racecourse in April 1917. Situated on land now known as the Ford Industrial Estate, the first meeting at the racecourse had taken place on 18 May 1869. Amongst those present at the final meeting was T.S. Coppinger of Midleton, who had been a steward at every meeting since 1869.

The reason for the closure of the racecourse was the proposal made by Henry Ford of Detroit to establish a tractor factory in Cork. Having initially negotiated with the British Government, he came to an arrangement with Cork Corporation for the purchase of the racecourse. An Act of Parliament in 1917, the Cork Improvement Act, facilitated the transfer of the property.

Although there was some sun it was bitterly cold and snow showers fell throughout the afternoon. There were no less than twelve races, including the Douglas Hurdle, Cork Plate, Munster Steeplechase, Ward Hunt Steeplechase, Ward Union Hunt Cup, King's Cup, Maiden Plate, and the highlight of the meet, the Irish Grand National, won by Mr W.P. Hanly's 'Pay Only'. The prize fund amounted to 200 sovereigns.

The final meeting at the Cork Park Racecourse began on 9 April 1917.

CORK-MACROOM TRAM

'This Company', began the advertisement in the *Cork Examiner*, in April 1861, 'intend applying for permission to lay down a Tramway from Great George's Street, Cork, to Macroom, using the common road all the way ... when the City Tramway is built, a Passenger need never leave his seat from the station at Macroom, until he is landed (if necessary) at the Great Southern and Western Station, Cork, or any other railway station in this City.'

The Cork and Macroom Tramway Company offered shares at £10 each, ('Fifty shares will entitle a member to be a Director'), and assured the public that, even if the shares were not sold, the company would complete the work using its own capital. It was pointed out that, while nearly all local railways, including the Cork/Youghal, Cork/Passage and Cork/Bandon lines were losing money, 'all the Tramway Companies in the United States pay a profit of ten to fifteen per cent'.

Although the tramway would be in opposition to the proposed railway line to Macroom, 'one great advantage claimed for the Tramway over the Railroad is, that it can stop at any House, Store, mile or furlong on the Road, without a moment's delay or inconvenience'. The Tramway Company proposed to run passenger cars every two or three hours all day, from each end of the line, with all goods, cattle and general business to be done at night.

The Cork and Macroom Tramway Company (Limited) advertised its prospectus in the *Cork Examiner* of 10 April 1861.

1861

11 April

ROYAL PROCLAMATION

Following the death of Queen Elizabeth in 1603, many Irish municipalities refused to recognise her successor, James I, when instructed to do so by Lord Deputy Mountjoy.

Sir George Carew, President of Munster, being absent in England, was represented by six commissioners, one of whom, Sir George Thornton, relayed Mountjoy's instructions regarding the proclamation of James I as king to Thomas Sarsfield, Mayor of Cork.

Mayor Sarsfield – mindful of the fate of a former Mayor, Waters, who had proclaimed the impostor Perkin Warbeck – argued that a City Charter allowed the Corporation time to consider the matter. Judge Saxey, Chief Justice of Munster, declared that all who opposed the proclamation should be committed to prison. The City Recorder, Mead, insisted that no one had the power to imprison Corporation members.

The Mayor and Corporation adjourned to consider the matter and, having kept Sir George Thornton waiting for some hours, informed him, in a manner that was perceived as insolent, that they had not yet reached a decision.

The Mayor and Corporation of Cork refused to proclaim James I as King on 11 April 1603.

1603

ROBERT BELL

Robert Bell, a magistrate's son, was born in Cork on 16 January 1800. Educated at Trinity, he was instrumental in establishing the Dublin Historical Society. He was one of the founders of the *Dublin Inquisitor* and the author of such dramatic pieces as *Double Disguises and Comic Lectures*. He also published a pamphlet on Catholic Emancipation.

After emigrating to London in 1828, Bell was appointed editor of the *Atlas*, a large circulation weekly journal. In 1829, he was indicted for libel but defended himself brilliantly, and distinguished himself by refusing to disclose his sources of information. Although he was found guilty, the jury recommended mercy and it would appear that Bell escaped any penalty.

He wrote numerous books including a *History of Russia*, and *Life of Canning*, and contributed to *Lives of the British Admirals* and a *History of England*. Bell became editor of the *Monthly Chronicle* and of *The Story-teller*. His work included three five-act comedies and two three-volume novels, but he is best remembered for his 24 volume *Lives of the English Poets*.

Bell continued writing into old age and became interested in spiritualism, contributing articles on that subject to *Cornhill Magazine*. An active member of the Literary Fund, he was very helpful to aspiring and struggling authors.

The much respected Robert Bell died on 12 April 1867, and was buried in Kensal Green Cemetery near his friend, W.M. Thackeray.

1867

SIR HENRY BROWNE HAYES

On 22 July 1797, Sir Henry Browne Hayes abducted Mary Pike, a Quaker and wealthy heiress, from the home of Penrose Cooper at Woodhill, Tivoli. He tried to persuade her to marry him. When she refused, he conducted some form of illegal marriage ceremony. Eventually Browne Hayes saw the futility of his actions and released Mary Pike. A reward of £1,000 was offered for Browne Hayes' arrest.

The authorities were loath to execute the warrant and while Henry Browne Hayes lived openly in Cork for three years, contemptuous of the law, and basking in the admiration of the citizens, Mary Pike was forced to seek refuge in London. Eventually Browne Hayes volunteered to stand trial, confident that no Cork jury would convict. However, when John Philpott Curran, the most respected lawyer of his time, was appointed to prosecute the case, Browne Hayes became anxious, as a guilty verdict carried the death penalty.

There was a huge attendance of the general public at the trial. When a member of the public greeted Philpott Curran with the encouraging words, 'May you win the day!', Curran replied, 'if I do, you will lose your knight'. Browne Hayes was convicted. The death penalty was commuted and he was transported to Australia. Mary Pike never recovered from the ordeal and spent the rest of her life in a convalescent home.

The trial of Sir Henry Browne Hayes for the abduction of Mary Pike commenced in Cork on 13 April 1801.

1801

14 April

MOZART'S MASS

In 1853, a severe storm did considerable damage to St Vincent's Church – then in the course of construction – sweeping away the unfinished roof. As a consequence the Vincentian Order found themselves £200.00 short the cost of the great stained glass window.

In April 1861, the London Grand Opera Company had a season in the Theatre Royal, George's Street, and it was arranged that the company would give a fundraising performance for the benefit of the church. The London Grand Opera Company agreed to join with the church choir in a performance of Mozart's *Twelfth Mass*.

Mr Elliott Galer, a principal in the opera company, assured the public that the orchestra and chorus, in addition to the leading members of the cast, would participate in the performance. The conductor, Mr W.M. Lutz, organist of St George's Cathedral, London, presided.

The charity performance of Mozart's *Twelfth Mass* was given on 14 April 1861.

1861

15 April

DANIEL MACLISE

Alexander MacLish, a British soldier serving in Ireland, married a Bandon girl, Rebecca Buchanan. He resigned from the army and the couple lived in Sheares Street, where MacLish worked as a cobbler.

A son, Daniel, was born in January 1806, and was baptised in the Presbyterian Church in Princes Street. From an early age he demonstrated a talent for drawing and sketching, studying the famous Canova casts then in the Royal Cork Institution. With the help of John Bolster he executed a famous sketch of Sir Walter Scott, 500 lithographed copies of which were sold. Maclise, the surname by which he was then known, set up a studio in Patrick Street. He was encouraged by Richard Sainthill who introduced him to Crofton Croker who, in turn, commissioned him to illustrate the second edition of *Fairy Legends and Traditions of the South of Ireland*.

In 1827, he went to study in the Royal Academy Schools in London and within a year was contributing character studies to *Fraser's Magazine*. He returned to Ireland to receive a gold medal from the Society of Arts and at a party in Blarney found inspiration for his 'Snap Apple Night or All Hallow's Eve in Ireland'.

Maclise is best remembered for his Norman Conquest series, particularly 'The Marriage of Eva to Strongbow', and the two murals in the House of Lords for which he received £10,000. The last painting completed by him was 'The Earls of Desmond and Ormond'.

Daniel Maclise died at his home, Cheyne Walk, Chelsea, on 15 April 1870.

1870

EDWARD V.H. KENEALY

Edward Vaughan Hyde Kenealy was born in either the Coal Quay or Sheares Street, Cork, on 25 July 1819. He was educated at Trinity College where he took an MA. He was called to the Irish Bar in 1840 and the English Bar in 1847, becoming a Queen's Counsel in 1868. He defended the Fenians, Bourke and Casey, but retired from the case after the Clerkenwell explosion.

Kenealy was a prolific writer, producing numerous works both religious and secular. His poems, published in three volumes, included translations from Latin, Greek, German, Italian, Portuguese, Irish, Persian, Arabic, Hindustani and Bengali. His work included a verse translation of Fr Mat Horgan's *Cahir Conri*.

Perhaps his greatest claim to fame was the manner in which he represented the 'Tichbourne Claimant', in a celebrated English court case that extended from 23 April 1873 to 28 February 1874. It concerned a claim on the estate of Lord Tichbourne. Kenealy, convinced of the probity of his client, conducted the case with extraordinary vigour. The jury held against his client and severely censured Kenealy's conduct. He was subsequently disbarred.

He was the publisher and editor of a successful newspaper and was elected to Parliament. However, he was temperamentally unsuited to politics and lost his seat. He befriended his fellow Corkman, William Maginn, who died in Kenealy's home.

William Vaughan Hyde Kenealy died on 16 April 1880.

1880

17 April

TOMÁS MACCURTAIN

Tomás MacCurtain, Brigade Commandant of the 1st Battalion of the IRA, was elected Lord Mayor of Cork on 30 January 1920. An order for his arrest was transmitted from Dublin to Major General Strickland, Commanding Officer, British Forces, Cork.

Between 1.00 and 1.15 am on 20 March 1920, a body of men with blackened faces roused the house. Two of them ran upstairs and shot the Lord Mayor. At the subsequent inquest the jury brought in the following verdict:

We find that the late Alderman Tomás MacCurtain, Lord Mayor of Cork, died from shock and haemorrhage, caused by the bullet wounds, and that he was murdered under circumstances of the most callous brutality, and that the murder was organised and carried out by the Royal Irish Constabulary, officially directed by the British Government, and we return a verdict of wilful murder against David Lloyd George, Prime Minister of England; Lord French, Lord Lieutenant of Ireland; Ian MacPherson, late Chief Secretary of Ireland; Acting Inspector-General Smith of the Royal Irish Constabulary; Divisional Inspector Clayton of the Royal Irish Constabulary; District Inspector Swanzy, and some unknown members of the Royal Irish Constabulary. We strongly condemn the system at present in vogue of carrying out raids at unseasonable hours. We tender to Mrs MacCurtain and family our sincerest sympathy in their terrible bereavement; this sympathy we extend to the citizens of Cork in the loss they have sustained by the death of one so eminently capable of directing their civic administration.

The inquest into the murder of Tomás MacCurtain concluded on 17 April 1920.

1920

PUBLIC HANGING

Francis H. Tuckey records the following incident in his book *The County and City of Cork Remembrancer* for the year 1767.

Jeremiah Twomey was executed at Gallows Green for robbing the dwelling house of Johanna Norton, at Crosses Green. Her husband was so ill-treated the night of the robbery that he died some time after. Twomey was convicted of the robbery alone. The general opinion was that he died innocent, in consequence of which the mob brought him from the gallows, in his coffin to the prosecutor's door, where they bled him, took the rope off his neck, threw it into the window, besmeared the door and window shuts with his blood, whilst showers of stones were pelted at the windows from every quarter; during this time Mrs Norton resolutely defended her house, threw the rope into the south river, and fired several shots at the mob, no person was, however, hurt; a party of soldiers soon came to her assistance, some of whom were left as a guard all night at the house. On the following day, as the executioner was passing through the Main Street, he was attacked by the populace, who followed him a mile out of town with sticks and stones by which he was desperately wounded; he was brought on a car by the sheriffs to the South Infirmary. What more particularly exasperated the mob against him was his having stripped Twomey's shoes off while the body was hanging, claiming them as a perquisite of his reputable profession.

This incident took place on 18 April 1767.

1767

19 April

A PREMATURE BURIAL

Up to quite recent times it was customary to inter corpses in shallow graves. This practice, while most unhygienic, had, on occasions, unexpected and fortunate consequences. One instance was the extraordinary occurrence recorded by Francis Tuckey in his *Remembrancer*.

One Francis Taylor was buried in St Peter's Churchyard, and the next morning was found sitting up in the grave, one of his shoulders much mangled, one of his hands full of clay, and blood running from his eyes, a melancholy instance of the fatal consequences of a too precipitate interment.

This event occurred on 19 April 1753.

1753

WILLIAM BURGES

William Burges, born on 2 December 1827, was the son of a civil engineer. He studied at University College, London and King's College, London, before deciding to become an architect.

In the nineteenth century there was a great interest in the study of medieval architecture and Burges applied himself to this subject with the greatest enthusiasm. He was influenced by Pugin, and considered the Gothic style, particularly early French, to be 'that noblest and truest of styles'.

Burges' first major commission was Lille Cathedral. Subsequently, he restored Cardiff Castle for Lord Bute and Castle Coch for himself. He won the commission for Brisbane Cathedral and executed two superb churches in Yorkshire for Lord Ripon. He was also interested in furniture design and insisted on designing all the decorative features of his buildings.

Described as 'the Lutyens of his generation', Burges prepared his designs for St Finn Barr's Cathedral in 1862, 'the most important ecclesiastical building which he ever carried out'. The cost was to have been £15,000 but Burges admitted that the design he submitted would cost at least double that figure. In fact the completed building cost £100,000.

William Burges died at his home, Melbury Road, London, on 20 April 1881.

1881

21 April

CONRADH NA GAEILGE

Bhí slua mór i láthair i seomraí an Cork Young Men's Society ar an 22ú lá d' Aibreán, 1894. Bhí idir cléir is tuath ann, baill don Bhárdas agus gnáth daoine na cathrach. Toghadh Augustus Roche, Maor na Cathrach, mar chathaoirleach ar an gcruinniú.

Fuarathas leithscéala ó mhórán daoine nach raibh i láthair, 'na measc an tOllamh Eoghan Ó Gromhnaigh. Bhí telegram ón Teachta Westminister, William O'Brien, ag moladh na hoibre a bhí idir láimhe. Dúirt sé go raibh eolas ar an Gaeilge chomh tábhachtach don intinn is a bhí lúthchleasa don cholainn.

Denny Lane a mhol an rún go gcuirfí craobh de Chonradh na Gaeilge ar bun i gCorcaigh. Bhí sé den bharúil gurb as ucht é bheith páirteach in eirí amach Éire Óg, breis is caoga bliain roimhe sin, gur tugadh an onóir sin dó. Bhí sé mar chuspóir ag Éire Óg spiorad na tíre a athbheochaint, fé mar a bhí sé de chuspóir ag Conradh na Gaeilge teanga na tíre a athbheochaint.

Luaigh sé sampla muintir na Breataine Bige, daoine a choimeád greim ar a dteanga féin d'ainneoin an brú a cuireadh orthu. Dúirt sé go raibh sé tábhachtach eolas a bheith ag daoine ar a dteanga féin cé go raibh sé riachtanach chomh maith eolas a bheith acu ar an mBéarla.

Foilsíodh an fógra, ag tabhairt eolais do mhuintir Chorcaí faoin gcruinniú seo, san Cork Examiner, an 21ú lá d'Aibreán, 1894.

1894

THE *AUD* IS SCUTTLED

Joseph Mary Plunkett made a secret visit to Germany in April 1915, and made an agreement with the German Government for the supply of a cargo of arms to Ireland in the spring of 1916. The Military Committee of the Irish Republican Brotherhood fixed the date of the uprising for Easter Sunday.

John Devoy, in America, instructed the Germans to land the arms in Limerick between Good Friday and Easter Sunday, presumably to allow time for the distribution of the weapons.

The vessel selected by the Germans to ship the guns – 20,000 rifles and some machine guns captured from the Russians at Tannenberg – was of 1,228 gross tons. It was built in Hull in 1911 and originally named the *Castro*. Captured by the Germans on the outbreak of war it was renamed the *Libau*, but for the voyage to Ireland the superstructure was reshaped for it to resemble a Norwegian tramp steamer, and the name changed to the *Aud*.

The captain was Lieutenant Carl Spindler who succeeded in evading the British blockade and brought the *Aud* through the North Sea to anchor in Tralee Bay on 20 April. Twenty-two hours later the British located the ship and commanded Captain Spindler to proceed to Cork Harbour.

On Saturday morning, 22 April 1916, Captain Carl Spindler scuttled the *Aud* at the entrance to Cork Harbour.

1916

HIBERNIAN CHRONICLE

Henry Sheares, father of the brothers executed for their participation in the 1798 Rising, was a descendent of Humphrey Sheares, an apothecary, who made profitable investments in land in the South Liberties. The family was wealthy and Henry Sheares was, in turn, banker, politician and newspaper proprietor.

He was a partner in the banking house of Rogers, Travers and Sheares, which later became known as Sheares' Bank, with premises at 29 Sheares Street. When the bank finally closed in 1793 the building became a maternity hospital.

Henry Sheares represented Clonakilty in the Irish Parliament from 1761 to 1767. He was involved in, indeed helped establish, many philanthropic organisations, one of which was the Relief of Small Debts Society.

In 1789, Henry Sheares launched a newspaper, the *Hibernian Chronicle*, which initially consisted of four pages of quarto size but later became an eight page folio production. It was printed by William Flynn at the 'Sign of the Shakespeare', near the Exchange. It was very much a paper of its time, rarely reporting local news, and Establishment in its views. It survived until 22 April 1802 when it became the *Cork Mercantile Chronicle*, an organ of Catholic opinion.

The first edition of the *Hibernian Chronicle* was published on 23 April 1769.

1769

24 April

ADVICE TO EMIGRANTS

His Lordship, John Sweeney, Catholic Bishop of St John's, New Brunswick, was deeply concerned at the plight of Irish emigrants to Canada during the 1860s. He noted their propensity to congregate in the urban areas and ignore the opportunities that obtained in the rural districts.

He contrasted the condition of those emigrants who had settled on the land, 'large and flourishing settlements consisting of farmers who have arrived at comfort ... (who) have succeeded in obtaining for themselves and their children respectable independence', to those who had remained in the cities, 'who do all the hard work in our saw mills, in our factories, in loading and unloading ships, in building railroads ... and who are no better off at the end of their period than they were at commencing ... a week's sickness leaves them often without the means of paying the rent of their poor tenements, and consequently exposed to be turned out on the highway to become with their children inmates of the Alms House.'

Bishop Sweeney informed would-be emigrants of the existence of the Emigrant Aid Association. This organisaation would reserve suitable tracts of fertile land adjacent to settlements, satisfy all the legal requirements, and meet the emigrants on disembarkation.

Bishop John Sweeney conveyed his advice to emigrants in a letter published in the *Cork Examiner* of 24 April 1861.

1861

RADIO CORK 6CK

In 1927, the old Female Gaol at Sunday's Well was chosen as the location of Cork's new radio station. Reconstruction work was carried out under the direction of the architect Mr G.J. Osborne, and Mr D.W. O'Callaghan of the Board of Works. The gaol was transformed into a magnificent studio, and fitted with the most modern equipment available.

At the inauguration ceremony the Station Director, Mr Seán Neeson, introduced the Minister for Posts and Telegraphs, Mr J.J. Walsh TD. The Minister said that since the Dublin Station had opened on 1 January 1926, the official policy had been to concentrate as much as possible on the cultivation and preservation of traditional Irish culture. In opening the Cork station he hoped that he was tapping a new vein of talent, Cork people having already achieved much in the fields of literature and music.

He did not want the Irish stations to be mere echoes of foreign broadcasting services. Irish culture had much to offer the peoples of other countries, and programmes emanating from Dublin had already been highly praised abroad.

The inaugural programme began at 8 pm, the content being entirely local. Well-known artists and personalities contributed, including Dan Hobbs, pipers Moynihan and Cronin, the choirs of the Christian Brothers, Blarney Street, and St Vincent's Convent. The programme also featured the Shandon Bells and Staff Gebruers on the carillon of Cobh Cathedral.

Cork Radio, using the call sign, 6CK, went on the air on the evening of 25 April 1927.

1927

26 April

NANO NAGLE

In his book, *Nano Nagle and the Presentation Sisters*, Fr T.J. Walsh tries to visualise the scene when Nano Nagle opened her first school. It was situated on the south-western corner of the playground attached to the Presentation Brothers' School on Douglas Street and was little more than a mud cabin. 'There was little difficulty in collecting children in Cove Lane and its vicinity – Pender's Alley, Willow Lane, Gould's Lane, Donovan's Lane and Maypole Lane. When they were counted they numbered 30 girls. The first prayer was recited and the great adventure was on.'

The adventure was, of course, the founding of the Presentation Order and the attempt to educate poor illiterate females, not only in Cork, but throughout the world. 'Nine months later 200 children were packed into the two or more cabin schools'. Soon a school was opened in the north side of the city; later the order spread to many parts of the globe.

Nano Nagle worked for 30 years educating the poor illiterate girls of Cork. On her death the *Hibernian Chronicle* reported: 'She died this day about noon and truly indescribable is the extreme of universal lamentation for the departure of a lady possessed of all that merit which for many years rendered her the object of unexampled admiration and acquired for her the most unlimited esteem of all ranks of people.'

Nano Nagle died on 26 April 1784.

1784

NORTH LUDLOW BEAMISH

North Ludlow Beamish, a member of the Cork brewing family, was born in Beaumont House on 31 December 1797. In 1816 he obtained a commission in the 4th Royal Irish Dragoons, and in 1823 he purchased his own troop.

Having become proficient in German, he published *Instructions for the Field Service in Cavalry*, a translation of a manual by Count F.A. von Bismark. In 1827, while in Hanover, he published another translation of a work by von Bismark, *Lectures in Cavalry*. Some of Beamish's suggestions were adopted by the British Cavalry.

Beamish was commissioned by the officers of the King's German Legion to write the history of the corps. His book so pleased the officers that they presented him with a silver vase and stand weighing nearly 900 ounces and valued at 1,000 guineas. He was made a Knight of the Royal Hanoverian Guelphic Order and became a member of The Royal Danish Society of Northern Antiquities.

In 1841 he published a summary of *Antiquitates Americana with Notes on the Early Settlement of the Irish in the Western Hemisphere*. In 1855 he wrote yet another work on cavalry, *The Uses and Application of Cavalry at War*.

North Ludlow Beamish died at his residence, Annmount, Glounthaune on 27 April 1872.

1872

UNUSUAL LAW CASE

In 1865, a 'numerously attended meeting' was held in the Chamber of Commerce Rooms, in order to devise ways and means of raising the sum of £500 to enable the Dominican Order to redeem the rent on Pope's Quay Church.

Mr James Simms, a butter merchant, had bequeathed £500 to the Dominican Order, Cork, for that purpose and a similar amount to two priests, the latter bequest being intended for the education of students for the Order. His son contested the validity of the will, and the Court of Chancery upheld his claim on the grounds that the bequest was for the benefit of a body, i.e. the Dominican Order, that did not exist under law!

The decision was based on the Catholic Relief Act of 1829, which provided, among other things, for 'the gradual suppression and final prohibition within the United Kingdom of Jesuits and other religious orders, communities and societies of the Church of Rome'.

The entire Catholic community was enraged by the judgement and by the fact that the provision still remained in force. Daniel O'Connell had promised that 'he would ride a troop of horse three times through it', and Pitt had given assurances 'that the section of the bill for the eventual suppression of all monastic institutions in Great Britain and Ireland should remain a dead letter on the Statute Book'.

The public meeting held on 28 April 1865, agreed to solicit subscriptions to compensate the Dominican Order. The people of Cork contributed £380 of the £450 raised nationally.

1865

THE SKIDDY CHARITY

In 1630, a meeting of Cork Corporation noted that, on 20 March 1584, by his last will and testament, Stephen Scudamore, alias Skiddy, late citizen and Vintner of London,

did demise that the Master, Wardens, freemen, and Commonaltie of the mysterie of Vintners of London, and their successors, should pay yearly for ever, after the death of Hellen, his wife, of the rents and profits of certain lands mentioned in said will the sum of 24 pounds ster., at the Common Hall of said Company, to the Mayor of Cork for the time being, or his sufficient deputy, at the Feast of the Annunciation of B.V.M., and at St Michael, to be distributed amongst ten of the poorest honestest people of said City, sole and aged 40 years at least.

A hostel having been provided for the destitute inhabitants of the city, the practice had arisen of dividing the Skiddy bequest equally among the inmates. However, it was pointed out at the meeting that successive Mayors had admitted a great many more people than the number stipulated in Skiddy's will. This, in effect, reduced the value of the allowance to which the recipients were entitled.

The Mayor and Members of the Corporation decided, on 29 April 1630, to reduce the number already in residence in the hospital and, for the future, to abide strictly by the terms of Stephen Skiddy's will.

1630

A MAYOR RESIGNS

A banquet was held in the Victoria Hotel on the evening of 27 April 1869, on the occasion of the departure of Messrs Warren and Costelloe to America. The Mayor, Mr Daniel O'Sullivan, presided. It was an emotional occasion, with patriotic speeches and songs, viz; 'The Harp that Once through Tara's Halls' and 'Fontenoy' being rendered.

During the course of his speech the Mayor lauded the sacrifice of the Fenians. He stated that when 'that noble Irishman, O'Farrell, fired at the prince (Alfred) in Australia, he was imbued with as noble and patriotic feelings as Larkin, Allen and O'Brien'. He believed that O'Farrell would be as highly thought of as any of the men who had given their lives for Ireland.

The Mayor's remarks caused a storm of controversy. He protested that, while not condoning the act, he could sympathise with the perpetrator's motives.

In London, Prime Minister Gladstone introduced a bill in the House of Commons, the 'O'Sullivan Disability Bill', seeking to have the Mayor removed from office. However, the Mayor resigned and the Bill was withdrawn.

Cork Corporation discussed the consequences of Mayor O'Sullivan's comments on the attempted assassination of Prince Alfred by O'Farrell on 30 April 1869.

1869

'MOTHER' JONES

Mary Harris was born on the north side of Cork in 1837, the daughter of Richard Harris and Ellen Cotter. The family emigrated to America in 1848 where Mary qualified as a teacher. She took up a teaching post in Munroe, Michigan.

Mary moved to Memphis, Tennessee, and married George Jones in 1861. He was a member of the Iron Workers Union, a factor which was to have a profound influence on her later life. Her husband and family perished in an epidemic of yellow fever in 1867, and her home was destroyed in the Great Chicago Fire of October 1871. She found refuge in the premises of the 'Knights of Labour' and her direct involvement in the cause of Labour dates from this time. She was active in most labour disputes throughout America, including the railway strikes of 1877 and 1886. In 1900, she was appointed organiser for the United Mine Workers' Union and travelled all over the country organising the workers.

'Mother' Jones, as she was known by then, was a founder member of the 'Wobblies', Industrial Workers of the World. She organised the women and argued that, ultimately, all strikes were won by the wives of the striking workers. At great personal risk, she investigated the employment of child workers in the southern states and organised a march to Washington in protest at their exploitation. The great American jurist, Clarence Darrow, said of her, 'she is a born cruasader ... Mother Jones is one of the most forceful and colourful figures of the American Labour Movement'. She died on 30 November 1930, and over 5,000 people turned out for her funeral at the Miners' Cemetery, Mount Olive, Illinois.

Mary 'Mother' Jones was born, on 1 May 1837.

1837

2 May

ST MARY'S PRIORY

At 1.00 pm the tolling of the bell announced the approach of the procession from the sacristy of St Mary's Church. In the background, higher up on the hill, the banners of the building trades, displaying religious motifs, imparted a picturesque effect to the scene. The *Cork Examiner* of the following day described the ceremony:

The foundations were traced out in lines of masonry of great extent. After the litany of the Saints was chanted, his Lordship sprinkled the first stone and foundation with holy water. A silver trowel, used at the foundation of the Metropolitan Church in Dublin, was then presented to his Lordship by the architect, William Atkins, esq., on a massive silver salver; when his Lordship, taking the trowel, signed the mark of the cross on the corners of the stone and laid the mortar. The stone was then let down into its berth, the foundations were again sprinkled with holy water, and the ceremony was concluded. In a hollow of the stone had been placed a bottle containing a parchment scroll and two beautiful medallions – one of the coronation of Queen Victoria; the other an exquisite specimen of art, of the installation of the reigning Pontiff, presented by Dr Delaney for the occasion. These two medals, as it were, typified the spiritual allegiance paid by the founders to the head of the Catholic Church and the allegiance due and paid to the temporal Sovereign.

The occasion was the laying of the foundation stone of the Priory of St Mary's, Pope's Quay, on 2 May, of the Famine year, 1848.

1848

3 May

FACTION FIGHT

On Thursday, 3 May 1879, as was their custom, the Fair Lane Fife and Drum Band and Blackpool Band paraded through the city streets. In the evening, as they made their way homewards, the bands met in Clarence Street.

One of the Fair Lane boys threw a stone and broke the skin of the big drum of Blackpool. Immediately a free-for-all began, during which the big drum was captured by Fair Lane and ripped into shreds. Some of the Blackpool musical instruments were also damaged. The police arrived and dispersed the factions.

However, on Saturday, another group from Fair Lane gathered on St Mary's Road and proceeded to shell showers of stones down on the houses in Blackpool, breaking windows and damaging roofs.

The following day the bands again paraded through the city and at 6.00 in the evening the Fair Lane contingent, men and women, collected near the North Cathedral. They were faced by 'only fourteen Blackpoolers armed with thick sticks (and other weapons with special skull-cracking properties)', as the *Cork Examiner* described the scene. However, 'the gallant fourteen, facing fearsome odds, were soon joined by the whole strength of the Blackpool party'.

The battle raged for hours. Police reinforcements arrived but were met with abuse and attacks from both factions. The injured were taken to the North Infirmary Hospital and one participant was so severely injured that his life was in danger.

As a consequence of the fight that started on 3 May 1879, the Mayor threatened to prohibit bands from marching through the city streets.

1879

CUSACK'S HISTORY

M.F. Cusack ('The Nun of Kenmare') offered her forthcoming book, *The History of Cork*, for sale when she forwarded the following letter to the *Cork Examiner*.

Sir

As the City and County of Cork are famous for their painters, poets and writers, I hope I may find as generous a support from them for my *History of the City and County of Cork* as I have had from the people of Kerry for theirs. Your readers have, I presume, seen the remarks made in 'Notes and Queries', a review which is in the hands of every literary man in Great Britain and Ireland, on the list of subscribers to the *History of Kerry*, and the credit that such a list reflects on the country. I hope a similar remark will be made on the list of subscribers to the *History of Cork. Agents* have already been appointed in different parts of the county, and our general agent and manager is at present in Cork, at Mrs Walsh's, 29 King Street. A complete list of subscribers, with the number of copies subscribed for each person, will be published at the end of the volume, and 25 blank pages will be left at the end for a Family Record, so that each person can enter his own pedigree, and such family circumstances as he may wish to hand down to posterity. This original and valuable arrangement has been much recommended.

This volume will necessarily be very much larger than the *History of Kerry*, and I have at present several persons engaged in Dublin, at considerable expense, in copying important and original documents in the Royal Irish Academy and other places. As all this will require an immediate outlay, and as I am anxious to get some good engravings in hand, I hope those gentlemen who can do so, will kindly pay their subscriptions in advance, and will order, if possible two copies. I would also request that subscribers will send in their names at once, as the work cannot be sent to press until the subscription list is closed, and the edition will be strictly limited to the number of copies subscribed for.

Yours respectfully,
The Author of the *Illustrated History of Ireland*.

The letter was printed in the *Cork Examiner* on 4 May 1871.

1871

PERKIN WARBECK

In the last decade of the fifteenth century, Perkin Warbeck laid claim to the crown of Henry VI of England. At various times he enjoyed the support of such personages as the Earls of Desmomd and Kildare, King Charles VIII of France, the Duchess of Burgundy, Archduke Philip, and Maximilian, king of the Romans. One of his most faithful supporters was Mayor John Walters (or Waters) of Cork.

Perkin Warbeck visited Cork no fewer than five times. On the second occasion, in July 1495, supported by the Earls of Desmond and Lincoln, he attacked Waterford but was defeated in a naval encounter. He returned to Cork and, according to Smith, 'he was received by Waters (Walters), then Mayor, who privately kept him till the arrival of the Citizens of Waterford. Then he conveyed him out of the city by night in a small bark, and he proceeded to Kinsale, from whence he stole in a Spanish bark'.

He was back in Cork for a fourth visit in 1496, but stayed only a short time before setting out for Scotland where he received the support of King James. He attacked the north of England but, a truce having been negotiated, Warbeck set out with a fleet of four small vessels, his wife and a party of 120 supporters. He arrived at Cork, for the fifth and final time, in 1497. On his return to England, having made an abortive attack on the city of Exeter, he surrendered and was eventually executed at Tyburn.

Perkin Warbeck, pretender to the English Crown, arrived in Cork for the first time on 5 May 1492.

1492

WHEAT FOR CORK

There were periods during the eighteenth century when, because of bad harvests wheat and other cereals were in short supply. Scarcity of food supplies was hardest on the poor, who were unable to pay the increased prices demanded.

In 1766, despite an embargo on the export of cereals, there was a serious shortage of wheat, threatening the poor with hunger. The Committee of Merchants in Cork met to consider what schemes might be implemented to relieve the situation. John Hely Hutchinson, Member of Parliament for Cork city, prevailed on the Lord Lieutenant to have a cargo of wheat shipped from Bristol to Cork and sold at a low price to the poor, any loss to be borne by the government.

Cork Corporation suggested that wheat aboard two vessels then in port be purchased for immediate distribution. The Corporation also suggested that two or possibly three more cargoes be purchased, the grain to be stored in city granaries as a stockpile against future shortages.

On 6 May 1766, John Hely Hutchinson prevailed upon the Lord Lieutenant to provide finance for the alleviation of hunger in Cork.

1766

SIR HUGH LANE

Hugh Percy Lane was born on 9 November, 1875, at Ballybrack House, in County Cork. He suffered ill health as a boy and consequently his education was severely curtailed. However, he acquired some knowledge of art while living in Jersey.

Through the influence of his aunt, Lady Gregory, he was employed as assistant in an art gallery and soon displayed the acumen that was to make him one of the great art experts of his time. He recognised works by Old Masters that other dealers had failed to identify. He later sold them at considerable profit.

On visits to Lady Gregory he met people like Yeats, Douglas Hyde and Edward Martin. After attending an exhibition of the works of J.B. Yeats and Nathaniel Hone, he became obsessed with the idea of acquiring and presenting to Ireland a collection of great paintings. His eventual contribution was staggering, including works by Orpen, Goya, El Greco, Veronese, Bordone, Romney, Turner, Hogarth, Constable, Stubbs, Lorrain, Chardin, Poussin, Lancet, Greuze, Rembrandt, Van Dyck, Bol, and many others.

Sir Hugh Lane is remembered chiefly, perhaps, for the controversy over a collection of French Impressionists bequeathed to Ireland but claimed by England because of a legal defect in his will. However, his contribution to Irish cultural life was immense and, in all probability, would have been even more generous had he not been one of the passengers who drowned when the liner *Lusitania* was torpedoed by a German submarine on 7 May 1915.

1915

CORK RECORDS

In 1721, Cork Corporation was experiencing some difficulty in gaining access to the various 'books, deeds, leases, etc.' held for safe-keeping in a locked chest. It appears that several individuals refused to hand over the keys of the chest. On 1 February 1721, a bye-law was enacted stipulating that all such records be kept in the possession of the Mayor, Sherrifs and Com. Speaker for the time being.

The Corporation summoned the people who were in possession of the keys to appear before them. The request was ignored, and the Corporation proceeded to take a firmer stand.

In order to prevent any objections to the validity of such a bye-law, it was decided to refer the matter to the Court of d'Oyer Hundred and have the terms of the bye-law of 1 February 1721, enacted into law. The matter was considered at the Court of d'Oyer Hundred and the jurisdiction of the Corporation over the said deed, etc., was enshrined in law. However, the people in possession of the keys refused to comply with the Corporation's demands.

At a further meeting, held on 8 May 1721, the Corporation directed that the chest be opened, and the contents be handed over into the possession of the Mayor, Sheriffs, and Com. Speaker, for the time being.

THOMAS KENT

The Kent family of Bawnard, near Castlelyons, had taken a prominent part in the land war of the 1880s. Three of the brothers were interned in Cork Jail. Another brother, Tom, on his return shortly afterwards from America, was also convicted of conspiring to evade payment of rent.

Tom Kent had been active in the Irish Volunteers from their inception. In January 1916, along with Terence MacSwiney, he was arrested and charged under the Defence of the Realm Act. Acquitted, he was re-arrested, found guilty of possession of arms and imprisoned for two months.

The Kents did not learn of the outbreak of the 1916 Rising until the Tuesday of Easter week. The brothers took the precaution of leaving home, but returned on the evening of 1 May. In the early hours of the following morning members of the Royal Irish Constabulary surrounded the house. In the ensuing gun-battle, during which military reinforcements were brought up, a member of the RIC was killed. David Kent was seriously wounded. Richard was fatally injured while trying to escape.

On 4 May, Thomas and William Kent were tried by court marshal for 'wilful murder'. William was acquitted, but Thomas was sentenced to death. He requested that no Irish soldier be chosen as a member of the firing squad, a plea that resulted in his firing party being chosen from the Scottish Borderers.

Thomas Kent was shot in Cork Detention Barrack on 9 May 1916.

1916

10 May

THE 'STAPLE' OF CORK

In 1376, the inhabitants of Cork were in great danger from their Irish enemies. The walls of the city have been described as being 'in great dilapidation, being by the hostile incursions of the Irish enemy, almost totally destroyed'. Trade was in disarray; merchants feared coming to Cork to sell their goods.

The English King allowed the citizens a remission, for a period of three years, of the annual sum of 36 marks. A few years previously an ordinance had been made, proclaiming that customs duty on wool could only be paid in the 'staple' or market cities of Cork, Dublin, Drogheda and Waterford.

Because of the state of unrest in the country the merchants of Galway petitioned that the staple of wool and other merchandise be held in that city, 'they being unable to come to Cork on account of the danger and difficulty of the navigation'.

It was ordered, on 10 May 1376, that the wool staple be held in Galway.

1376

REBEL CORK

Queen Elizabeth I of England died on 24 March 1603. The accession of James I to the throne revived demands for freedom of religion for Catholics. Mass was celebrated openly, cathedrals were re-dedicated for Catholic worship and in Cork, Smith has stated, the people 'had a person named a legate from the Pope who went about in procession with a cross and forced the people to reverence it. They buried the dead with Catholic ceremonies, and numbers took the sacrament to defend their religion with their lives and fortunes'.

The Mayor, Thomas Sarsfield, refused to proclaim James as king, and ignored an emissary, named Morgan, who arrived on 12 April with a copy of the king's proclamation. The inhabitants were in open rebellion. On Good Friday the Mayor and aldermen, priests and friars, walked in procession, singing hymns, from the South Gate to the North Gate. Shots were fired at the Protestant Bishop's palace.

The instigators of the rebellion threatened to resist the new king by force of arms if religious freedom was not granted. The rebels proposed to arm everyone between the ages of twelve and 24. They shelled Shandon Castle which was occupied by loyalists.

A ceasefire was agreed pending the arrival of Lord Deputy Mountjoy but many citizens threatened to continue to resist. However, wiser counsel prevailed and Mountjoy entered the city on 11 May 1603, effectively ending the rebellion which earned for Cork its title 'Rebel City'.

1603

WILLIAM K. SULLIVAN

William Kirby Sullivan was born in about 1822. His father, J.B. Sullivan, was an unsuccessful entrepreneur with interests in paper making, linen weaving, etc. Sullivan was educated by the Christian Brothers in Cork and showed an aptitude for chemistry.

Having studied chemistry under Professor Liebig in Giessen, Germany, he returned to Ireland and secured a position in the Museum of Irish Industry, later to be known as the Royal College of Science. There he worked with Sir Robert Kane, lecturing in Theoretical and Practical Chemistry. He joined the academic staff at Newman's Catholic University and edited the academic publication *Atlantis*.

In addition to his scientific accomplishments Sullivan was a renowned linguist, being familiar with many European Languages in addition to Irish and English, and translated works from German, French and Swedish. He contributed to *Two Centuries of Irish History* and *The Ireland of the Penal Days*. His outstanding work of scholarship was undoubtedly *Introduction to O'Curry's Lectures on the Manners and Customs of the Ancient Irish*, published in three volumes in 1873.

On the retirement of Sir Robert Kane, Sullivan was appointed President of Queen's College, Cork (now University College). He undertook the extension of the College Library and Museum, and was instrumental in having William Crawford sponsor the construction and equipment of the observatory. He persuaded the authorities to admit medical students to the Union Hospital in order to further their training.

William Kirby Sullivan, President of the Cork Literary and Scientific Society, died on 12 May 1890.

1890

BATTLE OF STARLINGS

A pamphlet published in London gives a contemporary account of one of the most bizarre incidents in Cork history. During May 1622, the citizens noticed the growing numbers of starlings gathering in the city. The birds appeared to be dividing into two flocks, one remaining to the east, the other to the west of the city, 'during which times their noise and tunes were strange on both sides to the great admiration of the inhabitants'.

From time to time, citizens noticed that a flight of some twenty or 30 birds would pass from one side to the other. Uttering strange sounds, they would hover over the other flock, which they seemed to be observing, before returning to their own side of the city. Then, at nine o'clock on a fine Saturday morning, the two flocks mounted into the air and encountered each other:

> ... upon this sudden and fierce encounter there fell down into the rivers multitudes of starlings, some with wings broken some with legs and necks broken, some with eyes picked out, some with their bills thrust into the breasts and sides of their adversaries, in so strange a manner that it were incredible, except it were confirmed by letters of credit and by eye witnesses with that assurance that is without all exception.

The battle continued for several days, the birds retiring each evening and returning the following morning to do battle again. Countless thousands of the birds were killed.

The Battle of the Starlings began in the skies over Cork on 13 May 1622.

1622

KUNO MEYER

Kuno Meyer, born in Hamburg, Germany in 1858, is one of the central figures in the Irish Revival and perhaps the greatest of the distinguished band of scholars who have devoted themselves to Celtic Studies.

While Professor of Celtic at the University of Berlin, he founded the School of Irish Learning in Dublin in 1903. He established the School's journal, *Ériú*, as well as other journals in Germany. His long list of publications includes *The Voyage of Bran, Stories and Songs from Irish Manuscripts, The Death Tales of the Ulster Heroes,* etc. In recognition of his commitment to Irish studies he was made a Freeman of Cork on 10 May 1912.

On 8 January 1915, however, during the First World War, Cork Corporation expunged the name of Kuno Meyer from the list of Freemen, on the pretext that he was inciting German-Americans to support Germany, and Irish-Americans to enlist in an Irish Regiment in the German Army. Some members of the Corporation voted against the resolution and several others abstained.

Kuno Meyer died in Leipzig in 1919. On 14 May 1920, the Corporation, with one member dissenting, decided to re-admit him to the list of Freemen.

1920

FIRE AT QUEEN'S

Between 5.30 am and 6.00 am, a warden in the County Gaol saw a fire raging in the adjoining Queen's College. He roused the College President, Sir Robert Kane, and the Vice-President, Doctor Ryall, who were in their living quarters adjacent to the conflagration.

The west wing of the College, a two-storeyed building about 120 feet long and 25 or 30 feet wide, was in flames. The Corporation fire-fighting apparatus arrived but was handicapped by the fact that no hydrant was in the vicinity. However, a hose was connected to a water main and efforts were concentrated on preventing the fire from spreading. At about 8.00 am, the fire brigade of the Royal Exchange Insurance Company arrived to add much-needed support. The military arrived and formed a bucket brigade from the river. The roof of the building fell in at shortly after eight o'clock.

Everything in the *Materia Medica* room, including the pharmacy equipment and the herborium, considered the finest in Great Britain and Ireland, was destroyed. The pathological room, which contained a collection of cinchona plants once owned by Napoleon, was gutted. Manuscripts, notes of experiments, gems, antique medals and shields were all consumed in the flames.

On the afternoon of the same day a private enquiry was held at the police office. Sir Robert Kane, Mr O'Connell, the Crown Prosecutor, and the three Magistrates, were of the unanimous opinion that the fire in the west wing of Queen's College had been started deliberately on the morning of 15 May 1862.

JOHN MILNER-BARRY

John Milner-Barry was born in 1768 at Kilgobbin. Having attended school in Bandon, he studied at Edinburgh University where he graduated in medicine in 1792. He returned to Cork and practised in the city until his death.

In 1800 he published *An Account of the Cow-pock, illustrated with cases and communications on the subject, addressed principally to parents, with a view to promote an extirpation of the Small-pox*. He contributed many papers on the subject; to the *London Medical and Physical Journal*; to *Harty's History of the Contagiousness of Fever Epidemics in Ireland in 1817-19*, and to *Transactions of the Irish College of Physicians*.

Impressed by the work of Jenner, Milner-Barry introduced vaccination into Ireland in 1800. A year later he published his *Report on the Infectious Diseases in Cork City*, which led to the foundation of the Cork Hospital House of Recovery on a site now known as Fever Hospital Hill. This initative led to the passing of two Acts of Parliament (43 & 54, George III), that provided the legislative support for the establishment of Fever Hospitals in Ireland.

Milner-Barry was an advocate of female education stating that he could see 'no reason why the education of women, particularly in literary attainments, should not be conducted in the same manner with that of the male sex'. He also called for legislation to compel habitual drunkards to reform.

John Milner-Barry died at his home inPatrick's Hill on 16 May 1822.

1822

MÍCHEÁL Ó LONGÁIN

Rugadh Mícheál Ó Longáin sa bhliain 1765 nó 1766. Ní fios i gceart cár rugadh é, cé acu i gCo. Luimní nó i dTobairín Maighir, i ngar do Charraig na bhFear. As Luimneach a mhuintir ach thréig siad a n-áit dúchais nuair a chaill an athair a phost.

Is dócha nach bhfuair Mícheál Ó Longáin aon oideachas foirmeálta, ach scoláire den chéad scoth ab ea é. Tá cáil air as ucht an athscríobh a dhein sé ar shean láimhscríbhiní Gaelacha, go háirithe ar son Sheáin Uí Mhurchú, Easpag cháiliúil Chorcaí. De bhárr na hoibre seo coimeádadh cnuasacht d'fhilíocht na 17ú agus 18ú aoiseanna slán don lá atá inniu ann. Tá breis is seachtó de na láimhscríbhiní seo in Ollscoil Mhagh Nuad, breis agus ochtó ins an Royal Irish Academy agus tá cnuasacht eile i gColáiste Fhear Muighe.

Nuair a bhí O Longáin ina fhear óg bhí sé mar bhall de na 'Whiteboys'. Sa bhliain 1797, fad is a bhí sé ag obair i gCorcaigh mar mhúinteoir, ghlac sé páirt i ngluaiseacht na nÉireannaigh Aontaithe. Scríobh sé an-chuid filíochta ag moladh na heagraíochta sin agus ag spreagadh mhuintir na h'Éireann. Bhí 150 baill cláraithe aige i gCarraig na bhFear taobh istigh d'achar gearr.

Nuair a theip ar Éirí Amach 1798 chuaigh sé ar a choimeád ar feadh tamaillín, ach sa deireadh d'fhill sé ar Charraig na bhFear mar a bhí sé 'na mháistir scoile. D'éag Mícheál O Longáin ar an 17ú lá Bealtaine, 1837.

1837

HONAN CHAPEL

The Irish University Act, 1908, decreed that no part of the finance made available for the new University College, Cork (formerly Queen's College) should be used 'for the provision or maintenance of any church, chapel or any other place of religious worship or observance'. Accordingly the funds required for building a University Chapel had to be provided from private sources. Fortunately the administrator of the Honan Bequest, Rev Sir John O'Connell, was in a position to provide the necessary finance.

The Honan Chapel was designed by James F. McMullen and built by John Sisk and Son. The idea was to create a building in the Hiberno-Romanesque style of the tenth, eleventh and twelfth centuries. It consists, like all Romanesque buildings, of nave and chancel, and approximates more closely to St Cronan's Church, Roscrea, than to any other ancient Irish church.

The Chapel is built of local limestone. A round tower stands at the north-east corner. The main doorway is richly ornamented with stone carvings and is surmounted with an image of St Finbarr, sculpted by Oliver Sheppard RHA.

Outstanding features of the interior are the mosaic floor and stained-glass windows. The mosaic depicts the sun and other heavenly bodies; a great beast lifts its head and the mighty river flowing from its mouth contains many strange creatures. Of the nineteen stained-glass windows eleven were designed and executed by Harry Clarke – the remainder were from the workshops of Sarah Purser. They are regarded as amongst the finest in the country.

The foundation stone of the Honan Chapel was laid on 18 May 1915.

1915

HUNGER IN CORK

No place in the United Kingdom of Great Britain and Ireland suffered more than Cork in the aftermath of the Napoleonic Wars, and no part of Cork suffered more than Blackpool. A newspaper of the time, *The Southern Reporter* stated the position: 'For a considerable period the greater part of the weavers and operatives of Blackpool have been thrown into the greatest state of destitution in consequence of the total absence of employment'.

Practically the entire industrial base of Cork had been committed to the war effort against Napoleon. The great slaughter houses; meat processing plants; cooperages and tanning yards; woollen, linen and cotton mills; sail and rope making sheds; all had helped victual and clothe the imperial army and navy, bringing great prosperity to Cork. But the defeat of Napoleon, followed by the reduction in size and eventual withdrawal of the British forces, threw Cork into deep recession. Unemployment was rampant, causing widespread poverty.

On Monday 15 May 1826, the weavers of Blackpool and other workers, with their wives and children, marched in the direction of the Mansion House to apprise the Mayor of their plight. They bore placards reading WE WANT EMPLOYMENT OURSELVES AND OUR CHILDREN ARE STARVING! The forces of law and order, ever fearful of the 'mob', confronted the starving marchers. A pitched battle ensued, the main guard from Tuckey Strret and a troop of cavalry combining with the sheriff's officers to inflict savage punishment on the people.

Four days later, on Friday 19 May 1826, the Mayor summoned a number of prominent citizens to a meeting in order to draw up schemes to alleviate the suffering of the destitute workers of Cork.

WATER SUPPLY

The Cork Improvements Act of 1852 empowered the Corporation to acquire the city water supply system, up until then owned by a private company. The Corporation, already owners of 25 shares in the company, purchased the remaining 75 shares for £13,875.

Regular extensions to the system were then made, including the provision of two new reservoirs and three pumping engines at a cost of £50,000. In 1858 a sum of £22,000 was expended to provide a supply of 2,000,000 gallons, the equivalent of 25 gallons per day, per head of population.

In 1876 it was decided to construct a filtering tunnel on land west of the pumping station in 'good, open gravel which forms the very best mechanical filter'. An expert's report, proposing the laying of a filter tunnel lined with red bricks parallel to the river banks, assured the members that a daily supply of 4,500,000 gallons of good and pure water, free from organic matter and without the aid of steam power, would be provided. The estimated cost was £4,000, but by 1880, over £8,000 had been expended, and the system was inefficient. Untreated water, as well as the water from the filtering tunnel, was getting into the turbines, and was being conveyed via the turbines to the consumer.

The Waterworks Committee met on 20 May 1880, to ascertain the exact cost of construction of the filtering tunnel, its degree of efficiency, and what remedial action was required.

RIVER CRUISES

During the 1820s Richard O'Driscoll and James Hayes initiated a series of river cruises aboard their steamer *Lee*. The vessel of 88 tons, 101 feet in length and fitted with salt water baths, was built in London. She was eventually to founder in 1840 off New Quay Head in St George's Channel.

The *Lee*, commanded by Captain Robert Sidney, cast off from her moorings near St Patrick's Bridge at 7.30 am, bound for Youghal on her inaugural cruise. The fare was five shillings and included breakfast and dinner. The first port of call was Cobh, where breakfast was served on board. Three hours later the *Lee* arrived at Youghal. The passengers, 'highly gratified at the beautiful appearance which the different seats and harbours on the coast exhibited', spent three hours in Youghal before returning to the vessel, 'on the deck of which dinner tables had been laid under an awning in the most perfect order'.

After dinner, 'an elegant and substantial repast, consisting of the primest variety the season affords', the tables were removed and 'great glee and cheerfulness prevailed, which continued uninterrupted by a single unpleasant occurrence until the return to the quay at Cork at 9 o'clock'.

The first cruise to Youghal on board the *Lee* took place on 21 May 1826.

1826

JOHN REDMOND

'Not since the visit of Charles Stewart Parnell in 1880 did the citizens of Cork witness a demonstration that could approach in dimensions, in fervour, in a whole-hearted unanimity of purpose, that which was seen in the streets of Munster's capital.' The *Cork Examiner* was reporting on the visit of Messrs Redmond, Dillon and Devlin to Cork in May 1910.

The party had arrived at Glanmire Station on Saturday night to unparalleled scenes of enthusiasm. A crowd estimated at not less than 20,000 people marched in a torch-lit procession from the railway station to Patrick's Street. Inside the Victoria Hotel, Redmond was greeted by a unique gathering of city dignitaries, civic, lay and dencal, led by Mr A. Roche MP.

From early Sunday morning special trains disgorged passengers from Fermoy, Youghal, Midleton, Dublin, Clonmel, Mitchelstown and Tipperary. The visitors were greeted by delegations of the United Party, accompanied by the bands of the Parnell Guard and the Hibernian Brass and Reed. The Tipperary contingent brought their own musicians, the Charles J. Kickham Brass Band, who gave a recital of stirring airs on the station platform before proceeding to Patrick Street.

Trouble flared in King Street (now MacCurtain Street) when the procession was attacked by a group of stone throwers at York Hill, but a sharp sally by the Parnell Guards put the attackers to flight. The Redmonites moved inexorably on their way and joined the great concourse of people in Patrick's Street.

The great crowd then marched to the Cornmarket to hear John Redmond speak, on Sunday 22 May 1910.

23 May

JOHN BOYLE

John Boyle was the editor of *The Freeholder* newspaper in the early nineteenth century. He was a controversial individual with strong views which he expressed forcibly, often at the expense of libel action. In December 1821 he commenced a series of articles, entitled 'New Voyages and Travels' in which he described his walks along the streets and laneways of Cork, leaving a valuable contemporary account of life in the city in the 1820s.

The Main Streets, North and South, being the oldest important thoroughfares within the old walled city, received particular attention. Mary O'Keeffe had an establishment there, where 'Dollars, Doubloons, etc,' were bought and sold. She was a money lender and money changer (at 40 per cent discount). She purchased a public house for her husband, and acquired a 'chateau' in Blackrock.

Boyle visited 'Pike's Inlet', now the site of Adelaide Street, but at that time a narrow laneway where most of the bankers lived, almost all of whom, including the Pikes, were Quakers. He discussed world affairs with one Tade Regan, in General Provisions. He viewed the Waterloo Glass House and regretted not having had an opportunity of inspecting the Terrace Glass House which was 'in the vicinity'. However, he did visit Beamish and Crawford's Brewery and, across the road, a rival in the trade, Lane's Brewery.

Boyle gave a graphic account of the sights and sounds of 'Fishamble Gut', where the ladies served fish and steaks 'which rose from a long line of musical Frying Pans with a harmonious accompaniment of knives and forks'.

John Boyle travelled the North and South Main streets on Thursday, 23 May 1822.

1822

MACROOM RAILWAY

In 1860 three separate proposals were put forward for the construction of a railway to connect Cork and Macroom. A northern route via Blarney and Coachford was decided upon, but the project failed for want of finance. A middle route along the banks of the Lee was suggested but fell through for various reasons.

The successful proposal was made by a consortium which included Sir John Arnott, Chairman, and Sir John Benson, Chief Engineer. The new company arranged with the Bandon Railway Company to use that company's terminus at Anderson's Quay, and to proceed along the Bandon line as far as Ballyphehane, where the rails of the Cork and Macroom Direct Railway would commence. On 1 August 1861, an Act of Parliament incorporating the Cork and Macroom Direct Railway Company was signed into law. Joseph Ronayne was appointed contractor, and work on the line commenced on 26 August 1863.

On completion of the railway the stage coaches which had provided a service between Cork and Macroom were auctioned off. On the following day 'a special train proceeded from Cork at 1.00 pm and took with it a large number of guests who were invited for the occasion. On arrival of the train at Macroom, the party was met with the most vociferous cheering. The Band of the West Cork Militia was in attendance.'

The formal opening of the Cork and Macroom Direct Railway took place on 24 May 1866.

1866

FIRST DEGREES IN UCC

The signing into law of the Irish Universities Act 1908, established the National University of Ireland with three constituent colleges – Dublin, Galway and Cork. Previously they had been known as Queen's Colleges, their examinations and degrees being under the jurisdiction of the Royal University.

The president of University College, Cork, Dr Windle, told a large representative gathering: 'You are now witnessing a meeting of the Senate of the National University of Ireland, the first Senate meeting of any university since the times of St Finbarr, which has been held in Cork'. He pointed out that while the courses for 1909 were set by the Royal University, those for 1910-1911 had been drawn up by the Academic Council of the College.

Dr Windle said that students of the College had already achieved high academic standards. Under the new independent administration, standards would be even higher. He pointed out that the new chemical and physical laboratories would be among the finest in Great Britain and Ireland.

On 25 May 1910, President Windle conferred the first degrees from the new University College, Cork.

1910

FRANKFIELD CHURCH

The Proprietory Church Act (6/7, William IV), provided for the construction of chapels of ease in Ireland. Mr Samuel Lane availed of its provisions to erect, at his own expense, a church at Frankfield, which would function as a chapel of ease to St Finnbarr's Parish.

Samuel Lane lived in Frankfield House. He was the proprietor of Lane's Porter Brewery, then situated on the South Main Street opposite Beamish and Crawford's, on the site of the present City Car Park.

On 3 May 1838, at a meeting of the Chapter of St Finnbarr's, a new parish of Frankfield was created. The church, in the Gothic style, was designed of Sir Thomas Deane and K.A. Deane, and was officially opened for services on 1 July 1838. The Rev John Alcock was appointed first incumbent.

The Church at Frankfield was consecrated 'as a chapel of ease to St Finbarry', by Samuel, Lord Bishop of Cork, Cloyne and Ross, on 26 May 1839.

1839

LAVITT'S QUAY

The name Lavit, Lavitt, or Lavitte – or even most correct, La Vitte – is of special interest in that it represents the only remaining public connection in Cork with the Huguenots. This predominantly French, Protestant sect was very successful in business, and played a prominent part in the civic affairs of Cork.

Joseph Lavit, a wealthy businessman who, in 1712, demised a plot of ground for the erection of a Huguenot church in the North-East Marsh, an area now known as French Church Street, was the first of the Lavits to become a member of the Corporation. He was made Sheriff in 1713 and Mayor in 1720. In 1723, he notified the Corporation of his interest in developing a section of the river bank, somewhere between the present St Patrick's Bridge and Emmet Place, into a quay.

The City Sheriffs were instructed to accompany Councillors Samuel Parker, John Browne and John Richards to inspect the works proposed by Alderman Lavit and ensure that the proposed work did not interfere with navigation rights on the river.

This decision, instructing the delegation to view the proposed works, was taken at a meeting of the Corporation of Cork on 27 May 1723.

1723

28 May

MARY OF THE NATION

Ellen Mary Downing, the daughter of the resident doctor of the Fever Hospital, Cork, was educated chiefly by her mother, who encouraged her delicate daughter's interest in religion and poetry.

The *Nation* newspaper appeared in 1842 and, under the editorship of Thomas Davis, it galvanised Irish public opinion with its advocacy of pride in country. The young Mary Downing was enthralled, and in 1845 her first poem was published in the paper. She used the pen-name 'Kate' for this poem but soon after signed her work with the name 'Mary'.

Her output was considerable: in 1845 she had five poems in the *Nation*; fifteen in 1846; twenty in 1847. However, on John Mitchell leaving the newspaper in 1848, she found the more temperate editorship of Gavan Duffy not to her liking. Thereafter she contributed patriotic verse and prose to the United Irishman, founded by Mitchell in 1848. She also wrote for the Fenian newspaper, the *Irish People*. Desolate at the collapse of the Young Ireland Insurrection and the arrest of Mitchell, she was gravely ill for some time. Her religious convictions led her to enter the North Presentation Convent as a novice in October 1849, but failing health compelled her to abandon her vocation. A collection of Mary Downing's verse, *Voices of the Heart*, was published in 1868. She died in the Mercy Hospital, Cork, on 27 January, 1869.

Sister Mary Alphonsus, 'Mary' of the *Nation*, was received into the North Presentaton Order on 28 May 1850.

1850

COUNCIL OF CONSTANCE

Patrick Foxe, known as Ragged or Ragget, may have been a native of Ballyragget in County Kilkenny. A graduate of Oxford and Cambridge, he was something of an authority on theology and canon and civil law. On 11 June 1400, he was appointed *clericus regis* or king's clerk, a position of some prestige under the Crown.

In October 1409, he was made Bishop of Cork by Pope Alexander V and the appointment was confirmed later by Pope John XXIII. There is no evidence, however, that Foxe officiated in the diocese, the bishopric being also claimed by Richard O'Hedian.

By reason of his achievements in theology and canon law and his position as *clericus regis* he was appointed a member of the English delegation to the Council of Constance, convened to resolve the Great Western Schism, which had ruptured both the religious and civil fabric of western society. In 1415 there were three claimants to the papacy: Gregory XII, who was prepared to stand down in the cause of unity; Benedict XIII, who retired without renouncing his claims; and John XXIII who was deposed.

The Council of Constance eventually elected Martin V as undisputed Pope. Patrick Foxe was the only Irish prelate present at the council and played an active role in its affairs, contributing to such subjects as communion under two species, examination of the privileges of the Franciscan Order, etc.

On 29 May 1415, Patrick Foxe was one of the five judges appointed to pass sentence on the fugitive, John XXIII, the Pope who had confirmed him in his appointment as Bishop of Cork.

1415

AN ANCIENT CUSTOM

From ancient times, possibly as far back as the era of the Danes, it was the custom of Cork Corporation to cast a dart into the waters of Cork Harbour, 'a shaft made of mahogany, about two yards long, adorned with bronzed feathers, and furnished with a bronzed head, which was weighted with shot'. The practice asserted the Corporation's rights to jurisdiction over the harbour, which jurisdiction extended to a line from Poer Head to Cork Head.

However, the first official confirmation of the ceremony did not appear in the Corporation minute book, as edited by Richard Caulfield, until 1759:

> Ordered that Mr Mayor do provide an entertainment at Blackrock Castle on the 1st of August next, and that the expenses thereof be paid out of the revenue of this Corporation; and it is ordered that the Mayor and other proper officers of the Corporation do go in their boats to the harbour's mouth, and other parts of the channel and river and assert their ancient right to the government thereof; and that the Mayor and other officers do land at convenient places in the said harbour and proceed to high-water mark, in evidence of the right of jurisdiction granted by Charter to the Corporation, in all creeks and strands within the harbour as far as high-water mark.

This decision was made on 30 May 1759.

1759

CORK BURNED

A Cork Corporation meeting of 30 September 1622, declared that

> Whereas the City of Corcke hath been often times afflicted with fyrings, and especially this year of our Lord, 1622, wherein 1500 houses in the city and suburbs were consumed, and the whole city put in extremity of danger to be totally burned, which mischief hath arisen by thatch houses, for prevention whereof in part it hath provided by former bye-laws, that no house newly built or re-edified chall be covered with thatch.

A contemporary pamphlet gives an eye witness account of the catastrophe.

> The last of May, being Friday, betwixt eleven and twelve of the Clocke the clouds over the Cittie began to gather thicke, which caused such a darkness in their houses, that they were amazed to behold sodaine darkness ... Whilst the Inhabitants stood thus wondering at the extraordinary darkness suddenly they heard a terrible clappe of thunder, and at the same instant they saw a dreadful lightning with flames of fire break out of the clouds and fall upon the Cittie at the same instant at the East and at the highest part of the Cittie ... there the first fire began with horrible flames, which the inhabitants of the West and lower parts of the Cittie Beholding, they began hastily to run towards the East part where the fire began. They were not runne halfway when as they heard a woeful cry of fire behind them, for the West side was also set on fire.

The intensity of the fire prevented the people from approaching and quenching the blaze. Some ran into the fields seeking shelter, others sought safety in the stone-walled, slated churches. Many hundreds were lost in the conflagration.

The 'Most Lamentable Burning of the Cittie of Corke' occurred on 31 May 1622.

1622

1 June

A CATHOLIC SEMINARY

The French Revolution had instilled in the Irish hierarchy a fear that seminarians, heretofore sent to the continent for their training, 'might be contaminated by the contagion of sedition and infidelity'. In an address to the Lord Lieutenant, in December 1793, they reiterated this fear, while expressing their 'unshaken loyalty and grateful affection' to his majesty.

Bishop Moylan of Cork was most anxious to provide a college for the education of the seminarians of his diocese, and in 1794 it was announced that Dr John O'Brien, a former Professor of Philosophy in Bordeaux University, would 'commence his general course in Philosophy, according to the method adopted by the most celebrated universities ... those who wish to profit of this opportunity, the first that has offered in the city'.

A report in *The Hibernian Chronicle* of 18 April 1795 stated that the first Catholic Seminary since the Reformation was scheduled to open in a house, later called 'Elm Grove' in Ballyvolane.

'The New Academy at Ballyvolane near Cork, For the Education of Young Gentlemen in Different Branches of Literature will be opened on 1 June 1795 for the reception of Boarders under the direction of Dr Moylan, RC Bishop of Cork'.

1795

AUGUSTINIAN CHURCH

A contemporary comment that 'the new chapel in Brunswick Street was consecrated', fails to reflect the antipathy between Bishop Butler and the Regular Orders, but especially the Augustinians, during the 1770s and 1780s.

In 1770, the Augustinian community began to consider the feasibility of constructing a church and friary in the city. In 1776, they 'unanimously resolved to lay up something yearly for the purpose of building a chapel wherever it shall please Providence to favour us'. A site, adjacent to the North Main Street, in the Parish of Ss Peter and Paul, was purchased in 1777. Bishop Butler reprimanded the community, insisting that they had no right to change from one parish to another, their ancient church, Red Abbey, having been in the Parish of St Finbarr; that there were already two convents, in addition to a parish church, situated in the parish and 'the greater convenience of the town would suffer from too great a proximity of chapels'.

The Augustinians replied by purchasing another site on Brunswick Street (now Washington Street) in St. Finbarr's Parish. The Bishop again objected, but the community leased the site and proceeded with the construction of the Church.

The Bishop continued his opposition but eventually complied with a mandate from the Holy See and blessed the new Augustinian Church on 2 June 1781.

DR BARRY O'MEARA

Barry Edmund O'Meara was born in Churchtown, Mallow, about the year 1786. He was educated in Trinity College and at the Royal College of Surgeons, Dublin, where he passed as an Assistant Surgeon on 12 January 1804.

O'Meara joined the British Army as an Assistant Surgeon in the 62nd Regiment, and served in Sicily, Calabria and Egypt. In 1807 he was involved in a duel and compelled to resign from the army. He joined the navy and served on both HMS *Goliath* and *Bellerophon*.

On his surrender, Napoleon was transported aboard the *Bellerophon* and became friendly with the ship's doctor, Barry O'Meara. When the British Government decreed that Napoleon be sent to *St Helena*, the emperor requested that O'Meara accompany him as his personal physician.

Barry O'Meara fell foul of Sir Hudson Lowe, Governor of St Helena, when he refused to disclose details of conversations he had with the prisoner. At Lowe's insistence, O'Meara was dismissed. In London, O'Meara charged that Napoleon's life was in jeopardy. A strong supporter of Daniel O'Connell, he embroiled himself in internal British politics and became something of a celebrity. He caught the eye of Byron who wrote of him, 'the stiff surgeon who maintained his cause Hath lost his place and gained the world's applause'.

O'Meara began a pamphlet war against Lowe and his work, *Napoleon in Exile or a Voice from Helena* became a best seller.

Barry O'Meara became a member of the Royal College of Surgeons and practised in London, where he died, in his Edgeware Road house, on 3 June 1836.

1836

4 June

GUARDIANS OF WORKHOUSE

The institution known as the workhouse emerged from the need to cater for the hordes of destitute poor who crowded the streets of the cities, towns and villages of Ireland in the eighteenth and nineteenth centuries. Previous initatives in Cork, the Foundling Hospital in 1747 and the House of Industry in 1776, in addition to other smaller private charities, had proven to be failures.

In July 1838, the Poor Relief (Ireland) Act became law. It provided for the establishment of places of refuge, i.e., workhouses for the poor and the destitute, by the imposition of local taxes (rates). Each workhouse was established to service several parishes, and thereby became commonly known as 'Unions'. Each workhouse was supervised by a Board of Guardians.

The Poor Law Union was declared on 3 April 1839 and the first meeting of the Board of Guardians of the Cork Workhouse was convened in June of that year. Mr Voules, a Poor Law Commissioner, opened the meeting in the House of Industry Board Room, and explained its functions to the members of the Board. After some discussion the following members, Messrs Crawford, Lane and Hayes, were unanimously elected to fill the positions of Chairman, Vice-Chairman and deputy Vice-Chairman.

The meeting agreed to fix the salary of the clerk at 80 guineas, decided to defer consideration of allowing members of the public attend meetings of the Guardians to a later date, and determined that the Board should meet at midday of each Monday.

The first meeting of the Board of Guardians of the Cork Workhouse was held on 4 June 1839.

1839

NOBLETT DUNSCOMBE

The names of streets, quays, even whole areas of Cork city, many altered over the centuries, were originally called after prominent citizens.

The South-East, or Great Marsh of Cork, an area bounded by the present Grand Parade to the west, Patrick Street and Merchants' Quay to the north, Parnell Place to the east and Lapp's Quay and South Mall to the south, was first called Dunscombe's Marsh in the seventeenth century. Edward Dunscombe came to Cork from London in 1596, settled in the parish of St Finn Barr's, and became a prominent merchant.

His grandson, Noblett Dunscombe, was born in 1628 and married Mary Hull of Cork in 1652. He became Mayor of the city in 1665. Dunscombe invested in land, leasing the North Strand (Pope's Quay), Pike's Marsh (now the 'Marsh'), a substantial portion of the North-East Marsh (in the vicinity of Paul Street) and the South-East Marsh in 1686.

Noblett Dunscombe suffered great losses in the course of the Williamite Wars and was compelled to surrender the land grants in 1690.

Noblett Dunscombe was buried on 5 June 1695 as his will dictated, 'in the ruins of St Mary's Shandon Church, having respect unto the station he filled in this city of Cork, and his great losses'.

1695

EUCHARISTIC PROCESSION

In 1926, the Catholic Church was engaged in the Eucharistic Congress in Chicago, USA. In Cork, Bishop Cohalan decided to honour the occasion by having the city's first Eucharistic Procession. He entrusted the task of organising the function to the well-known drill instructor, Mr Tim O'Sullivan.

It was estimated that not less than 30,000 adult males and boys participated in the procession, and countless others lined the streets of the route. Each parish was required to assemble locally and march to a predetermined location near the North Cathedral. The Butter Exchange, Barrack Street, Blackpool, Greenmount, Workingmen's and the St Vincent de Paul Augmented Bands, playing hymns, accompanied the marching men.

The procession started at 3.00 pm, following a route down Roman Street, Mulgrave Road, Camden Quay, Bridge Street, MacCurtain Street, Brian Boru Street and Bridge, Parnell Place and finally into the South Mall. An altar had been erected at the National Monument. Houses and shops along the line of the route were lavishly decorated and there were numerous emblems, shrines, statues, pictures, floral tributes and altars throughout the city.

At 7.00 pm a fanfare of trumpets, from musicians of the No. 2 Army Band, greeted the Bishop at the altar. A choir under the control of Professor Fleischmann, and the Army Band, performed *Pange Lingua* as Benediction was celebrated. At the completion of the services all the participants returned to the North Cathedral before dispersing.

The First Cork Eucharistic Procession, that had taken an estimated two and a half hours to pass a particular point, took place on 6 June 1926.

1926

BLACKROCK CHURCH

In 1811, Dr Jeremiah Collins was appointed to the parish of St Finbarr and immediately determined to construct a chapel of ease to the parish in the Blackrock district.

The lack of finance was a major impediment but two great philanthropists, Mr William Beamish and Mr William Crawford, of the brewing company, undertook to provide the cost of construction. A Mr Charles Barrington also generously contributed. Another benefactor, Mr Thomas Rochfort, bequeathed the sum of £1,100.00 for the provision of seating and other church furniture.

Fr Collins commissioned a Christian Brother, Michael Augustine Riordan, to design the church. Brother Riordan was a celebrated architect and also designed the churches in Kinsale, Dunmanway, Bantry and Millstreet.

The foundation stone of St Michael's Catholic Church, Blackrock, was laid on 7 June 1819 by Messrs Beamish and Crawford, assisted by Mr Charles Barrington.

1819

8 June

ARTHUR HILL

Arthur Hill, the son of Henry Hill, a prominent Cork architect, was born in Cork in 1846. He attended the School of Art, was educated privately and later attended the Queen's College Cork (now University College), where he graduated in engineering in 1869.

He went to Liverpool, served in the offices of Wyatt, the architect, and attended lectures in the University College. Hill enrolled as a student in the Royal Academy and was awarded a silver medal in 1871. An accomplished artist, he travelled extensively on the Continent, sketching in many countries, and in conjuction with Edmund Thorpe, produced *The Domed Churches of Charente*.

He was awarded two silver medals by the Institute of British Architects for his studies of Ardfert Cathedral, Temple Monaghan and Cormac's Chapel. He entered into partership with his father and was responsible for many of Cork's buildings.

Arthur Hill was architect for the extension to the North Infirmary, Victoria Buildings, the *Cork Examiner* Printing Works, the Science Laboratories in University College, Cork, the Technical Schools and the Munster and Leinster Bank. He was Lecturer on Architecture in the University and contributed articles to the *Journal of the Cork Historical and Archaeological Society*. He died on 4 February 1921.

Arthur Hill was born on 8 June 1846.

1846

9 June

EXCOMMUNICATION

On 10 May 1816, one year after his enthronement, Bishop John Murphy of Cork, speaking at a diocesan synod, fulminated against 'flagrant abuses and gross immorality' at places of worship on pattern days. The clergy of the diocese was admonished to prevent abuses.

It appears that all but one of the parishes, Gougane Barra, conformed; 'perversion has been so notorious at Gougane Barra that ... it annually exhibits such a scene of drunkenness, debauchery and rioting as to bring Religion into disrepute ... we suppress by the following Sentence of Excommunication the aforesaid patron of Gougane Barra.'

SENTENCE OF EXCOMMUNICATION.

In the name of Almighty God, and in virtue of the power that Jesus Christ left to His Church, and with which we are invested, we, by these presents, do excommunicate all sons of our Communion, who on St John the Baptist's Day, or on any day from the Sunday before it to the Sunday after it, both Sundays included; or on the 14th or 25th September (Feast of St Finbarr) shall presume to go to Gougane Barra to perform any work of Penance, any pious act, or any religious duty, or shall resort thither from motives of curiosity or amusement, or shall drink the water or shall bathe or dip in it by way of devotion, or in expectation of any corporal or super-natural cure, or wash or dip beasts or cattle theirin; and we declare all such persons excommunicated, in the Name of the Father and of the Son and of the Holy Ghost: THEY ARE EXCOMMUNICATED.

Bishop John Murphy issued the decree of excommunication on 9 June 1817.

1817

10 June

FRICTION AMONG FRIARS

With the admission of the native Irish into the ranks of the religious orders in the thirteenth century, it was inevitable that racial friction would develop between themselves and the English friars.

A contemporary analyst describes the situation that developed: 'At Cork in Ireland there was a general chapter of the Friars Minor, where the Irish Friars came armed with a papal bull; a dispute having arisen regarding this, they fought against the English friars; and after many had been killed and wounded here and there, the English at length gained the victory by the help of the city and with scandal to the Order'.

Another contemporary account relates that 'sixteen friars with their fellow friars were killed, some were wounded and some of them imprisoned by the King of England'.

The battle between the Irish and English Friars took place in Cork on 10 June 1291.

1291

MUTINY IN THE ARMY

Before armies were organised professionally, they were raised on an ad hoc basis. Many wealthy individuals organised, or purchased, their own regiments and were responsible for the training, clothing and upkeep of the troops. The maintenance of the soldiers was often neglected leading, on occasions, to unrest and even mutiny.

In 1716, a regiment of soldiers, billeted near Barrack Street, had not received pay for some considerable period of time. In protest, they marched out of the barracks and, with colours flying and drums beating, marched to Glasheen. Later they crossed the River Lee and proceeded to Dublin Hill where they encamped in a field belonging to a Mr Healy. They remained there for some days.

The military authorities, enraged at this perceived act of indiscipline, sent for reinforcements. The mutineers, meanwhile, had broken camp and marched to Glanmire. Loyal troops, dispatched from Dublin, landed at Cobh and immediately proceeded to engage the mutineers.

Led by a Dutchman, Christopher Curry, the protesting troops made a stand at Glanmire. However, their ammunition was soon exhausted and, while they used coat buttons instead of bullets as ammunition, they were forced to surrender.

Three leaders, Curry, Coffee and Holland, were tried by court-martial, sentenced to death and executed at Gallows Green, near the present Green Street. Many more soldiers were severely whipped as punishment.

The battle of Glanmire took place on 11 June 1716.

1716

12 June

SACRED HEART CHURCH

The Society of the Missionaries of the Sacred Heart, established by a Frenchman, Fr Jules Chevalier, was desirous of establishing a house in southern Ireland. In 1909 the order, with the permission of Bishop O'Callaghan, purchased Dyke House, situated at the western end of the Mardyke Walk, where they established a college.

Later the order was encouraged by Bishop Coholan to open a public chapel. Mr Dominic O'Connor was commissioned to design the building, and John Sisk and Son was entrusted with construction. Many local trades contributed to the work: S. Nolan &: Bros. were in charge of the lighting, installing the first flood lighting system in the south of the country; T. O'Driscoll of Ballydehob supplied the seating and furniture, including a fine vestment press in Austrian Oak; the marble holy water stoups were manufactured by J.A. O'Connell & Sons, Lower Road; the concrete rose window was constructed by Cotter's Concrete Works, Rocksavage; John Buckley, Half Moon Street, made the ornamental gates and railings.

The Church of the Sacred Heart was consecrated by Dr Coholan on 12 June 1931.

1931

COUNCIL BOOK OF KINSALE

Richard Caulfield, Librarian to Queen's College, was one of the most celebrated antiquarians in Cork. Among his many publications was *The Council Book of the Corporation of Cork* and in 1880 he produced another celebrated book, *The Council Book of the Corporation of Kinsale*.

'The process of amassing materials for history has been a labour of love with Dr Caulfield ... it does not the less entitle him to the gratitude of the intellectual world, while his own countrymen owe him their acknowledgements for the gigantic labour he has employed in the discovery and deciphering of the records of their early past.' This comment appeared in the *Cork Examiner* on the occasion of the publication of *The Council Book of the Corporation of Kinsale*.

'The volume is enriched with ancient maps and with appendices containing important charters and other documents ... we heartily commend this book as of great value to the historical student, but also as one which to the mere idler turning over its pages will be found full of attraction.'

Richard Caulfield's *The Council Book of the Corporation of Kinsale* was offered for sale on 13 June 1880.

PRISON ESCAPE

The conditions in the prisons of the nineteenth century were deplorable, with civil and criminal inmates, young and old, sharing accommodation. Many efforts were made to escape.

About one o'clock, a number of prisoners, chiefly convicts, exceeding 100, made a sudden attack on the keepers of the county gaol, for the purpose of effecting their escape; having supplied themselves with a quantity of stones, which the unfinished state of the yard afforded, they commenced this rash and desperate attempt; the moment the door was opened to distribute clean linen, &c., they began an attack on Mr Murphy, the gaoler, and his assistants, by a shower of stones, and succeeded in jamming the door so as to prevent it being closed, by which three of the most active ringleaders gained the passage leading to the inner yard; they were, however, almost instantly repulsed, and secured by the activity of two of Mr Murphy's principal assistants, whose timely efforts enabled him to compel the prisoners to return to their wards, and to secure the ringleaders in irons.

This attempt at escaping from Cork prison was made on 14 June 1818.

1818

15 June

CORK TO PASSAGE BY RAIL

It may have been the success of the Dublin/Kingstown Railway that stimulated Cork entrepeneurs to propose the construction of a railway to Passage via Blackrock in the 1830s. The initial proposal was made in 1836 but fell through because of the adverse economic conditions of the time.

The proposal was resurrected in the 1840s and, on 16 July 1846, a Parliamentary sanction was received for the project. A proposal to have the line extended as far as the Monkstown Baths was made in 1847 but almost immediately abandoned. However, one of the most eminent engineers of the day, Sir John MacNeill, was commissioned to design the railroad and Messrs Moore of Dublin were appointed to build the line.

Mayor James Murphy and many Cork celebrities were present when the first sod was turned by Sir John MacNeill's wife, at a site adjacent to Dundanion Castle. She performed the ceremony with an engraved silver spade, carrying the sod for some distance in an ornamental barrow. All the while the band of the 67th Regiment played 'God Save the Queen'. The party then adjourned to the castle to partake of dinner.

The line was opened for traffic in 1850, and the Albert Quay Terminus completed in 1873, but it was not until 1902 that the final section to Monkstown was completed.

The cutting of the first sod on the Cork/Blackrock/Passage Railway Line took place on 15 June 1847.

1847

16 June

THE PR SYSTEM

The local elections of 1922 were contested on the same day as the Draft Irish Constitution, the 'Treaty' was published. It was, significantly, the first election to be conducted under the Proportional Representation System.

A contributor to the *Cork Examiner* penned the following verse, explaining the system, on the morning of the election:

How to Vote
Put Figure 1 to the name of your favourite
And 2 to the next you prefer
Then put 3, 4 and 5 in the way you think right
Against three of the other names there.

Another anonymous correspondent gave his views on the likely outcome of the contest:
The Pleiades

Life, it seems, would run more gaily
If you vote early and vote for Daly.
And if on temperance you're not
squeamish
You might get well away on Beamish.
Or if to Labour you'd give sway
You'll vote to make a perfect Day.
Then, there's De Róiste, known as
Liam
As fine a boy as you or I am.
A Lord Mayor with a two year vogue
As fine a boy as you or I am.

A Lord Mayor with a two year vogue
Is stowed away in Donal Oge.
No eloquence can hold you back
From preference for Miss Mary
Mac.
And J.J. Walsh is sure almost
To be there first past the 'Post'.
All this of course is simply rot
Though I regret the fact, 'tis so
That seven into four won't go.

(Signed) The Man in the Moon.

The first election under the Proportional System was conducted on 16 June 1922.

1922

HURLING IN CORK

The game of hurling was one of the native Irish pastimes, the playing of which was illegal under the provisions of the Penal Laws. It appears, however, that the game was not suppressed and indeed enjoyed much popularity with the ordinary citizens of the city and suburbs. The establishment, in particular the Corporation, was not prepared to tolerate the game, and in 1631 adopted measures to prohibit the playing of hurling.

Whereas there hath been in former times used in this city a very barbarous and uncivil kind of sport upon Easter Tuesdays, May days, Whitson Tuesday, viz, tossing of great balls, and hurling in the open streets with the small ball, great mischiefs have oftentimes happened, as the death of men, and many wounded and maimed in these sports, and many quarrels have followed, which were like to break out into a general tumult within the City. We therefore, the Mayor &c., for abolishing these sports and preventing the mischiefs, and the rather that we have received directions from the Right Hon. the Lord President for abolishing of all such unlawful plays, ordain for a bye-law that said tossing and hurling in the streets shall not be used the days aforesaid, nor any other, upon pain of 40s. And likewise that any Mayor &c., that shall permit hereafter such sports shall forfeit 20li.ster., and every Sheriff 10li. Provided this bye-law shall not hinder any lawful sports, as to bring home the Summer and Maypole, or other lawful exercises that the young men of the City shall use hereafter, only the hurling upon the street to be given over.

This bye-law was adopted by Cork Corporation on 17 June 1631.

1631

FEVER IN CORK

The Dispensary and Humane Society was established on 23 March 1787 as a consequence of a public meeting called by the Mayor at the initative of Joshua Beale. It was one of the earliest attempts made to alleviate the sufferings of the poor people of Cork.

Premises were acquired in Hanover Street, six physicians and two surgeons gave of their services voluntarily, and the Society distributed medicine to the sick. On average 2,600 patients were treated annually.

The Society helped with the founding of the Fever Hospital, and contributed enormously to the care of the sick during the typhus epidemic of 1817.

At a meeting of the committee of the Dispensary and Humane Society, it was resolved that in consequence of the alarming increase in fever, the monks' school in Peacock Lane (North Monastery), and the benevolent offers of an individual (who concealed his name) to floor the room and provide 50 pallet beds, so as to establish an additional fever house, be received with gratitude by the committee. About a fortnight later, there were 200 patients received.

The Dispensary and Humane Society took this decision on 18 June 1817.

1817

MAYORALITY CHAIN

It appears that the first mayoralty chain was presented in 1511 by Queen Elizabeth to Mayor Maurice Roche for his services against the Earl of Desmond.

However, on 31 October 1755, the Corporation resolved 'that a Collar of S.S. and Gold Chains be bought for the Mayor and Sheriffs of this City, to be worn by them in their several offices for the honour and dignity of this City, same to be made like the Collar and Chains worn by the Lord Mayor and Sheriffs of the City of Dublin'.

The chain had obviously not been provided by 1787, as the Corporation passed another similar motion on 6 March concerning the provision of a mayoralty chain. On that occasion the Corporation's resolution was firm and a collar was commissioned. It is the collar in use to this day. The Mayoralty chain consists of links of sterling silver joined alternately by links of looped gold and enamelled. There are 53 pieces consisting of 26 S.S., thirteen Rosettes, twelve Knots, one Grill and a Medallion.

An inscription on the chain records the investment of the Mayor with the chain:

Cork 19th June 1787. The Right Worshipfull Samuel Rowlands, Esq. Mayor, was publicly invested by the Commons, in open Court of d'Oyer Hundred with the Gold Chain, and immediately after the Mayor conferred the like honour on the High Sheriffs, and lastly, the ceremony of Investing the Mayor with the Pendant and Collar of S.S. was performed by a Deputation from the Council.

1787

20 June

ENGLISH MARKET

The Charter of Henry III, granted in 1242, conferred the ownership of all markets in the City of Cork on the Corporation. Over the course of the centuries the Corporation had provided various markets, all located within the old walled city. However, in the latter half of the eighteenth century, they proposed to build the first market outside the walls. In 1786, they took a large tract of land on the Grand Parade and, in 1787, purchased a house from Mr Jappie, also on the Parade.

A fee of £500 was paid for a right of way into Princes Street and the market was officially opened for the sale of meat, fish, poultry and vegetables on 1 August 1788. Eighty years later the Corporation advertised for proposals for the major reconstruction of the market.

The architect, Sir John Benson, was awarded the commission and Mr Thomas Walsh was appointed builder. The main entrance was on the narrow Princes Street, a factor that prevented the public from appreciating its architectural features. It was described at the time as one of the showpieces of the city. All local materials were used, with limestone and red brick predominating. The interior was lofty, the high glass roof, supported on cast-iron pillars, giving a bright, clear, airy effect.

Over the years it has been known as the Princes Street Market, the Grand Parade Market, the Market, but most usually as the English Market. However, the reason for this appellation is unknown.

The English Market was severely damaged by fire on 20 June 1980.

1980

21 June

PURITANS AND THE POST

In 1850, the decision by the Prime Minister, Lord John Russell, to restrict the mail to only one delivery on Sundays infuriated many Cork citizens. 'This has been a great triumph for all blockheads and fanatics,' a correspondent to the *Cork Examiner* wrote. 'It is a surrender of the post-office,' the *Examiner* editorial commented, 'which a few stupid blockheads have been able to do to the public.'

The decision was brought about, the *Cork Examiner* insisted, as a result 'of the clamour of a small faction in favour of a Judaical observance of the Sabbath ... they (government) exhibited an example of dastardly and pusillanimous conduct, which has met the condemnation of their own supporters ... the community is called upon to express its practical power; and therefore we advise that a petition be prepared directly upon the subject, which cannot but receive the signature of every man of sense.'

'Men of this day', the *Examiner* thundered, 'will not submit to be placed under the iron yoke of external sanctimoniousness, which has always proved fatal to true religion and morality.'

The *Cork Examiner* fulminated against Lord John Russell on 21 June 1850.

1850

PAVING THE STREETS

In 1861, Cork Corporation began the process of paving the city streets with blocks. Patrick's Quay, as far east as the Steam Packet Office, had been initially treated. Citizens who had witnessed similar blocks being laid in England had commented on the unsatisfactory nature of the operation in Cork. Already deep ruts were appearing opposite the steamers' berths.

Mr J.W. Dyas, Cork Drug Hall, was concerned at the delay in the work of paving Winthrop Street. He complained that after three days the workers had only progressed as far as the third building in the street, and the spaces between the blocks had not been filled. Was it possible, he speculated, that only three men in the city were qualified to do the work? Had the workers any previous experience? Could other workers be found to expedite the work? How long would it take, considering the slow rate of progress in Winthrop Street, to block-pave Patrick Street and the South Mall?

In a letter to he *Cork Examiner* on 22 June 1861, J.W. Dyas, while complaining that business in the street had been suspended 'in order to test an experiment of the council', acknowledged that the streets were being block-paved for the first time as part of the Corporation's efforts to improve the condition of the city.

TRADE UNION LEADER

Con Connolly was born on Barrack Road (now Glengarriffe Road), Bantry, the eldest of thirteen children, in the last decade of the nineteenth century. He was educated locally but left school at eleven years of age, migrated to Cork, and worked as a messenger boy in Lady's Well Brewery. He attended night classes in Buckley's School, Washington Street, but returned to Bantry and worked in a timber yard owned by William Martin Murphy.

He became an apprentice carpenter and joined the Society of Carpenters and Joiners. He returned to Cork, became Chairman of his Union Branch in 1922 and was involved in the six-month lock-out in 1923. As a consequence of this strike, he was involved,with P.J. O'Brien, Jer Murphy (contractor) and John O'Connell (painter) in the establishment of the Joint Industrial Council for the Building Industry. With Jer Murphy, he acted as joint chairman for seventeen years. Council recommendations in disputed situations were required to be always unanimous and were invariably adopted. He became Chairman of the National Federation of Building Trade Operators and represented Ireland at the Trade Union Conference in Margate, England, in 1923. He was President of the Trade Union Congress in 1967.

Con Connolly was elected to Cork Corporation in 1935, and stayed politically active until 1967. He was an early supporter of Vocational Education and acted on various bodies advocating the development of the vocational school structure.

Con Connolly was born on 23 June 1892.

1892

MÍCHEÁL Ó CLÉIRIGH

Throughout the period of the Penal Laws, the application of which varied in intensity from one administration to another, the regular clergy apparently contrived to keep some representation in order to serve the Catholics still living in Cork city.

The Franciscan Monastery on the North Mall having been attained, its lands were disposed of to various people. However, in 1609, the friars succeeded in acquiring a rented house built, it appears, on some of their old lands on the North Mall. Mícheál Ó Cléirigh, the great Celtic scholar, one of the Four Masters, came to that house in Cork to copy manuscripts.

On 24 June 1629, he was engaged in copying the Life of Saint Finbarr, from a vellum manuscript belonging to Dónal O Duinín.

1629

RELEASE OF PRISONERS

On an evening in June 1917, members of the Irish Volunteers comman-deered Glanmire Railway Station. Large numbers of people congregated in the station yard. Outside the station gates, members of Gaelic Clubs, wear-ing their colours and carrying hurleys, were assembled. The Workingmen's Brass and Reed Band, the Blackrock Fife Drum Band, the Volunteers' Pipe Band and Brian Boni Pipers' Band were in attendance. The crowds were awaiting the arrival from Dublin of J.J. Walsh T.C., Diarmuid Lynch, David Kent, Maurice Brennan, Fergus O'Connor, William Tobin, C. Donovan and Thomas Hunter, all of whom had been imprisoned for their part in the Easter Rising.

On arrival, the freed men travelled by wagonette to the National Monument where they were introduced to the people. The party then pro-ceeded to the Victoria Hotel where a public meeting was held. J.J. Walsh said that it was not an occasion for speeches – their voices had been heard in Dublin in 1916. The other prisoners also spoke, expressing their grati-tude for having been given the honour of fighting for the freedom of their country.

Terence McSwiney, speaking initially in Irish, said that Irish must be the language of the Republic. What was important, he stated, was not the memory of the past but the state of preparedness for the future. 'If there was a miscarriage the last time there must be none next time; and when the flag goes up next time it must go up for good.'

The released prisoners arrived in Cork on 25 June 1917.

26 June

HISTORY AND ARCHAEOLOGY

A specially convened meeting of the council of the Literary and Scientific Society, held on 11 June 1891, considered the establishment of an historical and archaeological society in Cork. The objects of such a Society were to be: 'the Collection, Preservation and Diffusion of all available information regarding the past of the City and County of Cork, and to provide for the keeping of current events.' The officers were the Rev R.A. Sheehan, Bishop of Waterford and Lismore (President), Messrs Robert Day and Denny Lane (Vice-Presidents), Thomas Farrington (Hon. Treasurer), and J.P. Dalton and John O'Mahony (joint Hon. Secretaries).

In 1892 the Society initiated the publication of a periodical to which members could submit articles; this would be the primary medium through which the Society would fulfil its objectives.

The first volume of the journal was an ambitious undertaking. It contained a host of articles, ranging in subject matter from biographical notes on local celebrities and characters to an article on the past history of the diocese of Cork. The issue also contained a copy of Speede's Map of the city and notes on literary Cork. There was an introduction by Denny Lane, a brief account of the origins of the Society by the Honorary Secretary, a list of subscribers and the rules of the Society.

The Cork Historical and Archaeological Society was established on 26 June 1891.

1891

BAKERS' STRIKE

In 1842 the Operative Bakers of Cork began agitating for the suspension of night work. They were supported by such people as Fr Mathew and Messrs Lyons, Fagan, Hayes, etc. The campaign was hotly opposed by the master bakers who insisted that the public demanded, and was entitled to, fresh bread in the morning. The master bakers were supported by the business community, an attitude that was reflected in the contemporary newspapers.

In 1860, Cornelius Murphy, Secretary of the Operative Bakers of Cork, wrote a long letter to the *Cork Examiner*, outlining the case for the suspension of night work. He received trenchant, and unexpected, support in a newspaper editorial.

Bakers must still spend nights of blear-eyed, sweltering toil, over work which kills five out of six in eighteen years, in order that a few persons who are fond of indigestible food may have hot rolls for breakfast ... Fresh or hot bread is most deleterious food ... yet to produce that article, to diffuse it amongst the public before it is fit for use, is the sole tangible ground on which a large body of working men are compelled to turn night into day, to work when they should be asleep ... Not only is health destroyed, at the fearful rate to which we have alluded, but the mind is exposed to evil influences ... physical degradation, as a matter of rule, involves as a consequence moral degradation.

The correspondence appeared in the *Cork Examiner* on 27 June 1860.

1860

28 June

UNION RIOTS

At the end of May 1870, Cork tailors sought an increase in wages from three to three pence halfpenny an hour. The masters refused, the men went on strike and were joined by other workers. The strike proceeded in an orderly fashion until 22 June, when the tailors attacked and wrecked the homes of the masters.

Mounted police, armed with sabres, attacked the men and many combatants, workers and police alike, were injured. There were further confrontations: the strikers jeering the police resulted in renewed charges, in which the infantry supported the police force. The strikers retreated into the narrow laneways from where they mounted counter attacks, showering stones, bottles and iron bolts on the authorities. The military went berserk and attacked the workers with sabres, bayonets and clubs.

Day after day, night after night, the attacks and counter attacks continued, the police and military launching cavalry charges, the workers ambushing them in the narrow laneways, sabres and bayonets against stones and bottles. Other workers in the city – hackney drivers, women workers, iron foundry workers and seamen – supported the strikers, taking sympathetic action and joining them in their forays.

On 28 June 1870, the striking workers marched to where St Finnbarr's Cathedral was being built and prevailed on the construction workers, labourers and skilled operatives, to down tools and join them in the strike.

1870

DEATH OF A HISTORIAN

Timothy John Walsh was born on the South Douglas Road, Cork, on 11 February 1906. The family later moved to Marble Hall Park, Douglas Road. T.J. Walsh was educated in Farranferris Seminary before entering Maynooth College. He was ordained to the priesthood in 1930.

He spent a short time in Leeds, England, before returning to the diocese of Cork and an initial appointment in Kealkil. He was subsequently transferred to the chaplaincy in Coláiste Mhuire, Douglas, before ministering in the South Parish and Turner's Cross. He became pastor of Muintir Bhaire in 1965, Blackrock, in 1970, and a member of the chapter in 1979.

Canon Walsh was a celebrated historian. He was a regular contributor to such journals as: *The Capuchin Annual*; *The Journal of the Cork Historical and Archaeological Society* and *Archivium Hibernicum*. Canon Walsh was also the author of *In the Steps of Saint Finbarr and The Parish of Blackrock*. He was an acknowledged authority on the Irish Colleges on the continent of Europe, and was author of the book *The Irish Continental College Movement*.

Undoubtedly his outstanding work was the celebrated *Nano Nagle and the Presentation Sisters*. In this book he vividly recreates the appalling circumstances pertaining at the time, and details the herculean efforts made by Nano Nagle and her associates to bring education to the poor and to alleviate their terrible conditions.

Canon T.J. Walsh was buried in St Michael's Church, Blackrock, on 29 June 1984.

1984

MARY AIKENHEAD

Mary Aikenhead, the daughter of Dr David Aikenhead, a Protestant gentleman, was born in Cork on 19 January 1787. After her father had converted to Catholicism on his deathbed, she, aged sixteen years, also became a Catholic. When her mother died some years later, Mary Aikenhead was persuaded by Archbishop Murray, in 1815, to establish the Irish Sisters of Charity in Dublin.

Ellen Mahony, a wealthy Corkwoman, had bequeathed £1,500 towards the establishment of a convent of the Sisters of Charity in Cork's North Parish. Bishop John Murphy promoted the idea, but met with delaying tactics from the Archbishop of Dublin, both men contending for control of the convent. Eventually, in September 1826, Mary Aikenhead and Sister M.Regis Teeling arrived in Cork and were presented with a most unsuitable premises on Easons Hill.

Bishop Murphy refused to provide alternative accommodation and, despite strong protests, the Sisters of Charity opened their convent on St Mary's Road on 13 November of the same year. In the face of his continuing opposition, the Bishop was eventually prevailed upon to lay the foundation stone of the convent in St Mary's Road, on 6 August 1844.

At her death, on 22 July 1858, Mary Aikenhead left behind eight convents, an asylum and St Vincent's Hospital in Dublin. The Sisters of Charity, founded by Mary Aikenhead of Cork, received its Rescript, or Papal Approval, from Pope Gregory XVI, on 30 June 1836.

1836

THE 'DIRTY SHIRTS'

The Royal Munster Fusiliers was one of the most famous Irish regiments of the British Army. It consisted of five battalions, the first two being regular units, the 101st and 104th, with a lineage stretching back to India in the eighteenth century. There were three militia battalions: South Cork Militia, Kerry Militia and Limerick Militia.

The 101st was formed in 1759 and consisted of three companies of the East India Company's Bombay European Regiment. The 104th, originally raised in 1760 as the 'King's Volunteers', subsequently became the 104th Bengal Fusiliers. These units were eventually absorbed into a new regiment, The Royal Munster Fusiliers.

The regiment, extremely popular with Cork volunteers, saw extensive service especially in India, and participated in many of the most important actions of the eighteenth and nineteenth centuries. The 'Munsters' fought all through the First World War, in France, Gallipoli, Salonica and Egypt. Four 'Munsters', among them Corporal Cosgrove of Aghada, won Victoria Crosses.

The Royal Munster Fusiliers Regiment, known affectionately as the 'Dirty Shirts', was formed on 1 July 1881.

1881

2 July

PRESENTATION BROTHERS

In August 1821, friction developed between the newly-established Christian Brothers and John Murphy, Bishop of Cork. Although the Brothers had been granted an Apostolic Brief, placing the individual communities under the jurisdiction of their Superior General, Bishop Murphy opposed the arrangement.

The Bishop prevailed upon the Cork Brothers not to attend the first General Chapter of the congregation. A visit from Ignatius Rice, founder of the order, failed to resolve the impasse with the Bishop. A critical point in relations between the Bishop and Ignatius Rice was reached in 1826, when his Lordship sought to gain control of the Peacock Lane (North Monastery) premises. All the Cork Brothers, with the exception of Austin (Augustine) Riordan (Rearden), remained loyal to Rice and renewed their vows in Waterford.

Riordan, an accomplished architect who had designed at least five churches for the Bishop, was prevailed upon to accept the jurisdiction of Dr Murphy. With another brother, he severed his connection with the Peacock Lane community and established a school in Cat Lane, off Barrack Street, on the south side of the city.

Although Bishop Murphy did not formally confirm the rule of the new congregation until 18 April 1830, the Presentation Order was established for all practical purposes on the opening of Cat Lane School on 2 July 1827.

1827

EXHIBITION OF 1883

There was no little disappointment, in 1882, when Limerick succeeded in seeing off Cork's effort to attract the Agricultural Show of the Royal Irish Society. The very next day, 1 December, Alderman Nagle, mindful of the success of the National Exhibition of 1852, proposed that Cork host another National Exhibition. The United Trades of the city, appreciating its significance, adopted a motion in support of Alderman Nagle's proposal.

On 14 December, a meeting was held in the Mayor's Office, at which the *Cork Examiner* reported that 'a desire was exhibited to sink all political or sectarian differences in an earnest effort to promote the common good by stimulating the industry and commerce of the country'.

An executive committee, under the presidency of the Earl of Bandon, and the chairmanship of the Mayor, was immediately established. Members were allocated responsibility for various functions, viz. Finance, Industrial and Arrangements, Machinery, Raw Materials, Agriculture, Music, Fine Arts and a Solicitations Committee for the City of Cork. Members of the Committee travelled the country, soliciting financial support and participation in the Exhibition.

The Trustees of the Corn Exchange agreed to place their premises at the disposal of the Committee. After a public competition, Messrs R. Walker, architects, were selected to design the additional buildings required. Commendatore Delany was entrusted with the construction of the premises.

The National Exhibition was officially opened on 3 July 1883.

1883

4 July

ADMIRAL'S FLAG

The defeat of Napoleon had serious consequences for many communities, not least the city and harbour of Cork. The end of the war reduced, even eliminated, the need for many of the products that had been supplied by Cork industry. In addition the British Government, having decided to reduce the size of the armed forces, withdrew the Admiral's Flag from Cork Harbour, thus contributing even further to unemployment and poverty.

The withdrawal of the flag meant that the entire naval establishment in Cork Harbour, which contributed handsomely to the local economy – especially Cobh, but also the city – would be ordered to other stations. Protesters pointed out that the decision would not effect savings for the government as the forces would merely be transferred to other stations.

A meeting of the citizens was summoned, at which Mayor Garde presided. The original motion, a protest against the government's decision to withdraw the flag, was deemed to be inadequate. Speaker after speaker questioned the reason for the decision. Blame was laid at the door of absentee landlords and an absentee government.

A committee, consisting of Gerald Callaghan, John Moore Traverse, William Crawford, William Fagan, Bartholomew Venling, Horace Townsend and Richard Dowden, drew up the formal petition to Parliament. It was presented to the city MP, Dan Callaghan, for submission to the House of Commons.

The meeting protesting the withdrawal of the Admiral's Flag from Cork Harbour was held on 4 July 1830.

1830

EMIGRATE!

Such was the state of unemployment and poverty in Cork in 1842, that the Poor Law Guardians and rate payers attended a meeting in huge numbers to consider the consequences and propose a remedy.

Graphic pictures were painted of the plight of the working people; hundreds of coopers, weavers, hatters and sawyers being unemployed. The total remuneration of Cork's unemployed coopers amounted to £14.19s. per week, and with 1,500 dependants, each family was expected to subsist on less than 1s. per week.

The population of the country was fast approaching eight million and the solution proposed at the meeting was the emigrant boat. The prospective emigrants could not be expected to provide the fare themselves, so the Poor Law Commissioners and the rate payers proposed to levy a special rate to finance the scheme. Sir James Graham explained that any number of people could be sent out of the country at £5.00 per head – it cost £9.00 to maintain each person in the Workhouse. If the men remained unemployed at home, their familiies would spend the rest of their lives in the Workhouse. If a number from each trade emigrated those who remained could obtain work.

A levy of one penny in the pound on the rates would raise £1,000.00 in cash. Mr John Besnard announced his acquaintance with a man who would transport a great number to the Cape of Good Hope; the fare could be deducted from their labour.

At the meeting in the City Courthouse on 5 July 1842, a committee was formed to forward the decision – the levying of two and a half pence in the pound on the rates to facilitate the depopulation of Ireland – to the Poor Law Commissioners.

1842

JEREMIAH JAMES MURPHY

Burke's *Irish Family Records* provides details of one of the most extraordinary funerals in the history of Cork. Jeremiah James Murphy was the son of James Murphy, Ringmahon, Blackrock, the founder of James Murphy and Co., Distillers, Cork. He died in Pisa, Italy, on 29 November 1851.

Arrangements were made to have the body returned to Ireland but, on arrival at Naples, the sailors refused to handle the corpse, claiming it would bring bad luck. An ingenious scheme was devised whereby the cadaver was hidden inside an upright piano and thereby shipped to Cork. He was interred inside the piano, in Carrigrohane Cemetery on 18 January 1852.

Jeremiah James Murphy was born on 6 July 1795.

1795

A WATER SUPPLY

In June 1890, the residents of Togher petitioned the Vice-Guardians for a piped water supply. They pointed out that while other areas like Glasheen, Friars' Walk and Douglas Road had been serviced, the Togher area was dependent on water extracted from a polluted stream. The Togher residents were, however, expected to pay the same rates as their more fortunate neighbours. The Vice-Guardians promised to remove water fountains from the vicinity of the Lough and re-position them near Summerstown Lane, a proposal that was unacceptable to the residents of both Togher and the Lough.

A public meeting was called, and hundreds of people gathered after twelve o'clock mass in the yard of the Lough Church. It was pointed out that the proposal was not only inadequate for the residents of Togher but unsuitable for the people of the Lough. Mr D. Doyle, in proposing a motion, described the removal of the water fountains from the Lough as a work of vandalism that 'would be worthy of a Council of the Pigmies that Stanley tells of'.

Mr O'Regan, proposing a motion demanding a proper water supply for Togher, complained that the residents 'are exposed to great inconvenience and danger to health owing to the neglect of the sanitary authorities in not providing us with a proper water supply'.

The meeting was convened on Sunday 7 July 1890.

1890

THE MAIL COACH

In 1781 the Cork Committee of Merchants had indicated their displeasure to the Irish Parliament with the existing postal service. In 1782, John Palmer instituted the reform of the postal service in England, using coaches with armed guards to deliver the mail. On 2 August 1784, the new postal service was inaugurated between London and Bristol.

The Irish Government decided to introduce the new system. John Anderson, the entrepreneur who had constructed the town of Fermoy, undertook to provide the service. He faced daunting obstacles: raparees, like 'Brennan on the Moor', were a constant threat; the roads were so bad that he was compelled to virtually construct new ones; he had to provide a series of coaching inns where the passengers could obtain refreshments and the horses could be changed.

The departure point was on Patrick's Street, and the journey from Cork to Dublin took 31 hours and cost two guineas for passengers on the inside, and half that price for those on the outside of the coaches. Each passenger was permitted fourteen pounds of luggage. Small packages were charged at two shillings and two pence each.

The coaches were decorated in bright red and claimed precedence over other vehicles on the roadways. They were also exempt from all charges on the turnpikes.

Tuckey, in his *Remembrancer*, reports that the first royal mail coach from Dublin arrived in Cork on 8 July 1789.

1789

FLYING IN CORK

The highlight of 'Cork Week' 1914, was undoubtedly an exhibition of aero-gymnastics, given by Lord Carbery, in what the *Cork Examiner* erroneously called 'the first such demonstration ever given in Cork'.

From early afternoon crowds were making their way to the Mardyke fields, the venue for the event. The stands and enclosures were crowded. 'The gradual rise of Strawberry Hill made a fine free grand stand for a mass of people. In fact to the north of the grounds was a sea of faces.'

The Barrack Street Brass and Reed Prize National Band entertained the patrons until the arrival of Lord and Lady Carbery, who were greeted by the Lord Mayor, Alderman H. O'Shea and his wife. The aviator was presented with a green flag bearing the Irish harp, which he attached to his aeroplane.

The Moraine-Saultaire monoplane took off from the eastern end of the field and flew in a westerly direction before turning and circling the city. Lord Carbery obliged by making six flights, on each occasion taking a passenger. And then he thrilled the crowd on announcing that he would execute a series of manoeuvres: banking, steeplechasing and spiral switchbacking.

Unfortunately, a low cloud, at an altitude of 300 feet, had come in over the city, precluding Lord Carbery from executing the daring loop-the-loop, which feat required a minimum altitude of 1,000 feet.

Lord Carbery, pioneer aviator, performed for the citizens of Cork in the Mardyke fields on 9 July 1914.

10 July

ROBERT DAY

Robert Day FSA, MRIA, JP was born in 1836. From youth, he displayed a keen interest in archaeological matters. His interest was life long and he accumulated probably the finest collection of archaeological and historical artefacts pertaining to Cork history.

Day was President of the Cork Historical and Archaeological Society, of which he was a founding member, from 1894 until his death in 1914. He contributed regularly, on a variety of topics, to that Society's journal. He was a member of the Royal Irish Academy, Fellow of the Society of Antiquaries, London and Fellow of the Royal Society of Antiquaries, Dublin. He was a Fellow of the Royal Numismatic Society, Bibliographical Society, and Huguenots Society. He was a past president of the Cork Literary and Scientific Society.

Robert Day was active in civic affairs, being elected an alderman of the Corporation in 1880, and serving as High Sheriff in 1893. A trustee of both the South Infirmary and the Cork Savings Bank, he was also a member of the Court of Governors of the Commercial Buildings.

His most significant contribution to Cork local history was, arguably, his editorship of the Historical and Archaeological Society's reprint of Smith's *The Ancient and Present State of the County and City of Cork*, which he generously annotated from the manuscripts of Thomas Crofton Croker and Richard Caulfield.

Robert Day died at his home, Myrtle Hill House, on 10 July 1914.

1914

11 July

BRITISH LEAVE

British officers shook hands cordially with officers of the Free State Army and boarded the Saorstát, as both Irish and English soldiers cheered. The English force transferred to the M.V. *Innisfallen* and as the last of England's forces in the Free State sailed out of Cork Harbour, their national anthem was played.

Later, a simple, brief, ceremony took place on Spike Island to mark the historic occasion. The No. 2 Army Band played *Amhrán na bhFiann*, a 21 gun salute was sounded, a *feu de joie* was fired by troops in Cobh, the tricolour was hoisted over the three other forts in the Harbour (Camden, Carlisle and Templebreedy) and, the *Cork Examiner* reported a crowd estimated at 'forty thousand people, gathered in vantage points all round Cork Harbour last night, saw Mr de Valera, as head of the Irish Government, hoist the tricolour for the first time over Spike Island'.

The last English garrison departed from the Free State at eight o'clock on the evening of 11 July 1938.

1938

THE ATHENAEUM

The Great Exhibition of 1852 was one of the outstanding achievements of nineteenth-century Cork. It followed hard on the heels of the Crystal Palace, London, Exhibition and preceded the Dublin Exhibition by one year.

Because the Corn Exchange (near Anderson's Quay) was too small to contain all the exhibits, Sir John Benson was commissioned to construct a second exhibition hall. At the conclusion of the Exhibition the organising committee decided not to demolish Sir John Benson's creation: it was dismantled and re-erected on the site now occupied by the Opera House. The Athenaeum, as it was called, was perceived as a centre of learning and culture for all citizens.

At a public meeting, presided over by the Mayor, it was stated that the expense of transferring and erecting the building had been borne by the Exhibition committee. However, there was now a sum of £200 required to complete the work that would provide Cork with a magnificent public utility.

It was decided that a public subscription be opened. At the conclusion of the meeting, before the crowds had dispersed, over 30 shares were subscribed and many more reserved.

The public meeting took place in the Athenaeum on 12 July 1854.

1854

JOHN ANDERSON

John Anderson was born in Portling, a small village near Dumfries, Scotland, probably in 1747. In 1770, having accumulated about £500 in a business venture, he left Scotland and settled in Cork. The city was at that time one of the major trading ports on the Atlantic coast, a factor that probably attracted Anderson.

He established a business on Lapp's Island (near the present Parnell Place), and prospered. His ability was recognised and he became a member of the committee that planned the Harbour Commissioner's building. John Anderson was elected to the membership of the very influential and exclusive Committee of Merchants. The Corporation made him a freeman in 1787, and Anderson's Quay was named in his honour. He was a member of the consortium that built a coffee house – eventually to become the Imperial Hotel – on the South Mall.

John Anderson purchased a major portion of the Fermoy Estate and proceeded to build the town of Fermoy, transforming a dirty hamlet into a town with fine houses, military barracks and a population of 7,000.

The reform of the then rudimentary postal service was initiated in England in 1782, when stage coaches, known as the Royal Mail, were introduced. John Anderson undertook to provide a similar service in Ireland. It was an awesome task, in that roads had to be built, and inns and staging posts provided, to cater for the comforts of the passengers and to facilitate changes of horses. The first Royal Mail arrived in Cork, from Dublin, on 8 July 1789.

John Anderson, builder of Fermoy, and the man who introduced the Royal Mail to Ireland, died on 13 July 1820.

1820

LIBERTIES ARE WALKED

The Liberties of Cork were granted by King James 1 by letters patent, on 15 July, 'ann.regn.7th 1609, to remain a distinct county of itself to be forever called the County of the City of Cork; reserving nevertheless a place for a courthouse and gaol, for the County of Cork in the city'.

The bounds of the County of the City of Cork were set out from the rest of the county by Sir Dominick Sarsfield, knight, afterwards Lord Kilmallock, Sir Parr Lane, Knight, Sir Edward Fitzgerald and other commissioners. They were authorised to actually walk the boundary lines, thereby marking out the physical limits of the borough. The boundary on the northside of the borough was walked on 13 July.

To the north the boundary extended, generally speaking, from the city to Carrigrohane and thence east through Blarney, to Dunbulloge and to Glanmire and back to the city, and it was walked on 13 July.

To the south the boundary ran from the city to Carrigrohane, east through Ballincollig, Ballygarvan and to Rochestown and back to the city.

The south boundary of the County of the City of Cork was walked on 14 July 1906.

1906

OATH OF ALLEGIANCE

In the last quarter of the eighteenth century the British Government was coming under intense pressure to relax the impediments to the open practice of the Catholic religion. The government was also anxious to win the allegiance of the newly-emerging Catholic merchant middle class.

An Act of Parliament of 1774 (13/14, George III), aimed at securing this loyalty. It incorporated an Oath of Allegiance, formulated by the Archbishop of Dublin. The oath, requiring to be sworn before a magistrate, met with the approval of Archbishop Butler of Cashel, and the Capuchin friar from Cork, Arthur O'Leary, insisted in a pamphlet entitled, 'Loyalty Asserted', that the oath was compatible with Catholic doctrine.

The Archbishop of Cashel sought to persuade his suffragan bishops to take the oath. He summoned a provincial Synod of Bishops and Bishop Butler of Cork, together with the bishops of Kerry, Waterford, Cloyne, Killaloe and Limerick signed an undertaking, in Cork, on 15 July 1775, to accept the Oath of Allegiance to the British Crown.

1775

UPTON REFORMATORY

Alderman John George MacCarthy, Secretary, St Patrick's Reformatory, or House Agricultural Colony for Juvenile Criminals, informed the public that the institution was open for the reception of inmates.

The reformatory was provided to detain, for a period not exceeding five years, juvenile offenders under the age of sixteen years who had been sentenced to fourteen days and upwards. Only Catholics would be admitted. The administration of the institution was the responsibility of the Fathers of Charity of Market Weighton, Yorkshire, England. The government had been impressed by the success of the reformatory movement in England, France, Italy, Belgium, Holland, Switzerland, Austria, Prussia, Denmark and the United States. A good farm of 112 acres afforded ample scope for agricultural pursuits 'which are considered best as the staple employment of a Reformatory'. The sum of £2,500 had been expended on a plain substantial building.

The purpose of the reformatory was to 'convert into honest, virtuous, and industrious citizens, miserable beings, who under our present system, have nothing before them but a hapless career of wickedness and crime'. MacCarthy quoted Lord Brougham's assertion that 'there is nothing more certain than that their first offence may, by proper treatment of the offenders, be also made last offences'.

John George MacCarthy wrote to the *Cork Examiner*, informing the public of the opening of Upton Reformatory, on 16 July 1860.

1860

TOLL HOUSES

A principal source of revenue for local authorities, before the introduction of the rating system, was the collection of duties on imports and exports and tolls on goods brought by land into the city.

Rather than assume responsibility for the actual collection of revenues, Cork Corporation farmed out the tolls, leasing the collection to individuals in return for a fee. This system led to much abuse, the Corporation letting the tolls to fellow councillors and acquaintances at considerably discounted rates.

Toll houses were established throughout the suburbs, at every road leading into the city. Cork Corporation sanctioned the location of toll houses at the following locations: Dublin Road, Mallow Road, Fair Hill, Cattle Market, Blarney Lane, Youghal Road, Spring Lane, Leitrim Street, Lough Road, Gallows Green Road, Upper Glasheen Road, Lower Glasheen Road, Upper Douglas Road and Lower Douglas Road, on 17 July 1787.

CITIZENS' BAND

The two important influences on popular music in Cork in the middle of the nineteenth century were the Total Abstinence Movement and the British Military. Tens of thousands of people took Fr Mathew's pledge, formed themselves into clubs and sought means of entertaining themselves. Bands were organised, so numerous that there seemed to be one for every street in the city.

As a garrison city, Cork was familiar with the tradition of music in the British Army, each regiment boasting its own band. The bands paraded regularly through the city and represented the army at public and private establishment functions.

There were persons in the city, however, who felt that a band, independent of church and state, should be established, 'a band', the *Cork Examiner* commented, 'which will be always available on public occasions in the city, and which will play a class of music equal to those military bands which the commanding officers of regiments stationed here are so frequently chary in permitting the citizens to hear'. The idea met with the support of many of the respectable gentlemen of the city and Mr Howard, Band Master of Cork Artillery, was totally committed to the new band.

It was intended to have at least 30 musicians available at any time to perform at civic functions. Regular recitals would be given in the evenings on the Mardyke and on the New Wall (now the Marina).

The announcement of the formation of the Citizens' Band appeared in the *Cork Examiner* on 18 July 1860.

1860

19 July

WILLIE REDMOND RETURNS

William Redmond and J.J. O'Kelly, members of the 1891 Parnellite delegation to America, returned to Cork, having failed to raise vital finance. 'Parnellism, if such a thing at all exists in Queenstown,' the *Cork Examiner* commented, 'was evidently fast asleep on their arrival, for not a friendly voice was raised on their return to their native land. They came ashore practically unnoticed and unobserved.'

Redmond refused to be interviewed. He admitted, however, that there was great disunion and misunderstanding amongst the people of America, factors that interfered with the object they had been sent out to accomplish.

'It ought now be apparent to the Parnellites', the *Examiner* continued, 'what has long been obvious to everyone else, that Mr Parnell's effort to raise funds in America has been a disastrous failure, and has terminated just as most people anticipated it would.'

John Redmond and J.J. O'Kelly returned from America on 19 July 1891, and left Cork for Dublin, 'without having seen any of the local followers of the "Chief".'

1891

ST VINCENT'S CHURCH

The foundation stone of St Vincent's Church, Sunday's Well, was laid by Bishop Delaney in 1851. The Church, in the Gothic style, was designed by Sir John Benson and built in red sandstone – which may have come from the Glanmire Road railway tunnel – and limestone dressings. The contractors involved were Barry McMullen and E. and P. O'Flynn.

In 1853, when the church was partly built, a violent storm blew away the roof. However, the citizens contributed generously to have the work completed. The church consists of a nave, separated from the aisles by columns of Irish marble. The high altar at the eastern end of the church is made from marble and caen stone. The interior of the church was designed by Goldie and Child, London.

'This beautiful church', the *Cork Examiner* reported, 'which through so many difficulties and vicissitudes has now reached completion, and stands a noble monument to the zeal and piety of its founder, was yesterday consecrated solemnly to the service of religion.' The guests at the ceremony included bishops from all over the country, including the Primate of All-Ireland, Dr Dixon, who preached the sermon.

The church was thronged and huge crowds were gathered outside when the Bishop of Cork, Dr Delaney, solemnly blessed St Vincent's Church on 20 July 1856.

1856

21 July

BONS SECOURS CONVENT

The Bons Secours Nursing Order arrived in Cork in 1868 and established a convent in the Mardyke, a building subsequently used as the County Library. The conditions, however, were unacceptable, the house, situated in the Marsh, being subject to periodic flooding. The nuns were on the point of leaving Cork when they were prevailed upon to find an alternative site and construct a new convent.

A site was acquired on College Road at a cost of £1,200, which fee was paid by the head office of the order in Paris. Dominic J. Coakley, London, was commissioned to design the convent and John Delany of Great George's Street, Cork, was entrusted with the construction. The architect specified that the American technique of building be employed: hollow walls with stone on the outside and brick inside, bonded together with iron clamps. Decorative work was at a minimum, only the chapel displaying any signs of ostentation, Cork red marble and Bath stone being used to relieve the austerity of the building.

The Greenmount Industrial School Band played sacred music when the Bishop of Cork, Dr Delaney, laid the foundation stone of the Bon Secours Convent on 21 July 1879.

1879

THACKERAY IN CORK

During the early part of the week the city began to fill up with visitors from all over the country and from the kingdoms of England, Scotland and Wales. Prize farm animals and the newest of agricultural machinery were shipped into Cork. The city was the venue for the first meeting of the Royal Agricultural Society of Ireland.

The idea for the establishment of the Society came from an observation by Mr Purcell, the mailcoach entrepreneur. He argued that a Society, similar to the Highland Society of Scotland, bringing more knowledge, skill and mechanisation to the Irish farmer, would contribute handsomely to the fight against poverty. The idea was taken up with enthusiasm, and the Royal Agricultural Society was established.

One of the visitors to Cork was the distinguished writer, William Makepiece Thackeray. Although impressed by the organisation and splendour of the occasion, the great writer was overwhelmed by the ladies in Cork. 'They seem to excel the English ladies not only in wit and vivacity,' he wrote, 'but in the still more important article of the toilette. They are as well dressed as Frenchwomen, and incomparably handsomer; and if ever this book reaches a thirtieth edition, and I can find out better words to express admiration, they shall be inserted here. Among the ladies' accomplishments, I have heard … such fine music as is rarely to be met with out of a capital.'

William Makepiece Thackeray attended the first meeting of the Royal Agricultural Society of Ireland in Cork on 22 July 1842.

1842

23 July

THE 'DYKE'

After the siege of Cork in 1690 the marshes to the east and west of the city were reclaimed and the city began to expand. Edward Webber, the town clerk, undertook to construct a raised embankment through the marshes from Sheares Street, then known as Fenn's Quay, west to the point where the river Lee divides into two channels.

At the western end of the walk which was called Mardyke, apparently in imitation of a similar walk in Amsterdam, called *Meer Dyke*, a coffee house of red brick was constructed. The Mardyke was then, and for some time afterwards, known as the 'Red House Walk'. Webber died about the year 1735, and eventually the coffee shop was razed.

It appears that, after Webber's death, the walk came into the ownership of trustees. However, in July 1766, the Corporation made a grant of £50 to Henry Sheares, one of the trustees, 'to be applied by him and other managers of the Red House Walk in repairing same'.

The Mardyke Walk was landscaped by B. Wrixon: stone walls were erected to hold back the rising tide, seats were placed along the path, the surface was laid with gravel and the once famous elm trees were planted along its length. The public were regularly invited to subscribe to the upkeep of the walk and raffles, lotteries and various fundraising entertainments were held.

A public subscription was raised for the improvement of the Mardyke Walk on 23 July 1766.

1766

24 July

ELECTRO BIOLOGY

In 1851, two gentlemen, Fiske and Stone, advertised a course of lectures in the science of 'Electro Biology', at the Imperial Hotel. Mr Fiske explained that the nature and object of the science was 'confounded by unskilled persons with mesmerism on animal magnetism'. He reminded the audience, which included many religious and medical practitioners, that every great discovery had been at first denounced as impossible and absurd. He concluded with an appeal to their unbiased judgement.

Several gentlemen volunteered to participate in the demonstration, including Mr Dunscombe of Mount Desert and Mr George Crawford, citizens whose integrity was above suspicion. Mr Dunscombe was an especially good subject who, when hypnotised, failed to open his mouth or his eyes, sit or rise. He failed to take hold of a stick, or release it, save at the will of the operator. Many other experiments were performed, amongst them putting a large group of persons into a deep sleep.

The *Cork Examiner,* reporting on the performance, commended the skill of the operators, and while confessing to be nonplussed by the science, 'the nature of which it is most difficult, if not impossible, to explain', recommended that its readers should attend.

The exhibition of 'Electro Biology', now known as hypnotism, was given on 24 July 1851.

1851

25 July

JAMES MIRANDA BARRY

James Miranda Barry, whose father was probably a cousin of the artist James Barry, was born in Cork in 1799. In 1809, the young Barry, at ten years of age, entered the medical faculty of Edinburgh University.

Barry graduated in 1812, and after a period working in St Thomas' Hospital, London, enlisted as a surgeon in the British Navy and was posted to the Cape of Good Hope.

Barry was an extremely efficient, progressive medical officer, at various times proposing such innovations as cleanliness, regular changes of dressings, good drainage, sanitation and less overcrowding in hospitals. Barry introduced vaccination against smallpox and advocated regular sea baths and short hair cuts for the soldiers, the latter proposal not being implemented until Wellington, an Irishman, did so during the Peninsular campaign.

In 1826, Barry performed what may have been the first Caesarian operation in Africa. Always controversial, Barry was accused of having an 'unnatural' relationship with Lord Somerset who was challenged in the House of Commons with 'an unspeakable atrocity with his reputed son, the household physician'.

James Miranda Barry saw service in Jamaica, Malta and St Helena, being medical officer to Napoleon, and rose to the position of Surgeon General in the Navy. However, the controversy that surrounded Barry in life was nothing to that on death when an examination revealed that Barry was a woman and a mother!

James Miranda Barry of Cork, who died on 25 July 1865, was the first woman, 50 years before Elizabeth Garrett Anderson, to graduate in medicine from a recognised university, becoming the first woman doctor in western society.

1865

26 July

PRICE OF FOOD

There was considerable poverty in Cork in 1793. Food was both scarce and expensive. In April six bakeries closed their doors and no bread was to be had in the city. Potatoes were eight pence per weight, mutton was six pence per pound, beefstakes were eight pence per pound and coal was seven shillings and seven pence per barrel.

The position continued to worsen. In July, old potatoes had risen to one shilling per weight and new potatoes were one shilling and six pence per weight. Hucksters' meal was selling at sixteen pence per weight.

A great food riot broke out in Blackpool and the Mayor was forced to call out the 40th Regiment to quell the disturbances. Order was restored only when the Mayor agreed, on 26 July 1793, to allow the markets to remain open to give the citizens an opportunity to purchase the scarce items of food.

1793

27 July

THE MUNSTER ACADEMY

The Munster Academy was established by Thomas White in the early 1770s. It was one of the most distinguised private schools of that period, being mentioned by Francis Tuckey in his *Remembrancer*. Like the other schools, it catered for the sons of the emerging native merchant classes and prepared them for the European world of business.

The Academy was a series of schools, providing classes in languages, modern and classical, mathematics, geography and the fine arts. It had some of the finest teachers of the day, amongst whom were Rev Maurice Connor, Daniel Sullivan and Rev Giles Lee.

The departure of several teachers led to a decline in its reputation and in 1789, a Catholic priest, Rev David Daun, acquired the school. Fr Daun removed the school from 13 Grand Parade to 'a commodius house' in Academy Street, where he proposed to provide 'genteel accommodation for Boarders and different schools for the Sciences'. Subjects included 'Reading, Writing, Accounts, Algebra, Geometry, Trigonemtry, Conic sections, Geography, Chronology, Use of Globes and Maps, and every other branch of mathematics, adapted to Military, Naval and Mercantile Line. English Grammar, French in Parisian Purity, Italian, Latin Greek, Logic, Metaphysics, Physics and Ethics, Ancient and Modern History, Rhetoric (Oratory) with other fine Arts of Belles Lettres'.

Rev David Daun announced his acquisition of The Munster Academy on 27 July 1789.

1789

28 July

TRINITY PRESBYTERIAN CHURCH

Presbyterians arrived in Cork during the second half of the seventeenth century. The first minister, Rev John Brinkley, being mentioned in 1675. They erected a church on Dunscombe's, or the East Marsh, in the general location of Oliver Plunkett Street. Later they moved to Watergate Lane, near the present Hanover Street.

The Presbyterian Church was in some doctrinal confusion at this time and churches were built by different factions in Princes Street, and later, the 'Scots Church' in Queen Street, or as it is now known, Fr Mathew Street. In time, this church proving too small, the community acquired a beautiful site at the foot of Summerhill and commissioned an English architect, Mr Tarring, to design a new church.

Tarring elected to use a combination of local limestone and both Portland and Bath stone in the construction. The technique used was Kentish Rag Stonework, the only example of this system in the city. The spire, 140 feet high, is slightly off centre, a consequence, it is said, of the work of a drunken stonemason! However, the architect was apparently well satisfied with the quality of the work and he gave a dinner in the workers' honour in the Imperial Hotel.

In 1928, the re-union of the churches in Fr Mathew Street and Summerhill was effected and the joint congregation took the name 'Cork Trinity United Church'. The name survived until the 1950s when the word 'United' was dropped from the title.

The Trinity Church, Summerhill, was opened for service on 28 July 1861.

1861

CORK TUNNEL COMPLETED

When the directors of the Great Southern and Western Railway Company considered the final stretch of the route of the railway line from Dublin to Cork, they were faced with a dilemma. The direct route led immediately under Mayfield Hill and involved them in 'one of the greatest engineering enterprises which Ireland can exhibit'.

They considered alternate routes, the most obvious being through Blackpool, along the banks of the Kiln River. The line of this route led through a heavily built-up area involving the company in too high a level of compensation for property acquired. Another route lay up the Glen Valley and over Ballyvolane but the final descent into the station was too acute. There was no alternative but to tunnel through the hill, a distance of 1,340 yards with fifteen yards extra to accommodate a bridge.

The work, at two faces, was commenced in 1847, but it proved difficult and dangerous, proceeding at not more than three and a half feet per week. Several men were killed in an explosion near the Blackpool end of the tunnel. Work was proceeding simultaneously on four ventilation shafts, two near Assumption Road, a third near Old Youghal Road and the fourth in Bellevue Park.

Eventually, the two headings of the tunnel, being not more than a foot out of line, 'met most accurately', as the *Cork Examiner* reported, on 29 July 1854.

1854

THE IRISH WHIP

The Braves Field, Boston, USA, was filled to capacity on 30 July 1935, when Dan O'Mahony of Ballydehob, better known as 'Danno', defeated Ed Don George for 'what was almost unanimously recognised as the world final Heavyweight Wrestling Championship'. The referee was none other than Jim Braddock, the reigning Heavyweight Boxing Champion of the world.

Exactly one year later, Danno was in Cork to receive the acclamation of the citizens. A reception committee, which included the Lord Mayor, Alderman Sean French, J. Bennett, the well-known athlete and P. Kelly, Secretary, Reception Committee, travelled to Wilton to welcome Danno to Cork. From an earlier hour huge crowds thronged the route of the procession and thousands congregated at Victoria Cross. It was a reception, the *Cork Examiner* stated, 'of a size unique in Cork's history'.

The official party took their seats in an open landau, decorated with the tricolour and 'Old Glory', and led by ten bands, with another bringing up the rear. It proceeded down the Western Road, Washington Street and Patrick's Street to the Lower Glanmire Road.

There was a banquet in the Arcadia Ballroom, presided over by the Lord Mayor, during which a Tara brooch was presented to Mrs O'Mahony, and Danno received a silver tea set. Asked as to his future plans, Danno replied 'I do not know, or I do not care. I will fight anyone I am matched with'.

The reception for Danno Mahony was held in the Arcadia Ballroom on 30 July 1936, one year to the day on which he had won the Heavyweight Wrestling Championship of the World.

1936

ALL THEIR WORLDLY GOODS

In 1643, Thomas Abbott of Cork petitioned to have the brothers Robert and William King declared bankrupt. A warrant was issued by John Roche, Mayor, and Richard Gallawey and Robert Thyrry, Sheriffs, directing Dominick Copinger, Nicolas Skyddy, James Piersy and Jonas Morrishe to take possession of two trunks owned by the brothers, and perform an appraisal of the goods contained therein.

	£ s d
The first trunk contained:	
One dozen of half-worn French cloath napkins	0 08 00
One dozen and a half of old napkins	0 07 00
Eight old Pillowbears	0 10 00
Two pairs of sheets	0 18 00
Eight pairs of sheets, at 6s. per pair	2 08 00
Four old table cloaths	0 04 00
One pair of old sheets	0 07 00
Two short table cloaths	0 06 00
Four table cloaths	0 06 00
Nine silver spoons, containing thirtine ounces and a half a qr. of an ounce, at 4s. per ounce	2 12 6
In small silver	0 01 6
Eight pieces of bowed gold and 4 gold rings weighing three-quarters of an ounce and a dram	2 08 00
A Bracelet of pearl and an old bugle purse, at	0 02 00
Three quarters of an ounce and half a qr. of silver and gold berelace	0 03 00
The second trunk contained:	
One Cloake with an old loose taffits lining	2 00 00
One black gown and kirtell	1 05 00
Two silver bowes weighing 17 ounces and a half and a half a quarter, at four shillings per ounce	3 11 00
An old gown and kirtle	0 13 4
An other old gown and kirtle	0 13 4
A bearing blanket	0 3 4
The two trunkes	0 6 0
Total	19 13 0

The warrant, authorising officers of the Corporation to search and ascertain the value of the total worldly possessions of the brothers King, was issued on 31 July 1643.

1643

IMPERIAL CLARENCE HOTEL

At the beginning of the nineteenth century, when trade and business were booming as a direct result of England's foreign wars, the business people of Cork decided that the time had come to provide themselves with an 'Exchange', that is, a building wherein they could conduct their affairs with a degree of comfort commensurate with their pretensions.

On 20 March 1809, the Commercial Buildings Company was formed. Each member was required to contribute £100, and a sum of £12,000 was raised. Sir Thomas Deane was commissioned to design the Exchange, which consisted of a coffee room, a restaurant and some sleeping accommodation.

In 1814 the Company decided to extend the premises. When they sought governmental support, an Act of Parliament, (Chapter 196, 54, George III) was passed providing for the imposition of a tax on shipping using Cork Harbour, 'one shilling British on all entries, inwards and outwards in the Port of Cork, post entries and coal entries inwards only excepted'. The revenue therefrom would be divided equally between the Commercial Buildings Company and the Cork Harbour Commissioners.

Sir Thomas Deane was again retained to erect a hotel and tavern at the rear of the existing premises on Pembroke Street. On completion, the Imperial Clarence Hotel was leased to a Mr W. Joyce and opened for business on 1 August 1819.

1819

THE SOUTH INFIRMARY

Before the middle years of the eighteenth century the state did not provide hospitals; people had to fend for themselves when they became ill. The poor were totally dependent on the charity and philanthropy of concerned citizens.

In 1762 an advertisement appeared in the *Corke Journal* newspaper. It was in the form of a statement that four doctors, Messrs Farmer and Davies, physicians, and Messrs Hungerford Daunt and John Thomas Patrickson, surgeons, were prepared to establish an infirmary on the south side of the city. Their services would be free, provided a suitable premises were obtained. Ten days later four more doctors, Messrs Connell, Haly, Ferguson and Baldwin announced their readiness to do likewise. Within four weeks of the first advertisement the South Infirmary was opened in premises adjacent to the Sugar Factory, near the Red Abbey.

In 1765 an Act of Parliament (5, George Ill) provided for the establishment of two infirmaries in the city and for the payment of £50 to each. In 1861 the South Infirmary merged with the County Hospital, Mallow, a stratagem enabling the Grand Jury to grant £700 annually to the Infirmary. It was renamed the South Charitable and County Hospital. There was a major change in management in 1899 when the Sisters of Mercy assumed responsibility for the administration of the hospital.

The newspaper advertisement which led to the establishment of the South Infirmary Hospital appeared on 2 August 1762.

1762

3 August

VICTORIA VISITS

On 1 August 1849, Queen Victoria, accompanied by her consort, Albert, embarked on the royal yacht *Royal Victoria and Albert* for Cork. It was thought that the voyage would take a few days, but a following wind ensured a speedy journey – much to the relief of the Queen, who was not a good sailor.

A spectacular fireworks display greeted the flotilla of ships when they rounded Roche's Point and entered Cork harbour at 10 pm on 2 August. On the following morning an armada of ships and boats of every description travelled down river to greet the royal visitor. Queen Victoria condescended to step ashore in Cobh so that the name of the town might be changed to Queenstown. She then went aboard the royal yacht *Fairey* and proceeded up river to Cork. A halt was made at Blackrock to allow local fishermen make a presentation of a salmon to the Queen.

A pavilion had been erected at Custom House Quay where civic and other dignitaries were gathered to pay their respects. Overhead a huge banner proclaimed *Céad Míle Fáilte*. The Mayor, William Lyons, went aboard the *Fairey* and was knighted by the Queen. Victoria and Albert were escorted on a tour of the city, bedecked with flags and garlands. Huge arches towered over streets thronged with people. A statue of the queen was unveiled as she passed by the Queen's College.

Queen Victoria, the first reigning British monarch to visit Cork, arrived in the city on 3 August 1849.

1849

DEATH OF R. DOWDEN

Richard Dowden was born in Bandon on 12 April 1794. As a young man he studied medicine, but was persuaded to abandon his studies to assume control of the magnesia and mineral water manufactory of Jennings in Brown Street, Cork. He lived for a time in Pembroke Street, but in 1831 built a house, Rath Lee, in Sunday's Well.

It is virtually impossible to identify any educational or philanthropic organisation in Cork in the nineteenth century and fail to find the name of Richard Dowden associated with it. He was a Poor law Guardian, a governor of the lunatic asylum, and a prominent officer of the blind asylum. He was also a member of Cork Corporation and in 1845 was elected Mayor.

Richard Dowden was a member of the Cuvierian Society, the Cork Literary and Scientific Society, the Zoological Society of Dublin, the British Association and the '82 Club. He was one of the trustees and Hon Treasurer of the Independent Church in Princes Street. He was the author of an acclaimed booklet, *Botany of the Bohereens*, and of numerous articles on such diverse topics as 'Sacred Music on Sunday's Afternoon', 'Fresh Paint Pays its Way', 'Fatness, its Physiology and Morals', 'Prayer to put Horse Racing hors de Combat' and 'The Beautiful City'.

William Martin, a Quaker, and Richard Dowden, a Unitarian, established the Temperance Movement in Cork. Two years later Dowden persuaded his life-time friend, Fr Mathew, to assume the leadership.

Richard Dowden, one of the great philanthropists of Cork, died on 4 August 1861.

1861

ELECTRIC LIGHT IN CORK

It was a considerable achievement by Mr H. McNaughton-Jones, Professor of Midwifery at Queen's College (now University College) to persuade the British Medical Association to hold its Annual Meeting in Cork in 1879.

So many doctors attended – contemporary estimates were between 500-600 – that it was said that London and Dublin had been denuded of consultants! Spouses and friends also came, and an organising committee was kept busy catering for the interests of the visitors.

The travel agent, Thomas Cook, opened an office in the college to co-ordinate travel arrangements. Postal and telegraph facilities were specially provided and the Great Southern and Western Railway offered reduced excursion fares to the delegates. There were many entertainments on offer: a flower show, a *conversazione* in the Opera House, a dinner in the Assembly Rooms and excursions to the many beauty spots around Munster.

But of far more significance than the meeting of the Medical Association was the occasion of a demonstration of the new wonder of the age – electricity. The museum and halls of the college were wired specially for the occasion. The apparatus used was described as 'Jablochkoff Candles', and a lecture was given on the theory and practical use of electricity by Monsieur M.J.A. Berly of the Société d'Électricité, Paris.

Electric lighting was demonstrated publicly for the first time in Cork on 5 August 1879.

1879

WALTER RALEIGH DEPARTS

Walter Raleigh was born in Devon, England, in 1554. Educated at Oxford, he practised law in the Middle Temple. He went to sea, becoming one of many privateers who served Queen Elizabeth by preying on the Spanish and Portuguese ships returning with booty from the Americas.

Raleigh ingratiated himself with Queen Elizabeth, who presented him with vast estates in Counties Cork and Waterford. These he largely neglected, preferring the life of comfort and intrigue in the London court. He was knighted, appointed Lieutenant of Cornwall, and was responsible for the muster of troops in Devon and Cornwall when Spain threatened England with invasion.

Raleigh was intensely interested in colonising the Americas and established a colony in North America, which he named Virginia, in honour of the Queen. He organised and led an expedition to South America and journeyed up the Orinoco River. On his return he wrote a book, *Discovery of Guyana*.

He fell out of favour at court and was interned in the Tower of London. On his release he organised another expedition to find El Dorado, the fabled city of gold. His fleet initially consisted of thirteen ships and 1,000 men but it was dispersed in a storm and he continued the voyage with a reduced force.

Raleigh called into Cork Harbour and visited friends before sailing on his last ill-fated voyage from the Cork quays on 6 August 1617.

1617

7 August

CORRUPTION IN CORK

A contributor to the *Cork Examiner*, using the pen-name 'Cincinnatus', sought to expose the ineptitude and corruption of Cork Corporation in 1842. The passing of the Emancipation Act in 1829 and the Municipal Reform Act of 1840 had raised great hopes that a new era was beginning in the administration of civic affairs. 'Cincinnatus' found, however, that little had changed.

He expatiated on the abuses still current: inflated salaries and perquisites paid to the Mayor and other officials, the extravagant cost of maintaining the Mansion House, and the sumptuous hospitality which the Mayor lavished on judges and grand juries, 'who will not contribute to the support of any of the public charities, the price of even an empty claret bottle'. He accused the judges and grand juries of having manipulated the tax system so that the burden was removed from their own shoulders and imposed on the emerging middle classes.

'Cincinnatus' excoriated both the Corporation and the grand jury for having failed to maintain the Fever Hospital and the North and South Infirmaries, for leaving the poor destitute and failing to provide a supply of piped water to the city.

The anonymous scribe concluded that the civic authorities would be better employed if they were to rid themselves of the Mansion House, introduce financial reforms and apply the public resources for the benefit of the citizens and the city.

'Cincinnatus' expressed his trenchant criticisms in the pages of the *Cork Examiner* on 7 August 1842.

1842

DEATH OF CROFTON CROKER

Thomas Crofton Croker was born at Buckingham Square, Cork, on 15 January 1798. He was educated locally and then apprenticed to the Quaker firm of Lecky and Monk. Following his father's death in 1818, his mother managed to secure for Thomas a place in the British Civil Service.

He had already demonstrated an interest in antiquarian matters and had travelled extensively throughout west Cork collecting folklore. As early as 1815 some translations of his from the Irish were published in the *Morning Post* and in 1818 he sent old Irish airs to Thomas Moore.

Croker visited Ireland in 1821 and his *Researches in the South of Ireland* was published a short time afterwards. This was followed by *Fairy Legends in the South of Ireland*, the second edition of which was illustrated by Daniel Maclise. The German edition was translated by the Grimm brothers. Other works followed: *Legends of the Lakes or sayings and doings of Killarney and Songs of Ireland*. He edited the *Journey of a Tour through Ireland*, translated from the French of De La Boullaye Le Gouz.

Crofton Croker's work was not universally acclaimed. Sir Walter Scott was an early admirer, while William Butler Yeats held that he 'altered his materials without the word of warning and could never resist the chance of turning some nice fairy tale into a drunken peasant's dream ... nor could he quite desist from dressing his personages in the dirty rags of the stage Irishman'.

Douglas Hyde was not as critical as Yeats, conceding that Croker had been the first to delve into the rich traditions of Irish folklore.

Thomas Crofton Croker died on 8 August 1854.

1854

MACLISE AND SCOTT

In the early years of the nineteenth century Sir Walter Scott was widely acclaimed as the greatest living novelist. In 1825 he undertook an extensive tour of Ireland, having previously paid a few fleeting visits. He disembarked at Belfast, proceeded to Dublin to visit his son, and arrived in Cork via Killarney, Millstreet and Mallow.

Scott enjoyed a picnic in the grounds of Blarney Castle and, on his return to the city, found his hotel besieged by people eager to catch a glimpse of such a famous writer. A delegation from the Corporation waited on him and he was invited to dine with members of the legal profession. He also accepted an invitation to visit Bolster's bookshop.

This establishment stood at the junction of St Patrick's Street and Ss Peter and Paul's Place. The proprietor, John Bolster, was a well-known literary figure and editor of the magazine, *Bolster's Quarterly*. Unknown to the Scott party, Bolster had arranged for the fourteen-year-old Cork artist, Daniel Maclise, to hide himself in the shop. While Bolster engaged Scott in conversation, Maclise contrived to draw a portrait of the writer.

On viewing the completed work, Sir Walter Scott was amazed at the skill of Maclise, and encouraged him to develop his talent in London.

Daniel Maclise from Sheares Street executed the portrait of Sir Walter Scott on 9 August 1825.

1825

SS PETER AND PAUL'S

The task of replacing the old church of Ss Peter and Paul in Carey's Lane was entrusted to Fr John Murphy who commissioned the architect E.W. Pugin. Barry McMullen was appointed builder and the foundation stone was laid on 15 August 1859.

Ss Peter and Paul's Church is in the Gothic style. Constructed of local materials – rich red sandstone with limestone dressings – it consists of a nave, two aisles and a tower. There are ten columns, five on either side of the nave, the bases of which are of black marble from Foynes, at the mouth of the River Shannon. Over these, the plinths and columns are of polished red marble from Churchtown, County Cork. The columns around the side altars are in white Sicilian and Galway green marbles, and those under the choir are in red marble from the Little Island quarries. The church was opened for divine service on 29 June 1866.

In 1874, G.C. Ashlin of Dublin was commissioned to design a new altar. The work was executed in Samuel Daly's establishment, Cook Street, Cork, Michael Murphy being primarily responsible for the carving. The altar is 33 feet in height and 36 feet in length. The base is six feet from back to front and eleven feet in length, and the altar table is a splendid slab twelve feet long, two feet wide and over seven inches thick, and is executed in Sicilian blue marble. The statuary and more detailed carvings are worked out of pure white Italian marble.

The High Altar in Ss Peter and Paul's Church was consecrated on 10 August 1874.

1874

FREE STATE ARMY TAKES CORK

In August 1922, the Republican or 'Irregular' forces suffered a series of defeats at the hands of the Free State Army. The 'Irregulars' abandoned their entrenched positions in County Cork and retreated into the city, vowing to defend it against the advancing army.

On 9 August, troops of the Free State Army disembarked from the requisitioned B. and I. Line ship, *Lady Wicklow*, at Passage West and began an advance on Cork. The 'Irregulars' set fire to the police barracks at Union Quay, Empress Place (now Summerhill), Cornmarket Street and Tuckey Street as well as the Victoria (now Collins) Military Barracks. They also caused vehicles to be dumped into the river and attempted to destroy Brian Boru, Parnell and Parliament Bridges. Anticipating an attack from the south, via the Douglas Road, they commandeered and barricaded the Provincial Bank premises at the eastern end of the South Mall.

A great pall of smoke lay over the city as the Free State forces approached. But the 'Irregulars' abandoned Cork without offering a defence and General Ennis led the first platoon into the city, over the damaged Parnell Bridge. The citizens thronged the streets to greet them and the management of the Victoria, Imperial and other hotels provided refreshments for the soldiers.

The Free State Army regained possession of Cork City on 11 August 1922.

CHARLES GIBSON

Charles Bernard Gibson was born in 1807, probably in Dublin. A non-conformist, he became a minister of the Irish Evangelical Society in Mallow in 1834.

During the period of his residence in Mallow he owned a printing press which he offered to Thomas Davis and the Young Irelanders for use in furthering the Repeal Movement. He also published booklets which he distributed to children.

In 1848 he joined the Presbyterian Church and seven years later was appointed chaplain to the Presbyterian prisoners on Spike Island, during which time he lived in Monkstown. His experiences led to the publication of his *Life among Convicts*. He appears to have retained the incumbency of Mallow as, in 1860, he published a pamphlet, 'The Spike Island Chaplaincy and the Mallow Congregation'. Among his other works were *Historical Portraits of Irish Chieftains and Anglo-Norman Knights and Philosophy, Science and Revelation*. His last work, *Dearforgil*, was published in 1884.

In 1845 Gibson had been an unsuccessful applicant for the position of librarian in the new Queen's College, and he subsequently emigrated to England where he became lecturer at St. John's, Hoxton, and Anglican chaplain to Shoreditch Workhouse. However, he is best remembered in Cork for his *History of the City and County of Cork*, which was published in 1861.

The Rev Charles Gibson died in London on 12 August 1885.

THE MANSION HOUSE

In 1763, the Corporation of Cork decided by resolution to erect a public building that would reflect the growing affluence of the city: 'that a Mayoralty House be built for the habitation of the Mayors of this City, on the ground on Haman's Marsh, expenses out of the revenues of the City, and that Mr Mayor, Sheriff Travers, Aldermen Newman, Weterall, with those of the C.D.H., be a committee for approving of a proper plan for carrying out same.'

The contract for the design and construction was awarded to Davies Duckart. Of Italian-French extraction, he was responsible for the Limerick Custom House and several large private residences in the south-west part of Ireland. The Mansion House was designed in the Palladian style. The stucco work in the reception rooms was undertaken by Patrick Osborne. Construction costs came to £2,000.

The Corporation were not satisfied with either the quality of the work or the rate of progress, and claimed that Duckart did not spend sufficient time on the site. The building was eventually completed in 1773. For over 100 years it served as the centre of local administration before it was sold for use as a school. Later it was acquired for the Mercy Order of nuns. The original Mansion House is now incorporated into the Mercy Hospital and constitutes the north-west wing of the complex.

Cork Corporation resolved to construct the Mansion House on 13 August 1763.

1763

THE BLACK DEATH IN CORK

The Black Death, or the Plague, as it was called, ravaged Europe during the fourteenth century. A French chronicler, Jean Froissart, estimated that one-third of the total population of the continent perished as a result of the infestation. The Plague struck irrespective of rank. Among its victims were Eleanor, Queen of Peter IV of Aragon, two successive archbishops of Canterbury, Laura, who inspired the poetry of Petrarch, and his patron, Cardinal Giovanni Colanna.

The disease originated in China and inner Asia early in the fourteenth century. An Asian army catapulted corpses, infected with the Plague, into a Genoese trading post in the Crimea. The disease decimated the population and those who escaped by sea carried the Black Death to Europe. By 1348 it was in Ireland.

The Plague was carried by fleas which infested rats, and consequently it spread most rapidly in densely populated places. Particularly vulnerable were monastic settlements; friars, ministering to the sick, became victims themselves. The *Annals of the Four Masters* record the incidence of the Plague in Ireland. A local source relates that 'in this time of the great pestilence the greater part of Cork and other faithful men of the king dwelling there went the way of all flesh'. In 1350, the Mayor and bailiffs of Cork were petitioning the Crown for the relief of taxes because of the late pestilence in these parts.

The Black Death was rampant in Cork on 14 August 1348.

BOWL PLAYING

In their desire to defeat the Irish, English governments, and their supporters in Ireland, sought to eradicate all vestiges of an indigineous Irish society. The Irish language, the law code, the mode of dress, etc., were declared illegal. The Statutes of Kilkenny forbade the playing of Irish games, especially hurling.

In the seventeenth century Cork Corporation forbade the playing of hurling and another ball game in the city. In 1791 the Corporation attempted to stop bowl playing.

We are happy to hear that our active High Constables and Assistant Peace Officers are prepared to put a stop to this dangerous amusement in the Liberties of this City (Cork), and bring the offenders to justice. On the Passage Road about two years since, a boy twelve years of age was killed by a stroke of the bowl, and many similar incidents also happened, yet the practice is again renewed by some Ruffians. The exertions of gentlemen in the vicinity of the City must soon put a final stop to an illegal exercise so dangerous to society on the King's highway. N.B. A few days ago a boy eight years old was killed near the Lough by being struck on the head with a bowl.

The above article appeared in the *Cork Evening Post* newspaper on 15 August 1791.

1791

16 August

BALLINTEMPLE CORPORATION

In the early days of the nineteenth century the members of Cork Corporation were notoriously profligate with the city revenues. Once a year they indulged themselves particularly lavishly, wining and dining at Blackrock Castle at the city's expense, with a blatant disregard for public opinion.

Some citizens, concerned at the Corporation's autocratic behaviour, felt that subjecting the members to public ridicule might bring them to their senses. Thus, a group calling themselves the 'Ballintemple Corporation', convened regularly in a small building called 'Barrington's Folly' in Barrington's Avenue, Ballintemple. In 1811 the Ballintemple Corporation decided to ridicule the behaviour of the city fathers on the occasion of their annual junket to Blackrock Castle.

A number of people, dressed as knights of chivalry (who were dubbed 'The Knights of the Round Table'), accompanied by various lackeys, walked in procession to Ballintemple, followed by a huge throng of citizens. They were greeted by the members of the Ballintemple Corporation resplendent in mock civic regalia and attended by 'functionaries' bearing facsimiles of Corporation insignia. Both groups joined forces, and the combined party proceed to 'Barrington's Folly' where entertainments and a fireworks display had been organised.

The elaborate burlesque went on until a late hour on the evening of 16 August 1811.

1811

BRITISH ASSOC. IN CORK

The British Association was established to promote the sciences. In 1843 the cities of Cork and York were in contention as to which would host the annual general meeting of the Association's General Council. As a gesture of goodwill towards the incoming president (the famous scientist, the Earl of Rosse), Cork was selected.

The middle-class burghers of Cork anticipated the event with enthusiasm, but when the admission fees were announced they reacted vehemently. They objected not only to the charge – a guinea – but also to the fact that the tickets were non-transferable. Eventually, with the support of the *Cork Examiner,* they had their way on one issue: the use of the ticket was extended to family members.

The lectures were arranged at various venues, the principal location being the Corn Exchange on Albert Quay. The Exchange was decorated in a lavish style for the occasion. 'The Cork Arms are beautifully painted over the great entrance,' the *Cork Examiner* reported, 'the imperial crown with the letters V.G. are to shine radiantly high above the chair.' Mr McDowell of the Imperial Hotel was entrusted with the catering arrangements. He erected a supper room adjoining the main hall of dimensions, the *Cork Examiner* declared, 'unparallelled in Ireland'. Twelve hundred people could be accommodated at one time, and the hall was illuminated by 24 candelabras with waxed lights.

The Annual General Meeting of the General Council of the British Association began in the Corn Exchange on 17 August 1843.

1843

THE PRIMROSE LEAGUE

The political scene in Ireland, in the 1890s, was dominated by agitation for the repeal of the Act of Union and for Home Rule. The Irish Parliamentary Party led this reform movement but there were many associations opposing constitutional change.

One such organisation was the peculiarly named Primrose League which became more active and successful as agitation for Reform intensified. Between 1886 and 1891 its membership increased from 15,000 to over 1,000,000. Although the Primrose League had a quasi-democratic front it was controlled by the aristocrats and landlords. The League sponsored lectures, published posters and pamphlets, and organised fêtes, garden parties and theatricals to promote the cause of Unionism.

In 1891, Cork's St Patrick's 'Habitation', as the local units were somewhat oddly titled, organised a fête in the grounds of Blarney Castle. A full day's entertainment was provided, including a flower show and games of rounders and tennis. The outstanding attraction, however, was the refreshment tent and the *Cork Examiner* reporter was impressed by the vast quantity of tea and cakes consumed.

Speeches were delivered by, among others, Mr Martin, a Galway landlord and author of such humorous songs as 'Ballyhooley' and 'Killaloe', who was also renowned for telling stories of an 'Oirish' nature.

The Blarney fête was held on 18 August 1891.

1891

EDWARD HINCKS

Edward Hincks was the eldest son of Thomas Dix Hincks, who was instrumental in the establishment of the Cork Institution. He was educated at home and later at Trinity College, Dublin. He graduated with a BA in 1811 and was awarded a gold medal. He became a clergyman and, in 1825, was appointed rector of Killyleagh, County Down.

Despite residing in such a remote area Edward Hincks established a reputation of the highest order in the esoteric field of the decipherment of Middle Eastern scripts. Initially, he contributed to the Transactions of the Royal Irish Academy on the subject of Egyptian hieroglyphics: he was the first to employ the correct method for their decipherment. In 1846 he was studying Assyrian, in particular the Median, Persian, Babylonian and Van inscriptions.

Hincks is credited with the discovery of the Persian Cuneiform vowel system, simultaneously with Rawlinson's independent discovery at Baghdad. He was a regular contributor to the *Dublin University Magazine, Transactions of the Royal Irish Academy, Journal of Sacred Literature*, and *Melananges Egyptologiques*. He began *An Assyrian Grammar in the Journal of the Royal Asiatic Society*, but died, on 3 December 1866, before its completion.

Edward Hincks was born in Cork on 19 August 1792.

1792

CHIMNEY SWEEPS DISPUTE

In the early 1800s a period of prosperity in Cork, during the Napoleonic Wars, was followed by one of unprecedented hardship. Trade was virtually at a standstill and poverty was widespread, the poor experiencing extreme deprivation. Civil unrest was rife, for much of which the 'combinations' (as trade unions were then called) were blamed. As far as the 'combinations' were concerned they were doing no more than protecting their members' rights and welfare.

Morgan David, who was not a member of the chimney sweeps trade union, was employed by a Mr Fitzgerald to clean chimneys, using a machine which Fitzgerald had invented. This machine dispensed with the need for young boys (known as 'climbing boys') to climb up the inside of chimneys in order to clean them, a most dangerous and unhealthy practice. The sweeps warned David not to use the machine as it posed a threat to their employment.

David ignored the sweeps' warning, whereupon he was kidnapped, and forced to renounce the use of the machine. He was then enrolled as a member of the 'combination'. Subsequently, however, he acquired a machine for two guineas and persisted in using it. The sweeps forced an entry into David's house, attacked him and his wife and made off with the machine. David swore charges against his assailants.

Four men, two of them Falvey, and two others named Flynn and Fraser, described as members of the 'Sooty Corporation' (chimney sweeps), were charged with an assault on Morgan David and his wife in the Recorder's Court on 20 August 1819.

1819

WILLIAM MAGINN

William Maginn was born in Marlboro Street, Cork, on 10 July 1793. He was educated in his father's school and, at a very early age, went to Trinity College where he was awarded an LLD at 22 years of age, the youngest person ever to have been so honoured. After graduation he returned to Cork to teach.

His literary career began with contributions to *Bolster's Quarterly* in Cork, and then to *Blackwood's Magazine*. He emigrated to England to promote his career and wrote for *John Bull*, *London Literary Journal* and the *Quarterly Review*. He helped establish and edit *Fraser's Magazine* and prevailed upon his fellow Corkman, Daniel Maclise, to provide illustrations. A prolific writer, his output included several novels: *Whitehall*, *The Red Baron*, *John Manesty* and *Tales of Military Life*.

It was said of his *Homeric Ballads* 'that Maginn may be esteemed the first who consciously realised to himself the truth that Greek ballads can be really represented in English only by a similar measure. That is his great praise'. Matthew Arnold considered them as genuine poems in their own right.

Maginn could rarely suppress a barbed aphorism, and thereby lost friends as quickly as his talent attracted them. His intemperance led to loss of employment and poverty and he was imprisoned for non-payment of debts. Thackeray was among those who came to his aid.

William Maginn retired to Walton-on-Thames, to a house provided by a benefactor, and he died there alone, but for the company of his fellow Corkman, Edward Vaughan Kenealy, on 21 August 1842.

1842

THROWING THE DART

In August 1848, Cork Corporation decided to celebrate the ancient ceremony of 'Throwing the Dart'. This involved the Mayor and the Corporation in taking a journey by boat to the outer limits of Cork Harbour where a dart was hurled into the sea, thereby re-asserting the Corporation's jurisdiction.

Members of the Corporation and the Harbour Commissioners, accompanied by twenty guests, embarked on the steamer, *Royal Alice*, at Lapp's Quay. They were watched by a sullen, resentful crowd. At the Marina, workers employed on the construction of the 'New Wall' disregarded instructions and refused to cheer the party on its way.

The party was joined by officers from units of the British fleet which were then in the harbour. After the ceremony they adjourned to Haulbowline where they partook of a sumptuous champagne dinner. Various members of the British royal family and aristocracy were toasted and the band played 'Rule Brittania'.

Such a display of extravagance was felt to be wholly inappropriate at that time. It was 'Black '48' and the country was experiencing the worst effects of the Famine. Correspondents to the *Cork Examiner* excoriated the participants for their profligacy and psycophancy, one writer reminding them that both the army and navy had recently entered the city and intimidated the citizens with a formidable show of arms.

The custom of 'Throwing the Dart' was performed on 22 August 1848.

1848

PUBLIC LIGHTING

For much of its history Cork was a very small city, built on a series of islands. Its most distinctive feature was the number of streams that separated the islands. Many of the present city streets – Castle Street, Tuckey Street, Grand Parade, Patrick Street and the South Mall – were once water courses.

The unprotected rivers and canals posed a continuing threat to life, and contemporary records provide numerous accounts of deaths by drowning. The dangers were increased by the fact that streets and quays were unlit. This problem received regular consideration but there was a reluctance on the part of the Corporation, and the rate payers, to provide resources for a proper system of public lighting.

The position had become so critical in 1765 that several citizens volunteered to maintain lamps at their own expense if the Corporation would provide the standards. In 1766 the Corporation appointed certain people to assess the cost of erecting public lights in each parish. In the following years many schemes were advocated, but all failed for one reason or another.

Various Acts of Parliament were passed authorising the introduction of public lighting. An Act of George III provided for the erection of 1,500 lamps in Cork with 'a double burner in each lamp of good cotton wick yarn of 20 threads to each light'. The act provided for the lamps to be lit from 15 September to 15 May each year.

The Corporation agreed to implement the act and made provision for a scheme of public lighting on 23 August 1787.

1787

INDUSTRIAL UNREST

During the eighteenth century the development of Cork industry was habitually subject to external factors. Whenever Irish industry threatened English interests, in the woollen trade for instance, taxes or trade embargoes were invariably imposed on Irish native products. The consequence of those measures was the decimation of fledgling industries, mass unemployment, poverty and industrial unrest.

The outbreak of the American War of Independence had severe repercussions for Cork. English manufacturers of woollen goods and footwear, deprived of the American market, were left with substantial surplus stocks. An attempt was made to offload the goods at reduced prices on the Irish market. Native industries were threatened.

Contemporary reports indicate that two-thirds of the workforce were unemployed. Workers organised a boycott of shops and waylaid carriages transporting goods into Cork. On 3 March 1784, a protest march by the weavers ended in a riot in the city centre. In 1788 a huge crowd of the unemployed marched into the city and ransacked Main Street.

Legislation was introduced to inhibit the establishment of 'combinations', an early form of trade unions. Local groups of industrialists – like the Committee of Merchants, who controlled the Butter Market – prevented the coopers from forming a 'combination'. Workers avenged themselves on their fellows who refused to take part in strike action. On one occasion a shoemaker who scabbed on a strike was subjected to a new form of punishment.

He was tarred and feathered, the first recorded instance of this punishment, in Cork, on 24 August 1784.

1784

BISHOP CREAGH

In 1678, as a direct result of Titus Oates' allegations about a 'Popish Plot', the Penal Laws, which had not been recently invoked with either regularity or severity, were applied with renewed vigour. An edict was promulgated ordering the banishment of all Catholic bishops and priests from the country.

Bishop Creagh of Cork fled to the countryside for two years, but was arrested in 1680 and charged with taking part in a conspiracy. He was detained for a period in Limerick and then sent to Dublin. It was intended that he should be tried with Oliver Plunkett in London. However, due to illness and lack of evidence against him he was detained in Dublin. After the trial and execution of Oliver Plunkett, Bishop Creagh was returned for trial to Cork.

Chief Justice Davys presided when Manus Keeffe, Bryan Sweeney and others laid charges against the bishop. Under cross-examination Sweeney recanted, claiming that he had given evidence in order to procure employment. On the second day of the trial, the floor of the courthouse (a building now known as the 'Queen's Old Castle') collapsed.

Bishop Creagh, in an account of the incident, relates. 'And behold all, judges and advocates, nobles and common people ... went in all directions, one through the roof, one through the window ... but through the Grace of God no one was killed but hundreds were injured in the collapse'. Apparently Bishop Creagh and the Judge were the only two to escape unhurt. Justice Davys proclaimed that heaven had intervened to demonstrate the innocence of the defendant and he acquitted the Bishop.

The trial of Bishop Creagh took place on 25 August 1682.

1682

FREEDOM OF THE CITY

The custom of conferring the Freedom of the City on people who had distinguished themselves by public service dates from the fourteenth century. Over the years the custom had become debased and the honour was conferred freely and indiscriminately. Corporations conferred it to curry favour with people of influence.

The reformed Corporation of 1841 attempted to reform the system but it was the signing into law of The Municipal Privileges Act, 1875, that standardised the conditions whereby the honour could be conferred. And yet the Freedom of Cork was granted to many people of some temporary fame but now long since forgotten.

In 1877, the Corporation went to some inconvenience to confer the Freedom on a visitor to the city. A native of Cork, Mr Shea was on a visit to Ireland, but could not find the time to disembark from the Cunard steamer, *Bothnia*, to accept the honour in the Corporation Chambers. Accordingly the Mayor and members of the Corporation went to Cobh and boarded the *Bothnia*.

Unfortunately the recipient of the honour had already disembarked and gone to visit the Member of Parliament, Mr N.D. Murphy, at his residence in Currabinny. Emissaries were dispatched to expedite the return of the visitor and eventually the party assembled in the saloon of the steamer. The Mayor praised the achievement of Mr Shea, originally from Cork, who had achieved the exalted position of Chief Justice of the Marine court, New York.

The Freedom of Cork was conferred on the Chief Justice on board the *Bothnia* on 26 August 1877.

1877

ST LUKE'S CHURCH

To cater for the growing number of Church of Ireland members living in Douglas during the latter half of the nineteenth century it was decided to replace the old building, which had been consecrated on 25 October 1786, with a new church. Mr O.C. Edwards was appointed architect and Mr Edward Fitzgerald, Youghal, was the contractor.

This church is cruciform and consists of nave, vestry, south transepts and porches. There was provision for a tower, but this feature was not added until a later date. Several of the parishioners made substantial donations: Mr Seymour presented the organ, which was built by Murphy's of Duncan Street; the cost of the chancel was borne by Messrs J.W. and Hugh Pollock of Douglas; Mr John Lane provided the communion table, kneeling stools and Glastonbury chairs; the lectern was a gift of Captain Lunham and the great central light was donated by Valentine Tomkins. The rose window was a gift of the architect.

The gable windows on the south transept were made by Messrs Clutterbuck, the eastern and western windows on the northern transept by Saunders and Co. of London. All the other windows were manufactured by Waites and Co. of Newcastle-on-Tyne. In 1885, the nave was lengthened by twelve feet and a fifteen foot bell tower was added. The work was completed in 1889, the bell being presented by Miss Reeves.

St Lukes, Church of Ireland, Douglas, was consecrated on 27 August 1875.

1875

JOHN WINDELE

John Windele was born in Cork in 1801 and lived at Blair's Hill, Sunday's Well. From his youth he developed a keen interest in antiquarian matters and travelled the countryside examining ancient monuments, churches and ruins. A consummate artist, he left a substantial corpus of illustrations.

Windele was particularly interested in identifying and preserving Ogham stones, and he transferred many that were in danger of destruction to his own garden. He was accompanied on many of his journeys by Abraham Abell, William Willes and Fr Matt Horgan, who was responsible for the decipherment of the Ogham script. Windele was a noted linguist, fluent in Irish, English, French and Latin. He employed elderly Gaelic scribes, and prevailed on many of his friends to do likewise, in the translation and transcription of ancient documents.

He was a regular contributor to periodicals: *The Bagatelle*, which was published in Cork; *Dublin Penny Journal*; *Ulster Journal*; *Kilkenny Archaeological Journal* and the *Kilkenny Journal*. He collaborated with John Francis Maguire in the writing of *Irish Industrial Movement* and with the Halls in *Ireland and its Scenery*. He was editor of *Bolster's Quarterly*.

John Windele was author of *South of Ireland Guide*. He is, however, best remembered for his *Historical and Descriptive Notices of the City of Cork and its Vicinity, Gouganebarra, Glengarriff and Killarney*, which was published in three editions, and in facsimile.

John Windele, antiquarian and writer, died on 28 August 1865.

1865

CHRIST CHURCH

Churches have stood since earliest times on the site in the South Main Street where the building currently housing the Cork City and County Archives is located. The present structure, originally Christ Church, replaced an earlier church which had been badly damaged during the siege of 1690.

The Corporation of the time, having decided to replace the church, petitioned for help. An Act of Parliament was passed levying a tax on coal and cuim, the proceeds to be applied towards the construction of the new church. The body of the church, which was designed by Coltsman, was completed in 1720. Work began on the spire which, it was envisaged, would rise to a height of 170 feet. At 136 feet, however, it was noticeable that the spire was already beginning to lean to one side. Shortly afterwards the tower was reduced to 100 feet and capped. Unfortunately, it still continued to lean.

The condition of the tower was the cause of much concern. In 1747 the Assizes ordered that the tower be removed, but no action was taken and twenty years later, Chief Justice Willis noted that the tower lay 32 inches out of plumb.

The leaning tower of Christ Church was notorious, Pococke commenting in 1758 that it overhung as much as the tower in Pisa. It was also the cause of a new figure of speech being introduced: a person displaying partiality was said to be 'all to one side like Christ Church'. Eventually the Corporation ordered an investigation into the condition of the tower.

The decision by the Corporation to take down the leaning tower of Christ Church was taken on 29 of August 1823.

1823

30 August

THE *CORK EXAMINER*

John Francis Maguire was a firm supporter of the Reform Movement and of Daniel O'Connell. He was a journalist with several books to his credit, he became the owner and editor of a newspaper and he represented Cork as a Member of Parliament until his death in 1872.

Maguire, the politician, saw the need for an organ that would not only counteract establishment propaganda, but that would also advocate the aims of O'Connell. Maguire, the journalist, perceived that a newspaper would best meet those needs. The *Cork Examiner* was the result.

As editor he set out the aims of the new paper in the first edition. The *Cork Examiner* was established 'not to personal or private ends but to the welfare and interests of the whole community ... Regardless of all else save the liberty of our country, unmindful of all else save the happiness and prosperity of our children, there is one paramount interest, the service of Ireland, the liberty of Ireland. Hurrah for Repeal!' John Francis Maguire went on to commit the paper to support for O'Connell, the Catholic Church and Fr Mathew's Temperance Movement.

The first edition of the *Cork Examiner* was published on 30 August 1841.

1841

DICKENS IN CORK

The *Cork Examiner* reporter could hardly be accused of overstatement when he described Charles Dickens as being 'both personally and in his writings the most popular of living novelists'. The occasion was Dickens' visit to Cork in 1858.

Charles Dickens achieved fame with the appearance of *Pickwick Papers* in 1836. Subsequent novels ensured his reputation as one of the greatest of all writers. He travelled extensively giving readings of his work; one such tour brought him to Cork.

The *Cork Examiner* reported that there was a huge audience for the reading, especially in the galleries where 'the cram showed intellectual entertainment to be most favoured amongst the democracy'. The paper continued: 'the peculiarities of his appearance, the extreme elegance of his toilette, his handsome yet careworn features, his American moustache and beard, and those large wonderful eyes which seem to fascinate everyone's attention ...'

Charles Dickens was, according to the reporter, a consummate actor. 'His voice is full and mellow, strong without being noisy, and of the most versatile quality. Then he can speak with every muscle and line of his face and though he does not make much use of his hands, now and then he does startle with a somewhat vehement or fantastical action. All these aids are combined to make Scrooge more miserly, hard and exacting; his nephew more good humoured, forebearant, the ghost of Marley more transparent.'

Charles Dickens was in Cork on 31 August 1858.

1858

BLACKROCK IN 1843

Colonel North Ludlow Beamish, 4th Royal Irish Dragoons,was born on 31 December 1797, at Beaumont House, Blackrock, Cork. He became an acknowledged expert on military theory and translated from the German many of Bismark's manuals on cavalry.

In 1843 Ludlow Beamish presented a paper, 'Statistical Report of the Parish of St Michael' (Blackrock), to a meeting of the British Association. Having defined the parish boundary he reported that the population stood at 2,630, consisting of 457 families living in 413 houses: 2,187 of the population were Catholic, 443 being Protestant or Dissenters; 90 families lived in one-room accommodation, 260 in two rooms, 207 in three rooms or more; the average number of persons to a bed was three; there were fifteen carpenters, fourteen masons, twelve slaters, ten tailors, fourteen shoemakers, nine smiths, three coopers, two cabinet makers, 32 gardeners, 53 farmers, thirteen gingle (jarvey) drivers, eighteen lime burners, 56 brickmakers, 111 fishermen, 79 male servants, 212 labourers, 46 aged and infirm and 426 children.

The average weekly wage of a tradesman was £1.00, five shillings for labourers. Women and children were paid as little as two shillings per week. The diet of the poorest families consisted of potatoes and milk or potatoes and salt fish, the cost of which was about nine and a half pence per person per day. The fishermen worked for only six months of the year and were in poor circumstances. Only three people had accounts in the Savings Bank. There was no supply of fresh water in the houses. Although few of the adults were members of the Total Abstinence Association there was no record of drunkenness. There were only two illegitimate children in the parish.

Colonel North Ludlow Beamish read his report on the Parish of Blackrock to a meeting of the British Association on 1 September 1843.

1843

BALLOON ASCENT

In a field on the outskirts of Cork, on the afternoon of a September day in 1816, a balloonist by the name of Sadler prepared for an ascent. He released a trial balloon in order to gauge the direction and strength of the wind. Satisfied that the weather was suitable, he entered the basket at twenty minutes past four, a gun was discharged and the balloon rose into the sky.

Many thousands of the citizens witnessed the unusual event and Sadler waved to the crowds before disappearing temporarily into a cloud. To allay the fears of his friends on the ground, he reduced height as the wind drove the balloon away from the city in a southerly direction.

His view of the surrounding countryside was he, he reported afterwards 'sublime in the extreme': the coastline, from Bantry in the west to Waterford in the east, lay stretched out below him. As Sadler had not intended to remain aloft for a long period, he opened the valve at twelve minutes past five and prepared to make his descent. He made a safe landing in the countryside, thereby causing some alarm amongst the local farmers. He was, however, offered hospitality and accommodation by two gentlemen, Messrs Hodder and Foote.

Mr Sadler made his successful flight on 2 September 1816.

1816

WILLIAM PENN VISIT

William Penn was born on 14 October 1644, at Tower Hill, London, the son of Admiral Sir William Penn. He was educated at Chigwell School and Oxford, from which university he was expelled for nonconformity: at this early stage Penn had come under the influence of the Quakers. He went to France and studied for two years at the Protestant University of Saumur, before returning to London to study law at Lincoln's Inn.

Cromwell had rewarded William's father, Admiral Penn, with a considerable estate, the castle and manor of Macroom, then producing an income of £300.00 per annum. On the accession of Charles II, however, he lost that property to Lord Muskerry, but was compensated with lands in Shanagarry, County Cork. In 1667, the Admiral sent his son to Ireland to take charge of the estate.

While in east Cork, William Penn renewed his friendship with the Quaker, Thomas Lee (or Lowe), and converted to Quakerism. His father did not approve but Penn remained adamant.

On a visit to Cork city in 1667, William Penn attended a Quaker meeting in their premises, located in the area now called Grattan Street. The Mayor, Timothy Tuckey, had all who attended arrested and lodged in gaol. Penn succeeded in having a letter sent to Lord Orrery, Lord President of Munster, who ordered his immediate release.

William Penn subsequently distinguished himself as a man of letters, becoming the author of some 100 works. He went to America and was instrumental in establishing the State of Pennsylvania, which was named after him.

William Penn, Quaker, was arrested and gaoled in Cork on 3 September 1667.

1667

BÁS AIRT Ó LAOIRE

BÁS AIRT Ó LAOIRE
Mo ghrá go daingean tu!
Lá dá bhfaca thu
Ag ceann tí an mhargaidh,
Thug mo shúil aire dhuit,
Thug mo chroí taitneamh duit,
D'éalaíos óm charaid leat
I bhfad ó bhaile leat.

Eibhlín Dhubh Ní Chonnaill, gaol le Dónal Ó Connaill, a chum an dan álainn seo ar ócáid dhúnmharú a céile, Art Ó Laoire, ag saighdiúirí tiarna talún darbh ainm Abraham Morris.

Is amhlaidh gur tharla easaontas idir Morris agus Art Ó Laoire faoi chapall breá a bhí ag Art. 'San am sin, as ucht na bPéindlithe a bheith i bhfeidhm, bhí sé ceadaithe ag Protastúnaigh capall a cheannach ó Chaitiliceach ar chúig phunt, cuma cén luach a bhí ar an ainmhí. Do thairg Morris cúig phunt do Art Ó Laoire agus ní hamháin gur dhiúltaigh Art Ó Laoire an airgead ach thug sé fé Abraham Morris. Chuir Morris an dlí air.

I ndeireadh na dála tháinig Abraham Morris agus a shaighdiúirí ar Art Ó Laoire, scaoileadh urchair agus maraíodh é. Tamaillín 'na dhiaidh sin thug deartháir le Art Ó Laoire fogha fé Morris agus d'éalaigh sé ón dlí go dtí na Stáit Aontaithe. Bheartaigh Morris go rachadh sé féin chun dlí as ucht bháis Airt Ó Laoire.

Fuaireadh Abraham Morris neamh-chiontach i ndúnmharú Airt Ó Laoire sa chúirt i gCorcaigh ar an 4ú Meán Fomhair, 1773.

1773

HAULBOWLINE DOCKYARD

It had long been the ambition of the burghers of Cork and Cobh to persuade the British Government of the desirability of constructing major naval facilities in Cork Harbour. In the middle of the nineteenth century plans for a dockyard on Haulbowline Island were prepared by an engineer, Mr James, for the Harbour Authority.

A delegation from the Harbour Authority, which included Mr William Moore Drew the Chairman and Mr George Scott, visited the Admiralty to present the case for the dockyard. They argued that Cork Harbour was a strategic location for the Royal Navy, especially since the advent of steam-powered vessels.

If a dockyard were established, naval vessels and merchant ships, damaged and in distress, could be repaired in Cork rather than having to proceed further in a dangerous condition to English ports. Timber for ship repairs, currently imported from America, and coal from Wales, could be delivered to Cork at a cheaper rate than to English ports.

John Francis Maguire, Member of Parliament for Cork, supported the case for a dockyard. In 1864 he was instrumental in having the sum of £300,000 voted for the project.

The plans for the construction of a dockyard at Haulbowline were presented to the Admiralty on 5 September 1856.

1856

JOSEPH MAINZER

Joseph Mainzer, originally from Treves, claimed that at ten years of age he could read music, irrespective of its degree of complexity. He appears to have been a precocious child and to have grown into a man of many talents. He was in turn, priest, political activist, writer and musician.

He had travelled extensively in Europe before arriving in Cork in 1842. His mission in life was to bring music to the masses, he announced to an audience of 1,400 members of the Temperance Movement, which included Fr. Mathew, packed into the South Presentation School in Douglas Street. He suggested that in future the motto of the Temperance Movement should be 'music and sobriety, sobriety and music'. He was especially interested in teaching music to the working classes, for 'national strength and prosperity is based on the working class', and there is among the working class, 'more generosity of soul, more true nobleness of disposition, more real and exalted virtue than in the higher and richer classes of society'.

Mr Mainzer proceeded to demonstrate his method, the *Cork Examiner* reporting that 'in a very short time clear and harmonious sounds rose on the ear, as the vast numbers caught the note struck on the piano, and gave it back with precision and perfection of tone'.

Within a week of the meeting a committee was set up to promote and superintend the progress of Joseph Mainzer's system in Cork and the South of Ireland. The following music teachers were appointed: Mr Uglow, 2 York Street; Mr Orr, Member of the Cork Cathedral Choir; Mr Hazell, organist of Upper Shandon; Mr J. Seymour, Jun., Organist of St Patrick's; Mr Tomkins, for Bandon.

Joseph Mainzer lectured in Cork on 6 September 1842.

1842

JOHN GEORGE MACCARTHY

John George MacCarthy was born in South Main Street, Cork, in June 1829. The family was comfortable and cultured, French and Italian being freely used in the home. He was educated at Fr Michael O'Sullivan's School in the Mansion House (now the Mercy Hospital). Having qualified as a solicitor he became principal in the firm of MacCarthy and Hanrahan.

On 1 November 1852, he was elected first President of the Cork Catholic Young Men's Association and held that position until he moved to Dublin in 1880. Elected to the House of Commons in 1874, he distinguished himself as an advocate of land reform. MacCarthy was appointed a Land Commissioner, and published several books, viz., *Letters on the Land Tenure of Europe, Irish Land Questions plainly Stated and Answered* and, *The Farmer's Guide to the Land Act*. He was also the author of the following works: *A Plea for the Home Rule of Ireland; Henry Grattan, A Historical Study; Speeches on Irish Questions* and *The French Revolution of 1792*. He also wrote a *History of Cork*, published in 1869.

John George MacCarthy was a member of the Society of St Vincent de Paul and was made a knight of the Order of St Gregory the Great in 1880. He was the owner of the Athenaeum, which became the Opera House in 1877, and he was elected chairman of the company.

His health began to fail in 1892 and he went to Hamburg to recuperate. John George MacCarthy fell ill, however, on the journey home and died in London on 7 September 1892.

1892

8 September

THE NEW CITY HALL

During the War of Independence units of the British occupation forces burned a considerable part of Cork, including the City Hall. The British Government accepted responsibility and agreed to pay compensation.

Eventually it was decided to erect a new civic office and a competition was organised to select a design, the architectural concern of Jones and Kelly being successful. John Sisk and Co. were appointed contractors. Mr Eamonn de Valera laid the foundation stone on 7 July 1932.

The building was completed in 1936 and Mr de Valera was once again invited to perform the opening ceremony. The Lord Mayor, Seán French, and the city councillors proceeded to Tivoli to greet Mr de Valera and escort him to the City Hall. The military guard of honour consisted of a mounted troop of army cavalry, attired in blue and gold uniforms, black bearskin headgear and orange plumes.

The Lord Mayor hosted a lunch in the Victoria Hotel at which there were 130 guests, including the former Head of Government, Mr W.T. Cosgrave, General Mulcahy and Mr Frank Aiken. After lunch the party adjourned to the City Hall where the President was greeted by a fanfare of trumpets. Three thousand guests were present.

The building is constructed of limestone from the Blackrock quarries. The stone was cut and dressed in the contractor's workshops under the supervision of William Ellis. Practically all the fittings were made locally.

The President of the Free State Government, Mr Eamonn de Valera, declared the City Hall officially opened on 8 September 1936.

1936

9 September

INQUISITION IN CORK

Charles Smith, in his celebrated work, *The Ancient and Present State of the County and City of Cork*, writes of the FitzGeralds of Desmond: 'Maurice, the first Earl of Desmond, raised the greatness of his house by Irish exactions and oppressions; so Gerald, the last Earl, reduced it to nothing by the same means, fell into rebellion, where he perished, with numbers of his followers'.

In the latter half of the sixteenth century the Desmonds held sway over a huge area of Munster, encompassing 574,628 acres of English measure. The last Earl had 'all wrecks of the sea, through all the ports and creeks out of the County of Kerry ... 13s.4d. out of every fishing boat in the Port of Ventry and Ferriter's Island'. He had 'a great number of vassals, and of his kindred and surname above 500 gentlemen'. It was said that he was able to raise 600 horse and 2,000 foot soldiers. When the rebellion failed all his property and wealth was declared forfeit.

Anyone suspected of having supported Desmond was called to account before inquisitions (judicial enquiries) to prove their innocence or plead for clemency. A large number were found guilty, and their property attained by Act of Parliament. The confiscated property was divided out among the Elizabethan adventurers.

An inquisition was held in Shandon Castle on 9 September 1588.

1588

10 September

1ST NATIONAL EXHIBITION

The great exhibition in London in 1851 captured the imagination of the Victorian world. The magnificent glass hall, the Crystal Palace, designed by Paxton, appeared to symbolise a new era of enlightenment and prosperity. Among the thousands to visit the exhibition were many of Cork's leading citizens, including Daniel Corbett, John Francis Maguire, and Sir Thomas Deane.

Corbett, a dentist described by Fr Prout as 'the kindliest of human beings and sincerest of Corkmen', was a stalwart of the Apollo Society, a dramatic group that performed for charity. He made a modest proposal that an exhibition of Cork's industrial products be organised. The proposal was developed, at the initative of Sir Thomas Deane and Mr Beamish, into the concept of an All-Ireland Exhibition. John Francis Maguire explained its objects:

> to display to the country its own resources and capabilities; to inspire confidence, to remove doubt, to awaken interest in what materially concerned the welfare of all classes, to induce every person who entered the Exhibition to resolve on doing as much as possible to give employment, diminish poverty, lessen taxation, promote happiness and elevate by the practical encouragement of native industry.

The chosen site for the Exhibition was the Corn Exchange which stood near the present City Hall. Sir John Benson, the architect, was commissioned to adapt the Corn Exchange Building and to provide whatever additional buildings were required. The whole covered area eventually embraced 42,525 square feet.

The First National Exhibition, which opened in Cork in June, was ceremoniously brought to a successful conclusion on 10 September 1852.

1852

HUGH CARLETON

Hugh Carleton was born in Cork in 1739, the son of Francis Carleton, who was so pompous that he was known as 'King of Cork'. The young Carleton went to Trinity College, Dublin, studied law and was called to the Bar. He achieved rapid promotion, becoming Solicitor General in 1779 and Chief Justice of the Common Pleas in 1787. He was a member of the Irish Parliament for fifteen years. In 1789 he was made Baron Carleton of Amer, and was elevated to the Viscountcy of Clare nine years later.

Carleton supported the Act of Union in 1800, and was rewarded by being named one of the 28 representative Irish peers in the British House of Lords. His manner in court was lugubrious, and John Philpott Curran commented that 'Carleton was ever plaintiff in every case that came before him'.

Carleton was the presiding judge at the trial of John and Henry Sheares, friends of his in youth, for their involvement in the 1798 Rebellion. When John Sheares pleaded for a stay of execution that his brother might attend to his affairs, boyhood memories did not influence Carleton. 'It does not rest with us,' he declared, 'to hold out mercy. It will be difficult to grant even that indulgence which you, John Sheares, so pathetically request for your brother to arrange his affairs. Unfortunately, it could be of no use, because by the attainder he will forfeit all his property, real and personal; nothing to be settled will remain.'

Hugh Carleton, Viscount Clare, was born in Cork on 11 September 1737.

1737

CARNEGIE LIBRARY

In 1855, Cork Corporation voted to establish a Free Public Lending Library. It was not, however, until 1892 that a committee was nominated to make the necessary arrangements. The first Free Public Library was opened at Emmet Place on 24 October 1892. The premises proved unsuitable and efforts were made to acquire more commodious accommodation.

A suggestion that the Corporation solicit help from Andrew Carnegie, the philanthropist, was rejected. However, in 1902, Sir Edward Fitzgerald approached Carnegie in a private capacity. He agreed to provide £10,000, provided that the Corporation make a site available. In accepting the offer, the Corporation decided to confer the Freedom of the City on Carnegie; the ceremony of conferring took place when the donor laid the foundation stone on 21 October 1903.

The site chosen by the Corporation was to the rear of the City Hall, facing Anglesea Street. The building was designed by the Corporation Engineer, Henry A. Cutler, and construction was carried out by Patrick Murphy. All the materials and fittings, with the exception of the terazzo flooring, which was executed by Italians, were of Irish origin. The library had only a brief lifespan: it was burnt to the ground by British forces during 'The Troubles'.

Andrew Carnegie was unable to attend the official opening of the Carnegie Free Library, which was performed by the Lord Mayor, Alderman Joseph Barrett, on 12 September 1905.

1905

THOMAS DIX HINCKS

Thomas Dix Hincks was born of English parents in Dublin on 24 June 1767. He was apprenticed to an apothecary, but abandoned that after two years and studied for the Church at Trinity College, and later in England. On the recommendation of a tutor he accepted an offer to minister in Cork, where he was ordained in 1792.

Hincks was a prolific writer. His published works include *Letter in answer to Paine's Age of Reason; An Introduction to Ancient Geography and Rudiments of Greek Grammar*. He also contributed to *Cyclopedia and Transactions of the Royal Irish Academy*. He fathered a talented family: one son, Francis, became Premier of Canada; another, Edward, a Minister of Religion in County Down, was instrumental in deciphering the ancient cuneiform writings of the Middle East.

His most valuable contribution to Cork life began with a pamphlet, 'A Plan for an Academical Institution', in which he argued for the establishment of a seat of learning and research in Cork. The proposal was widely welcomed, and the Royal Cork Institution was established in premises on the South Mall. A Parliamentary Grant was arranged, the Institution purchased land and established a Botanic Gardens on the site where St Joseph's Cemetery is now located. Hincks left Cork in 1821 and was classical headmaster in the Belfast Academical Institution from then until 1836. He died in Belfast on 24 February 1857.

'In consideration of his great exertions in establishing a Society for bettering the conditions of the poor, which is likely to prove of great benefit to this City,' the Corporation made Thomas Dix Hincks a Freeman of Cork on 13 September 1799.

1799

HARBOUR SOVIET

In September 1920 a committee, appointed by the Corporation to investigate the cost of living in Cork city, reported that a 'living wage' was not less than 70 shillings per week. The report was ratified by the Corporation in February 1921, whereupon the dock workers lodged a claim with the Harbour Commissioners for an immediate increase of seven shillings and six pence, which would bring their weekly wage to 70 shillings.

Councillor Bob Day, Branch Secretary of the Irish Transport and General Workers' Union and a Harbour Commissioner, proposed that the dockers' claim be referred to arbitration. The proposal was rejected. He repeated his proposal a week later and again it was rejected. The dockers struck on 26 August 1921. The harbour pilots came out in sympathy and the port of Cork was brought to a standstill.

The dockers marched in procession through the city preceded by a man carrying a huge red banner. They took control of the offices of the Harbour Commissioners, hoisted a red flag and through their spokesmen, Bob Day and William Kenneally, declared themselves a Soviet and expressed their intention of assuming control of the operation of the harbour.

Bob Day claimed that the dockers, operating the port themselves, could earn their weekly wage, and demonstrate how the harbour could be managed more effectively. The movement of all ships, unless authorised by the Soviet, was prohibited. Even though the Soviet was short-lived, the dockers' action was successful in that the rise in wages was conceded – at a time when the pay at other ports was being reduced by a shilling per week! Control of the harbour, however, reverted to the Commissioners.

The Cork Soviet dock strike ended on 14 September 1921.

1921

RICHARD BOYLE

Of the many Elizabethan adventurers who came to Ireland to carve out their fortunes, none was more rapacious or acquisitive than Richard Boyle. Born in Hertfordshire, England, his first ambition was to become a lawyer. Perceiving, however, that lack of patronage would inhibit his career, he determined to seek his fortune in Ireland.

Boyle arrived in this country with, he tells us, 'the sum of twenty seven pounds, three shillings and a diamond ring, a gold bracelet, a taffety doublet cut with and upon taffety, two cloaks; competent linen and necessaries, with my rapier and dagger'. He obtained a post as deputy to the Escheator General, which involved the enforcement of claims by British subjects to lands confiscated from the Irish. Boyle availed of his position to acquire much property for himself. When a charge of acquiring property by illegal means was proved unfounded, Queen Elizabeth promoted him Clerk of the Council of Munster and recommended him to Sir George Carew.

Richard Boyle gained more royal favour when he was the first to bring Elizabeth the news of the defeat of the Spanish and Irish forces at Kinsale. He had an insatiable hunger for property; that which he could not steal or confiscate he bought, acquiring, for a pittance, Walter Raleigh's enormous estate.

He was, in turn, made Privy Councillor for Munster and for Ireland, knighted and created Lord Boyle. In 1620 he was given the Viscountcy of Dungarvan and Earldom of Cork. It was rumoured that he had laid out £4,000 in order to acquire the earldom.

Richard Boyle, Earl of Cork, died on 15 September 1643.

1643

ASYLUM MEETING

Down through the centuries the mentally handicapped were treated in an inhuman fashion: at best ignored, at worst incarcerated in dreadful conditions with scant regard for their condition.

Towards the middle of the eighteenth century provision was made for the establishment of a lunatic asylum in Cork, but it was not until the passing of the Gaol Act in 1787 that a premises was provided, an annexe to the House of Industry. In 1817 it was recommended that the Cork institution be enlarged to cater for 250 inmates. An Act of Parliament of 1825 allowed for the change of designation, from City and County Asylum to the Cork District Asylum.

An Act of Parliament (8/9, Victoria), empowered the Board of Governors to acquire land for new premises. Fourteen sites were offered, including Shanakiel, Belvedere, Dodges Glen and Springville. The Shanakiel site owned by Lord Cork was finally selected. Additional land was also acquired, the total cost of the site amounting to £10,076.

The Governors of the Cork District Lunatic Asylum met for the first time on 16 September 1845.

1845

OPERA HOUSE OPENS

The Great National Exhibition, held in Cork, ended on 10 September 1852. The magnificent structures that had been erected to supplement the accommodation in the Great Hall of the Corn Exchange now stood vacant. The Executive Committee of the Exhibition decided on 'the carrying out of the plan of re-erecting the Fine Arts Hall as an Athenaeum'.

The proposal was to be financed by the raising of a sum of money, not less than £500, by way of debenture. A proviso was added that 'the same Hall to be in legal connection with the Royal Cork Institution'. A site was acquired between the Old Custom House and the north channel of the River Lee, where the present Opera House is now situated. The structure that had served as the Fine Arts Hall was dismantled and re-erected on the new site.

It was intended that the Athenaeum, as it was called, would be a centre for the arts in Cork, in particular the spoken word. However, it was soon obvious that the building was unsuitable for the purpose, the acoustics being most unsatisfactory. Accordingly it was decided to replace the Athenaeum with an Opera House and a company, formed under the chairmanship of Mr John George McCarthy, proceeded with the venture.

Mr C.J. Phipps of London, who then was responsible for about twenty theatres, including the Gaiety Theatres in both Dublin and London, was commissioned to design the Cork Opera House. Mr Terence O'Flynn of Cork was appointed contractor.

The opening performance in the Cork Opera House, Mr Byron's comedy, *Our Boys*, was given on 17 September 1877.

1877

THE URSULINES

Nano Nagle was born into a wealthy and influential North Cork family; among her cousins were Edmund Burke and Fr Theobold Mathew. She was educated privately, and later in Paris. While in France she perceived that the condition of the poor there was no different to that of the poor in Ireland, and she was particularly distressed by the poverty of the children. She considered joining a French convent but returned to Ireland, living with her brother in Cork.

In 1754 or 1755, she opened a small school in Cove Lane (now Douglas Street), her pupils coming from the vicinity: Pender's Alley, Willow Lane, Gould's Lane, Donovan's Lane and Primrose Lane. A second school for girls was opened, followed by a boys' school. The probable model for her schools was the French system of *petites ecoles*, established as early as 1357.

Nano Nagle received encouragement from the future Bishop of Cork, Dr Moylan, and his uncle, Fr Doran. It was probably the latter who suggested that Nano Nagle invite the French Order of Ursulines to teach in her schools. Dr Moylan approached the Ursulines in Paris and arrangements were made for four Irish girls to travel to Paris, at Nano Nagle's expense, for training. In the meantime Nano Nagle acquired a site in Douglas Street and proceeded to build a convent.

The Ursulines took formal possession of the convent in Douglas Street on 18 September 1771.

1771

JEREMIAH CALLANAN

There is a green island in Lone Gougane Barra,
Where Alloa of song rushes forth as an arrow:
In deep-vallied Desmond – a thousand wild fountains
Come down to the lake from their home in the mountains.
There grows the wild ash, and a time-stricken willow
Looks chidingly down on the mirth of the billow;
As, like some gay child, that sad monitor scorning,
It lightly laughs back to the laugh of the morning.

Thus runs the opening stanza of 'Gougane Barra', a poem by Jeremiah J. Callanan, who was born in Cork in 1795. He was educated in O'Sullivan's Academy on Sullivan's Quay, and later attended the Reddington Academy in Cobh as a boarder. He then went to Maynooth, but finding that he lacked a vocation, he left and subsequently entered Trinity College, Dublin, to read law. He was a poor student and did not take a degree, his only accomplishment being a prize for a poem honouring the accession of George IV to the English throne.

Callanan abandoned Trinity and returned to Cork. A poem of his, 'And we must part', was published in the *Cork Mercantile Chronicle*. Several of his poems, adaptations and translations of traditional Gaelic verse were published in *Blackwood's Magazine*. He proposed to publish a major collection of his work but the volume never appeared. He took positions as tutor in many houses around County Cork and announced his intention of starting a school in Cork city. This project failed through lack of finance.

He accompanied a Cork family to Portugal, acting as tutor to the children. He wrote home professing his intention to return to Ireland. Jeremiah J. Callanan died in Lisbon on 19 September 1829.

1829

DOMINICK ROCHE

William Roche was Mayor of Cork in 1633 and, at a meeting of the Corporation, found himself in the invidious position of having to adjudicate in a case concerning his son, Alderman Dominick Roche.

Alderman Roche was a contractor who built a market house in New Street. In 1633 he contracted with the Corporation to build bridges in the city, which work resulted in a loss of £200. He claimed compensation from the Corporation. Eventually, it was agreed to refer the matter to arbitration, and Sir Walter Coppinger and Henry Gould were nominated as arbitrators. They found in favour of Roche, awarding him £200. The Corporation was, however, unable to reimburse him in cash and chose to give him the benefit of 'the customs of the ports of the City for one year.

Dominick Roche is distinguished in being, in 1618, the first whiskey distiller of whom we have a record, having a 'maulte-house' adjoining his garden. At his death he left 'a barrel and a-half of aqua vitae, worth £15 sterling; thirty barrels of maulte, worth twenty shillings the barrel; also, one great kettle for brewing, one aqua vitae pot, and one brass pan'.

Dominick Roche, who was Mayor in 1609, and Member of Parliament for Cork in 1639, presented his case against the Corporation of Cork on 20 September 1633.

1633

21 September

HARBOUR COMMISSIONERS

In 1729, an Act of Parliament (3, George III), placed responsibility for the upkeep and conservation of Cork Harbour on the Mayor, Sheriff and Commonality of the city. It was not an effective piece of legislation; the condition of the harbour deteriorated, silting occurring on an extensive scale. Although Parliament voted additional sums of money in 1773 and 1784, the situation remained critical.

In 1813, yet another Act of Parliament, which became known as the 'Butter Weighhouse Act', provided for the imposition of taxes on goods entering or leaving the port. Half of the money collected was allocated to the development of the harbour. The act was significant in that for the first time a regular source of finance was provided, and a named group of individuals were designated as Commissioners responsible for the upkeep of the harbour.

The following year, an act which became known as the 'Commercial Buildings Act' provided additional finance but also stipulated the 'Mayor, Sherriffs and Common Council and to the other Commissioners for the time being duly appointed', as being responsible for the harbour. It was obvious that the two groups could not function independently, and accordingly a compromise was reached under the influence of the Mayor, Sir David Perrier, whereby the parties nominated in the Statutes of 1813 and 1814 agreed to form a joint committee. Thus the Cork Harbour Commissioners came into existence.

The first meeting of the Cork Harbour Commisssioners took place on 21 September 1814.

1814

PARLIAMENT BRIDGE

Until the middle years of the eighteenth century the island city of Cork was connected to the mainland only by the ancient North and South Gate Bridges.

However, the growth of new suburbs, in the Tivoli and Montenotte areas, and in the South Mall and Douglas Street districts, intensified the demand for new river crossings. The location most favoured for the latter crossing was from the southern end of Princes Street across to George's Quay. The situation really demanded the construction of two bridges: one from Princes Street to Lavitt's Island, which was in the area of the present Parliament Street, and the second from Lavitt's Island to George's Quay. The plans were frustrated, however, when Mr Lavitt refused permission for a right of way over his island.

In 1760, a group of citizens received permission from the Corporation to build a bridge from a place known as Pellican's Corner to George's Quay. The following year, however, an Act of Parliament (7, George III), provided 'for building a Stone Bridge from the Quay opposite Princes Street to Lavitt's Island and a stone bridge from thence to the Red Abbey Marsh with a drawbridge'. Parliament allocated the sum of £4,000 for the work. In 1764 another Act of Parliament authorised the removal of the recently erected private drawbridge from Lavitt's Island to George's Quay and the construction of a three-arched stone bridge.

That bridge, now known as Parliament Bridge, was opened for use on 22 September 1764.

1764

BISHOP JOHN ENGLAND

John England was born on the north side of Cork city in 1786. At fifteen years of age he entered Carlow seminary to study for the priesthood, and while a student he was instrumental in the establishment of a female penitentiary and schools for the poor. As he was under the canonical age, a special dispensation was required for his ordination, which took place in the North Cathedral, Cork, on 10 October 1808.

He was appointed President of St Mary's Seminary and was deeply committed to the concept of education for the poor. He was a member of the Committee of the Catholic Poor Schools and General Superintendent of the schools in the control of the Charitable Society. In 1809 he founded a magazine, *Religious Repertory*, and was also editor of the newspaper, *Cork Mercantile Chronicle*. He is reputed to have been the author of *School Primer of Irish History*, considered to have been a manual of political action.

John England was the organising genius of the anti-veto campaign when the English Government, aided by some Catholic bishops, tried to obtain a veto on the appointment of Catholic bishops. His stand on this matter met with the displeasure of Bishop John Murphy. When Rome considered him for elevation to Bishop, Murphy considered him unsuitable for the Irish scene, but recommended him for the American missions. On 21 September 1820, he was consecrated Bishop of Charleston, which comprised the states of North and South Carolina and Georgia.

Bishop England established a seminary and published the first Catholic paper in America, United States Catholic Miscellany. In January 1826, he addressed the joint houses of the American Government. He was particularly attentive to the cause of negroes, for whom he conducted regular services in his cathedral. He introduced the Ursuline Order of nuns into America.

Bishop John England, who died on 11 April 1842, was born on 23 September 1786.

1786

24 September

JOHN WESLEY IN CORK

John Wesley was born at Epworth, Lincolnshire, England, on 28 June 1703. The son of a rector, he was educated at home, and subsequently at the Charterhouse School, London, before going up to Oxford in 1720. He graduated in 1724 and on 22 September 1728, was ordained a priest of the Anglican Church.

He went on a mission to the natives of the State of Georgia in America, but it was not a success and he returned to England. At 35 years of age Wesley came to the belief that salvation would come through faith, and he travelled the country preaching wherever a pulpit was provided. On his journeys he covered over a quarter of a million miles throughout Great Britain and Ireland, preaching an estimated 50,000 sermons.

John Wesley kept a detailed diary of his peregrinations, and in it noted that he attempted to give his first sermon in Cork in 1748. The location was the Military Guard House in Blackpool. He met with a hostile reception: pelted by a mob, the city authorities declined to protect him. He returned, nonetheless, on several occasions, and on 20 May 1750, he preached on Hammond's Marsh. 'The congregation was large and deeply attentive,' he wrote in his diary. 'I have seldom seen a more quiet and orderly assembly at any church in England or Ireland.'

He was again in Cork in 1752, and recorded the occasion in his diary: 'in the evening I proposed to the Society the building of a preaching-house'. As a result of his proposal a sum of money was collected, and a plot of land purchased.

John Wesley arranged for the erection of the first Wesleyan 'preaching-house' in Cork on 24 September 1752.

1752

ST FINBARR

Some time about the year 550, Amergin, a master smith from Connacht, came south to work for the Lord of Muskerry. He was given land and married. About the year 560, a son, Loan, was born. When Loan was quite young three clerics, Brendan, Lochan and Fidach, travelling through the district, offered to take the boy on fosterage and educate him. One of the monks, admiring his fair hair, gave him a new name, Fionn Barra, the fair-haired one. The party continued to Gowran in County Kilkenny where Finbarr received his education.

It is possible that Finbarr established his first church near Coolcashin in County Kilkenny. He founded a second church near Aghaboe, but made a gift of this church to St Canice, who prophesied that Finbarr would establish a monastery which would be famous for the quality of its students. He founded another monastery in Gougane Barra before continuing on his travels, setting a foundation at a place called Cill na Cluaine (the Church of the Meadow), now incorporated with Ballineadig, in the parish of Aglish in the Barony of Muskerry.

Once again he was persuaded to leave, on this occasion by two monks, Cormac and Buichin, and he continued into Corcach Mór Mumhan (the Great Marsh of Munster) where he established a monastery. It is not possible to identify precisely the location of this foundation but it was on the southside of Cork city, somewhere between Elizabeth Fort and Gillabbey.

The school associated with the monastery was famous and students flocked there from all over Europe. Secular subjects, such as general literature and science, were taught in addition to religious matters. In his old age Finbarr returned to Cul na Cluaine, where he died, probably in the year 630. His saint's day is on 25 September.

THE *NIMROD*

Henry Bell, a Glasgow carpenter, installed a steam engine in a trading vessel on the Clyde River in Scotland, and thus inaugurated the age of steam ships. He was responsible for freeing the mariner from dependence on the vagaries of wind and currents.

The next major development in sea travel was in the use of iron, instead of wood, in the construction of ships. In 1843 the Cork Steamship Company commissioned the Liverpool firm of shipwrights, Thomas Vernon and Company, to build an iron-clad vessel. The ship, *Nimrod*, so called because of its figurehead of a huntsman, was 177 feet long, 25 feet broad and had a draught of sixteen feet. The power was supplied by double direct cross-head engines built by John Kennedy. The *Nimrod* served on the Cork-Liverpool service.

On 25 February 1860, the *Nimrod*, with Captain Lyall in command, sailed from Liverpool for Cork. She carried a mixed cargo and a number of passengers, including Sir John Fitzgerald and Henry Goold. A fierce gale blew up, the *Nimrod* engines failed, and even though it proceeded under sail, it was in serious difficulty. Captain Lyall refused help from another ship, *City of Paris*, as he considered that the fee being demanded was too high. The captain tried to take his ship around Saint David's Head but the *Nimrod* was driven onto the rocks. The total complement of crew and passengers, some 45 people, were lost.

The *Nimrod*, the first iron-clad ship built for the port of Cork, was launched on 26 September 1843.

1843

27 September

THE SMA IN CORK

A French missionary society, 'Missions Africaines de Lyons', (known in Ireland as the SMA or 'African Missions'), found itself, in 1870, ministering in English-speaking territory in South Africa. It was imperative that the SMA, a French-speaking order, recruit English-speaking priests.

Fr James O'Hare, an Irish priest working in the Cape, suggested that English-speaking priests be recruited in Ireland, and volunteered to undertake the task. He returned to Ireland, and by November 1876 had sent four students to the SMA seminary in Lyons, France. He also obtained permission from Bishop Delaney of Cork to open a house in the city. This development met with considerable opposition from the local clergy. Following a disagreement with the French order, Fr O' Hare resigned, being replaced by a Frenchman, Fr Deveucoux.

The SMA purchased St Joseph's Cemetery from the Capuchins and then acquired property on the Blackrock Road which was converted into a church and school for the education of students. The Bishop, however, refused to give permission for the celebration of mass there. Without the support of the local clergy, the SMA found it extremely difficult to recruit suitable candidates, and the Society was compelled to resort to advertising in the newspapers. The French authorities did not have a high opinion of the Irish students, and the Cork school was downgraded to concentrate on the teaching of English to foreign students.

The Society of African Missions established their first college in Ireland at Blackrock, on 27 September 1878.

1878

SIEGE OF CORK

While William of Orange was conducting the siege of Limerick in 1690, the army in England was under the command of John Churchill (later Duke of Marlboro), who took the decision to lay siege to Cork. William approved of the plan, regretting that he could not send artillery support, his own guns having been spiked by Patrick Sarsfield at Ballyneety.

Churchill's fleet set sail on 17 September, arriving at Crosshaven four days later. It consisted of '80 ships great and small' and included 42 capital ships, ten fire ships and seventeen Dutch vessels. The troops, eight infantry regiments, disembarked at Passage West on 23 September and advanced on Cork. The Duke of Wurtemberg, with 2,900 Danish, Dutch and Huguenot infantry and 390 horse, marched to his support.

The Governor of Cork was a Kerryman, Colonel Roger MacElligott. The commander of the Jacobean Forces in Ireland, the Duke of Berwick, advised MacElligott to burn the city and withdraw to the west. The Governor, however, chose to defend Cork. Although the walls of the city were 50 feet high and in parts ten feet thick, the city was vulnerable to cannonade from the hills to the north and south, and was considered by most experts to be indefensible.

The siege of Cork began on 25 September. Churchill's forces took up position on the heights to the north, at Shandon, and to the south, at the Cat and Elizabeth Forts. Supported by the guns of a man-of-war, *Salamander*, the bombardment began. It was soon obvious that Cork could not hold out. MacElligott at first refused favourable terms of surrender, but after four days was compelled to capitulate.

The siege of Cork ended on 28 September 1690.

1690

29 September

ST MICHAEL'S

In 1825, the Chapter of St Finnbarr's Cathedral prevailed upon a Mr Coburn to sell a half-acre plot of land at Church Road, Blackrock, as a site for a chapel of ease. The church, St Michael's, remained a chapel of ease until 9 January 1873, when it was constituted a parish church. It remained a single parish until 1975, when it was joined by St Nicholas and Christ Church parishes to form St Michael's Union.

There has been some controversy as to the identity of the architect of St Michael's. It has been credited to George Pain, but a plaque in the vestry, dated 1856, states that Mr W.H. Hill was the architect. It is thought that while the church was designed by Hill, the construction was undertaken by Pain. On the night of 29 January 1856, the spire was destroyed by lightning, and during reconstruction the chancel was extended and two transepts were added. The stained-glass windows were contributed by the Hall and Harris families.

The outstanding item of ornamentation in the church is John Hogan's sculpture, 'The Morning of the Resurrection', a memorial to William Beamish of Beaumont. The monument consists of two marble slabs, representing 'the Archangel in the act of blowing the trumpet of the Resurrection, whilst a cherub holds the Book of Life in which are written the names of the Blessed Dead. Beneath, the tomb has been rent, and an angel summons away the rising form into which the life of God is passing'. The monument is considered to be one of Hogan's most important works.

The Church of St Michael's, Church Road, Blackrock, was consecrated by the Lord Bishop of Elphin on 21 August 1828, the foundation stone having been laid on 29 September 1826.

1826

EDMUND SPENSER

Edmund Spenser was born about the year 1552, and was educated in London before going up to Cambridge. However, he did not remain long at the university. Under the patronage of Sir Philip Sidney, who admired his poetry, he became a courtier and, in 1580, was appointed Secretary to Lord Grey, the Lord Deputy of Ireland. Thus Spenser arrived in this country, where he spent the last nineteen years of his life.

Spenser married in Cork and wrote his celebrated poem, *The Faerie Queen*, and other works of a poetic and literary nature while in Ireland. Yet he despised the Irish. In his view the only solution to the Irish problem was the extermination of the native people. He described their condition after an insurrection:

> Out of every corner of the woods and glens they came creeping forth upon their hands, for their legs could not bear them; they looked like anatomies of death; they spoke like ghosts crying out of their graves ... yet, sure, in all that war, there perished not many by the sword but all by the extremity of famine which they themselves had wrought.

Spenser was present at Smerwick, County Kerry, when the English murdered 600 Spanish soldiers who had surrendered at 'Fort del Oro'. Although he never admitted to having taken part in the slaughter, he did concede that he had been 'as near them as any'.

Edmund Spenser was named Sheriff of the County of Cork on 30 September 1598.

1598

EDMUND BURKE

Edmund Burke was born in Dublin on 12 January 1729. His father was a Protestant, his mother a Catholic. He entered Trinity College, Dublin, in 1744 and six years later was in the Middle Temple in London studying for the Bar. It appears that he soon lost interest in his law studies and went on a European tour. In 1756 he published his first book, a satire on both revealed religion and the 'return to nature' school.

In 1759 he edited *The Annual Register*, a yearly survey of world affairs, and was associated with this publication for 30 years. Burke became associated with the Whig Party and entered the House of Commons. He was critical of the Crown and published *Thoughts on the Cause of the present Discontents* in 1770.

Edmund Burke was sympathetic to the American colonists and argued that it was absurd to treat universal disobedience as criminal; the revolt of a whole people argued serious misgovernment. As regards Ireland, he was always concerned at the condition of the country, advocating relaxation of the economic and penal regulations and concessions to legislative independence.

Burke became much alarmed at the conduct of the French Revolution. His book, *Reflections on the French Revolution*, provoked Tom Paine to reply with *Rights of Man*. His continued opposition to the French Revolution gained for him a European reputation. He retired from parliament in 1794, never having achieved high office. Burke continued to write until his death on 9 July 1797.

Edmund Burke was presented with the freedom of Cork on 1 October 1766.

1766

THOMAS DEANE

Thomas Deane was born on 4 June 1792 into a family of architects and builders. His working career started when he had a minor involvement in the construction of the great water storage units on Haulbowline Island.

Deane was only 21 years of age when he designed the Commercial Buildings (now the Imperial Hotel) on the South Mall. Subsequently he was commissioned to design some of the finest buildings in the city: the old and new Savings Banks and the classical portico of the Courthouse, work that Macauley considered worthy of Palladio. Deane was also responsible for the lunatic asylum in Killarney.

With his young partner, Bernard Woodward, Deane produced an extraordinary extension to Trinity College, Dublin. It was designed in the Venetian style and the masons had to be specially trained to cut the stone carvings. This partnership also produced the Museum at Oxford. Deane's greatest architectural legacy to Cork was the design for Queen's College (now University College), which Macauley praised highly, considering it fit to stand in the High Street, Oxford.

Deane, active in the civic life of the city, was High Sheriff on several occasions. In 1830 he was knighted by the Lord Lieutenant. He was a patron of the arts and a benefactor of young artists like Maclise and Foley. He was President of the reconstituted Cork Society for Promoting the Fine Arts.

Sir Thomas Deane was married three times and left a large family on his death, which occurred on 2 October 1871.

1871

SEÁN Ó RIADA

Rugadh Seán Ó Riada i gCorcaigh sa bhliain 1931. Fuair sé a chuid oideachais i gColaiste Fhearann Phiarais i gCorcaigh, agus i gColáiste Naomh Muinsin i Luimneach. D'fhill sé ar Chorcaigh agus d'fhreastail sé ar Choláiste na hOllscoile, mar a bhain sé céimeanna amach, san ealaíon agus sa cheol.

Chaith sé tréimshe i bParis sarar chuaigh sé ag obair le Radio Éireann mar leas-stúrthóir ceoil. Thug sé sraith léachtanna radio, gur teideal dóibh 'Our Musical Heritage', sa bhliain 1958. Dhá bhliain 'na dhiaidh sin bhunaigh sé an banna ceoil Ceoltóirí Chualann, agus chuaigh an ceol go mór i gcion ar cheoltóirí thraidisiúnta uilig na tíre.

Dhein Ó Riada cóiriú ar an cheol dos na scannáin Mise Éire agus Saoirse. Mar a dúirt léirmheastóir amháin, 'his orchestrations of traditional themes have been so superb that he has given Irish people a completely new insight into the beauty and dignity of their heritage'.

Bhí ar chumas Sheáin Ó Riada ceol dá chuid féin a chumadh agus tá Nomos 1 agus Nomos 2 chomh maith le Hercules Dux Ferrariae ar chinn des na ceapacháin ba cháiliúla a chum sé.

Ainmníodh Seán Ó Riada mar Léachtóir Cheoil in Ollscoil Chorcaí sa bhliain 1960. Chuaigh sé chun cónaithe i nGaeltacht Chúil Aodha agus dúirt sé i dtaobh na háite seo, 'it is one of the richest sources of traditional songs'. In onóir na háite chum sé aifreann, ar a dtugtar Aifreann Chúil Aodha, atá scríofa sa stíl tradisiúnta.

Cailleadh Seán Ó Riada ar an 3ú la Deireadh Fomhair, 1971.

1971

WILLIAM LYON

William Lyon was one of the Elizabethan adventurers, like Spenser, Raleigh and Boyle, who sought their fortunes in Ireland. Lyon, however, chose a career in the church rather than in the army.

After an education at Oxford, Lyon was appointed vicar of Naas in 1573, and seven years later was granted the vicarage of Bodenstown. In 1580 he was named as the first Protestant Bishop of Ross diocese in west Cork. A diligent worker, he won the support of the mayor of Cork, who petitioned for Lyon to be made bishop of the diocese of Cork. William Lyon was appointed by special charter to the bishopric of the combined dioceses of Cork, Cloyne and Ross in 1587, in consideration of his 'diligence in well instructing the people of his diocese as also the hospitality which he keepeth among them'. He was awarded an annual allowance of £200.

Lyon built his palace in Bishopstown. He provided bibles in Latin and English, and bemoaned the fact that he had failed to convert the Irish to Protestantism, attributing much of the blame to 'the disorder of the soldiers among the people which breedeth great hatred of our nation and not without cause'.

He was familiarly known as the 'sailor' bishop though there is no evidence that he had any nautical experience. William Lyon, Bishop of the combined dioceses of Cork, Cloyne and Ross, died on 4 October 1617.

1617

DERMOT BREEN

Dermot Breen was born in Waterford in 1924. While he was still young the family moved to Cork, where he was educated at Sullivan's Quay School and Presentation College.

He began his business career as a commercial traveller. In 1956, however, he became manager of the Palace Theatre. He was interested in the theatre and helped found the Presentation Theatre Guild. He acted and directed with the Cork Little Theatre and the University College Drama Society.

Dermot Breen became involved with tourism and was a key figure in An Tostal, a national tourism promotion organisation. His enterprise led to the inauguration of the Cork Film Festival, of which he became Director. The success of the Film Festival owes much to Dermot Breen's organisational skills. He became a member of the Film Appeal Board, and was appointed National Film Censor in June 1972.

Dermot Breen died unexpectedly on 5 October 1978.

1978

6 October

BLACKMOOR LANE CHURCH

The Capuchin Order of Friars arrived in Cork in 1637 to serve the beleaguered Catholics of the city and county. The Penal Laws were being imposed spasmodically; at times not enforced at all, at other times rigorously applied. In such circumstances it was virtually impossible to maintain regular services in recognised churches.

The once celebrated Fr Arthur O'Leary arrived in Cork in 1771. He described the church in Blackamoor Lane as being no better than a hovel, 'buried between salt houses and stables'. Blackamoor Lane was a narrow thoroughfare running parallel with Sullivan's Quay. He contrived to have a new church built in Blackamoor Lane, a building which is still standing to this day.

In 1814 Fr Mathew, the Apostle of Temperance, lived in a small loft over the little church until he moved to a new home, at 38 Cove Street. The Passing of the Act of Emancipation in 1829 permitted the Catholic Church to operate in public and Fr Mathew led a campaign to have a new church constructed. As a result the Church of the Holy Trinity on Fr Mathew Quay was solemnly blessed on 10 October 1850.

Four days previously, on 6 October 1850, the Capuchin Friars had closed their little church in Blackamoor Lane.

1850

7 October

GLEN ROVERS' FIRST 'COUNTY'

In April 1916, a group of men gathered in the premises of the Glen Boxing Club in Spring Lane, Blackpool, and decided to form a hurling team which they called 'Glen Rovers'. They chose green, white and gold as their club colours, later adding black as a sign of respect for those who had died during the Easter Rising.

Teams were entered in both minor and junior grades, but without immediate success. In 1922, however, the Thomas Davis Hurling Club amalgamated with 'The Glen' and the combined team won the minor hurling championship in that year. Two years later they won the junior championship. The club moved to the intermediate grade a year later and, in 1926, Glen Rovers entered the senior championship. Their opponents were the famed Blackrock and the result was a heavy defeat for 'The Glen'.

They played their first senior county final in 1930, but lost again to Blackrock. In 1934, 'The Glen' advanced to the county final, defeating Blackrock at the penultimate stage, and met the renowned St Finbarrs in the final. Glen Rovers won a famous victory on the score of three goals and two points to six points. It was a remarkable achievement, and 'The Glen' then proceeded to retain the trophy for the next six years. This feat, winning seven consecutive finals, has never since been equalled.

Glen Rovers won their first County Senior Hurling Championship on 7 October 1934.

1934

8 October

POSTAL ARRANGEMENTS

In 1827, difficulties arose between the influential Committee of Merchants and the man contracted to deliver the post by stage coach from Dublin to Cork, Sir James Anderson. The contractor (the son of John Anderson who had inaugurated the first passenger-carrying service in Ireland), proposed to alter the schedule of the Dublin-Cork service.

He informed the Committee that he was abandoning the fast service of 22 hours and replacing it with a 24 hour timetable, and that the coaches would leave Dublin at ten o'clock in the morning. This arrangement posed a serious problem for the Committee of Merchants; the English mail would arrive in Dublin after the coach had departed for Cork and, accordingly, the Cork Merchants would not receive their post until the following day.

The Committee of Merchants invoked the help of Sir Edward Lees, Secretary of the Post Office. His reply was so equivocal that *The Southern Reporter* commented, 'there must be some special place for the letter in the archives of non-communication'.

Eventually Sir James Anderson relented and agreed to re-introduce the 22 hour service, 'though the sacrifice to me and my partners will be very considerable'.

The Meeting of the Committee of Merchants, at which issue was taken with Sir James Anderson, was held on 8 October 1827.

1827

9 October

ST PAUL'S CHURCH

In September 1719, Cork Corporation decided to offer for rent, for a period of 999 years, a portion of land as a site for a church and school. The location was, roughly speaking, in the present Paul Street area. On 20 February 1720, the Corporation rescinded that decision and agreed to present the land to the Bishop of Cork and Ross for the purpose of building a church and graveyard. The gift was forever and provided for a free passage, eighteen feet wide, leading from the church to the Custom House (now the Crawford College of Art). The Corporation also agreed to provide £100 towards the cost of 'so pious a work'.

The church, named St Paul's, was built by public subscription and the first incumbent was Dr Henry Maule. The building, at the junction of Paul Street and St Paul's Avenue, is Grecian in style and rather plain on the exterior. However, the interior was lavishly decorated, a notable feature being the stucco work on the ceiling, said to have been the work of Italian soldiers taken prisoner during the Napoleonic Wars. St Paul's was familiarly known as the 'seamen's church'. The Corporation exercised the right of free burial in the graveyard for strangers dying in the parish, which was then the centre of a thriving shipping trade.

Divine service was celebrated for the first time in St Paul's Church on 9 October 1726.

1726

FR MATHEW

Theobold Mathew was born in Thomastown, County Kilkenny, the fourth son in a family of nine boys and three girls. His family was related to the powerful Butlers and to the Earl of Llandoff.

He was educated privately at Thurles and Kilkenny before entering Maynooth. He left Maynooth prematurely, fearing expulsion for indiscipline, became a Capuchin novice, and was ordained on 17 April 1813. He ministered in Kilkenny for a period, but transferred to Cork and lived over the 'Little Friary' in Blackamoor Lane before moving to a house in Cove Street. Fr. Mathew learned Irish in order to preach to the poor, and distinguished himself during the outbreak of cholera in 1832 when he ministered unselfishly to the sick.

In 1836, the Total Abstinence Movement had been established by William Martin, a Quaker, Rev Nicholas Dunscombe, and a Catholic, James McKenna. The Society sought to improve the lot of the poor people ravaged by the consumption of alcohol. Fr Mathew, through his work among the poor, was conversant with the evils brought about by the abuse of alcohol, and accepted leadership of the movement on 10 April 1838.

Fr Theobold Mathew, known as the Apostle of Temperance, was born on 10 October 1790.

1790

JAMES BARRY

James Barry, the son of John, a seaman, and Juliana (nee Roerdan), was born at Water Lane, Blackpool. He showed an aptitude for painting from an early age and was probably educated by a Dr Sleigh in Cork. Later, he studied at West's Academy, Dublin. In 1763, Barry won prominence when he displayed the work, 'The Conversion by Saint Patrick of the King of Cashel', a painting that brought him to the notice of Edmund Burke, who took Barry to London and introduced him to well-known artists, including Sir Joshua Reynolds. Burke later arranged an allowance so that Barry could study in Rome.

While in Italy his painting 'Philoctus on the Isle of Lemnos' won him membership of the Academy of Bologna. On his return to England his 'Venus Rising from the Waves' ensured his election to the Royal Academy. In 1771, Barry undertook the incredibly ambitious task of decorating, gratis, the Great Room of the Society of the Encouragement of the Arts in the Adelphi. This herculean labour went on for seven years and for it he was voted 250 guineas and a gold medal. In 1782 Barry was appointed Professor of Painting at the Royal Academy.

James Barry was irascible by nature, alienated some of his friends, and made many enemies. His outspoken criticisms of the Royal Academy led eventually to his expulsion, and his career was thereafter virtually at an end. He became a recluse. Some of his remaining friends feared for his health and arranged for an annuity to be paid to him. He died penniless on 5 February 1806, and Sir Robert Peel gave £200 for his funeral. He was buried in the crypt of St Paul's.

James Barry was born on 11 October 1741.

1741

CHARLES STEWART PARNELL

Charles Stewart Parnell, Freeman of Cork, was at the apex of his power when he visited the city in 1885. No fewer than 45 parish priests and over 100 curates were among the delegates who gathered in the Assembly Rooms on the South Mall to select seven candidates, including Parnell, to contest the impending general election.

Some weeks previously he had met, secretly, with Lord Caernarvon. While Caernarvon stipulated that there could be no repeal of the Act of Union, he appears to have given the impression that some form of Irish Assembly would be considered. Parnell assumed that Caernarvon spoke with the authority of the British Government. The election, accordingly, was of paramount importance. It was essential that the Irish Parliamentary Party elect a substantial number of members to parlaiment so that, in the event of a hung House of Commons, the Irish Party would hold the balance of power.

All seven nominated candidates were selected with an impressive show of unanimity and discipline. After the meeting 'one of the most multitudinous assemblages of the people of Cork', as the *Cork Examiner* reported the event, gathered outside the Victoria Hotel in Patrick Street and clamoured for the 'Uncrowned King' to address them.

'In dark times, in gloomy times you have come to cheer me,' he told his audience. 'I am sure that soon we will win Ireland legislative independence, and we shall win as well for the teeming masses of Cork as well as all classes of our people whether they live by the labour of the brain or of the hand and the arm. We shall win for all the right to live and thrive in their own country.'

Charles Stewart Parnell addressed the people of Cork on the evening of 12 October 1885.

1885

MAHONY'S OF BLARNEY

In 1751, Timothy Mahony established a small woollen mill at Rochestown. Within a short time he had transferred the business to Glanmire and thence to Blackpool. Later on, when the firm was controlled by the brothers Martin and Timothy, grandsons of the founder, it was known as the 'Cork Stuff Factory'. In an advertisement in the *Cork Hibernian Chronicle* of 4 January 1798, the brothers claimed that the manufacturing and finishing of all goods was carried out entirely by their own workforce.

One of the brothers, Timothy, died in the typhus epidemic of 1818. In 1821, the company was involved in an industrial dispute with the Cork Worsted Weavers, who claimed that the weekly wage of four shillings was inadequate. Three years later the business was transferred to Blarney. Mahony's claimed to have introduced the spinning of worsted by steam power to the south of Ireland.

The Blarney factory occupied a three-acre site and employed a considerable number of workers. A gas works was installed in 1869. On 1 December of that year, a fire destroyed the premises and many houses nearby, making 125 people destitute. Mahony's immediately began reconstruction, which was carried out by the factory workers. By 1871 some 200 workers were again employed, and in 1881 the number had risen to over 600.

In 1881, the managing director, yet another Timothy Mahony, organised a fête for the workers to celebrate the forthcoming marriage of his son, Frank. He took the opportunity to recall to those present the history of the family business. The date was 13 October 1881.

1881

14 October

CORK STREETS

The close, damp and unhealthy weather is coming upon us, and we are preparing for it in such a way as to render it certain that we shall have as accompaniments, disease and contagion. The wise projectors who introduced the MACADAMIZATION of our Streets, by strewing broken limestone as a substitute for pavement, may find the exposure of their ignorance in every place where the experiment has been tried; and if there are such things as books of account kept at the Wide Street Commissioners Office, it will be seen at what an enormous cost this mode of street making is sustained. The end of Patrick Street near the Bridge – one of the widest avenues in the City – is an undulating mass of mud, in which any pedestrian who has the hardihood to attempt to cross from one side of the street to another runs some risk of being dangerously immersed. The Commissioners have contracted with persons, it seems, to sweep the streets, who, of course, get the manure which they collect; but as the sweepings from limestone are quite useless, those streets which are laid down with it are extremely neglected. And then comes the mockery of fining the Contractors – mockery, we say, since if they were anything else, the penalties said to be inflicted would have produced some attention, but no such result has been experienced.

Such were the trenchant comments expressed by the *Southern Reporter* and *Cork Commercial Courier* with regard to the introduction of macadam and the condition of Cork streets on 14 October 1827.

1827

CHARTER OF 1303

The rights and privileges enjoyed by the citizens of towns came direct from the king by way of the grant of charters. In accepting the charters, however, the citizens also acknowledged the sovereignty of the monarch.

The charters conferred many diverse rights, from provisions for defence and administration of towns to regulations concerning trade. They often reveal a great deal of information. The charter granted to the citizens of Cork in 1303 empowered them to collect customs duty on specified items and indicates, indirectly, the variety of trade carried on through the port. Imports were restricted to wine, cloth, spices and rice. The bulk of the trade appears to have been exports of fish (salmon, ling, conger and mussels), timber, Irish cloth, honey, skins of animals (rabbits, sheep, fox, squirrels), and hides of stags, horses and goats.

The charter stipulated that the collected fees be expended on the upkeep of the city walls, and contribute towards the expense of providing a piped water supply to the city.

King Edward I of England conferred the charter, the thirty-first of his reign, on the city of Cork on 15 October 1303.

1303

16 October

CORK AIRPORT

In 1914, Lord Carbery took off from the Mardyke fields and flew his aeroplane to Clonakilty, one of the first times that a powered machine was seen in the skies over Cork. In the following years, aeroplanes appeared at infrequent intervals over the city. In 1927, Lindbergh flew solo from east to west across the Atlantic Ocean. Later on, an Irishman, Major James Fitzmaurice, with the Germans, von Hunefeld and Kohl, made the first west/east crossing of the Atlantic.

In 1928, Cork Harbour Authorities commissioned a study as to the feasibility of the use of the Cork Harbour area as a base for either aeroplanes or seaplanes. However, despite the efforts of the Cork County Surveyor, Richard O'Connor, and the preparation of several studies, no progress was made. The establishment of Aer Lingus in 1936 rekindled hope, but the outbreak of the War in 1939 halted any development.

In 1947 the Cork Aero Company was established by George Heffernan and Dan Cullinane. On 8 May 1948, Farmers' Cross Airfield was opened by Mr Liam Cosgrave. Local authorities and other organisations pressed for the upgrading of the airport to full international standard, but successive governments refused to issue a scheduled service licence. The point was finally conceded in 1957, when it was agreed to provide an airport in the Ballygarvan area.

The Taoiseach, Mr Sean Lemass, declared Cork Airport officially open on 16 October 1961.

1961

17 October

THE HUGUENOTS

In April 1598, Henry IV of England proclaimed the Edict of Nantes, giving freedom of religion to all citizens. Its purpose was to protect the religious freedom of Protestants living in France. Louis XIV of France revoked the Edict in 1685.

Louis was particularly hostile to the members of the Huguenot persuasion and ordered that their temples be levelled. Their ministers of religion were to quit France within fifteen days, and all the children of the Huguenots were to be baptised into the Catholic religion. This led to the exodus of 50,000 Huguenots from France.

They sought sanctuary in countries where Protestanism was dominant – Switzerland, Germany, Holland and England – from where some came to Ireland. A small group eventually arrived in Cork. They were skilled in weaving wool and silk, in the manufacture of gingham and tapestries, were consummate horticulturalists and skilled silversmiths and goldsmiths. They introduced new surnames into the city, Besnard, Hardy, LaTouche, Daltera, Lavitte (remembered in the name of Lavitt's Quay), and Perrier, whose family gave several mayors to the city. Many translated their names into the English equivalent: Le Roy became King; Le Croix became Cross; Delappe is now known as Delap; Duclos became Dukelow. The Huguenots' Church was in St Paul's Parish in a street now known as French Church Street.

The Revocation of the Edict of Nantes, which led to the arrival of the Huguenots in Cork, was proclaimed by King Louis XIV of France on 17 October 1685.

1685

DUBLIN / CORK TRAIN

In 1849, William Lyons, the first Catholic mayor of Cork since the reformation, accompanied by many civic dignitaries, went to Blackpool and took a special train to Mallow. The party awaited a train from Dublin which carried Lord Clarendon, the Lord Lieutenant, and the directors of the Great Southern and Western Railway. The occasion was the inauguration of a train service between Cork and Dublin.

There was a great concourse of people at Mallow to celebrate the occasion. Charles Bianconi, of stage coach fame, joined the party for the final stage of the journey. Many stops were made on the way to Cork, the visitors being afforded an opportunity to view the great engineering feats along the route: the Mallow Viaduct, 75 feet high with ten arches 45 feet apart; Ballygiblin embankment, 110 feet high, constructed, according to the *Cork Examiner*, 'with all the precision of a flower bed in a gentleman's garden', as well as Monard Viaduct and Rathpeacon cutting. The contractor, Mr William Dargan, who had insisted on a minimum wage of one shilling and sixpence per day for the workers, accompanied the party.

The first train from Dublin arrived in Cork on 18 October 1849.

1849

JOHN SWINEY

John Swiney, the son of Daniel and Elenor (nee Anglim), was born in Cork and baptised in the North Cathedral on 10 August 1773. He became a woollen draper and had a large shop at Goulnasporra, at the foot of Shandon Street.

He joined the United Irishmen and became one of that society's most active and senior members. The government issued a warrant for his arrest and he was captured on 28 March 1798, while visiting Roger O'Connor in the County Gaol at the South Gate Bridge. Timothy Conway, one-time friend of Swiney turned informer, described him as 'a blood thirsty traitor, planned the insurrection of the Dublin Militia, publisher and circulator of the handbills exciting the soldiers of that regiment to mutiny, and this garrison to murder'.

Swiney was taken to Dublin and lodged in Newgate Prison. He was never tried, but was one of the twenty leaders of the insurrection sent to Fort George in Scotland where they were interned for three years and three months. In June 1802, the prisoners were taken to Cuxhaven, in Germany, and there liberated. Swiney, in the company of Thomas Addis Emmet, went to Holland, but the following year returned to Ireland to help Robert Emmet. After the failure of the 1803 insurrection, Swiney experienced great difficulty in effecting his escape.

In France Swiney became an officer in the Irish Legion but, having killed an officer in a duel, resigned his commission. He went to live in Morlaix where he married Marie Victorie Pezron.

John Swiney died at Morlaix in France on 19 October 1844.

1844

SAINT ANNE'S, SHANDON

A Decretal Letter of Pope Innocent III, dated 2nd ides April, 1199, refers to 'the place itself in which the church is situated, with all the appurtenances within and without the city, the Church of St Mary on the Mountain'. It would appear, however, that religious establishments had stood on the site of Shandon since before recorded history.

The fort and church at Shandon were destroyed during the siege of Cork in 1690. Services were conducted in another church at the foot of Shandon Street for some years until the present church of St Anne's, Shandon, was erected in 1722.

The church is rather plain, the distinctive feature being the 170 foot tall tower. The walls are seven feet thick. The south and west faces of the building are of limestone, quarried on the south side of the city, the north and east sides of local sandstone. As a rhyme puts it;

Party coloured, like its People
Red and white stands Shandon Steeple.

The tower is surmounted by a lead dome and a weather vane in the design of a gilt salmon, symbol of the fishing industry. It is eleven feet three inches long. The famous clock, a gift of the Corporation, is known as the 'Four-faced Liar', the dials having a propensity to show different times, except on the hour. It was built and installed by Mangan's of Cork in 1847. The bells, weighing over six tons, are hung on a fixed structure and were cast by Rudhall of Gloucester in 1750. They rang out for the first time on 7 December 1752.

The Church of St Anne, Shandon, was opened for service on 20 October 1722.

1722

MURDER IN CORK

Michael O'Callaghan, a teacher from County Limerick, stated, at his trial in Cork in 1830, that he had been a sergeant and schoolmaster in the 21st Fusiliers. He had served in the West Indies where he contracted a fever, and had been discharged on the grounds of 'imbecility of mind'. He was in receipt of a pension of sixteen pence per day.

O'Callaghan came to Cork to have his pension re-assessed. He entered the house of Mary Denny, who kept a brothel in Bridewell Lane, paid a fee of six pence to Mary Denny's daughter, and insisted on staying the night. A struggle ensued, O'Callaghan injuring two of the girls. When Mary Denny became involved, he struck her with a bedpost and fractured her skull.

He attempted to flee the scene, but was captured by clients of the brothel who had witnessed the fight. O'Callaghan was charged with the murder of Mary Denny.

Michael O'Callaghan was found guilty of the murder of Mary Denny on 21 October 1830.

1830

ELECTRIC TRAIN

'In the electric railway visitors see a present novelty and a possibility of the future,' wrote the correspondent of the *Cork Examiner*. He was referring to the application of electric power to trains. The occasion was an international exhibition organised by the North Monastery School in the Corn Exchange premises at Anglesea Street. The year was 1889.

The promoters of the experiment were an unusual pairing: Brother Dominic Burke of the North Monastery and Gerald Percival, a Unitarian and electrical contractor. Brother Burke had already displayed his interest in electricity when, to celebrate the silver jubilee of the episcopacy of Pope Pius IX, in 1877, he lit a great electric bulb in the grounds of the monastery. Brother Burke and Gerald Percival organised a demonstration of an electrically powered railway as a feature of the exhbition.

Gerald Percival apparently laid the rails, and Brother Burke manufactured the rolling stock in the school workshops. Although the famous Giants' Causeway Electric Tramway had been functioning for some time, the system devised by Brother Burke and Gerald Percival was revolutionary. An overhead electric cable supplied the power, rather than the third rail conductor principle then in use in Great Britain and France.

The electric railway proved an enormous success at the exhibition. It made its first journey on 22 October 1889.

1889

23 October

RELIGION IN CORK

Cork fell to the Cromwellian forces on 16 October 1649. The inhabitants who had returned to their city were now faced with a cruel choice. Catholics were to abjure their religion or leave the city. Those who would renounce their religion and accept Puritanism would be permitted to retain their property. A signal was to be given; three canon shots would be fired and after the last shot, Catholics remaining in the city did so at their own risk.

There was not even one in the city who would accept the impious conditions offered, to try and keep his property and goods at the cost of his faith. 'Before the third signal, all went forth from the city walls, the men and women, yea, even the children and the infirm ... abandoning their houses and goods, their revenues and property and wealth, choosing rather to be afflicted with the people of God on the mountaintops and in caverns, in hunger and thirst, in cold and nakedness, than to enjoy momentary pleasure and temporal prosperity with sin.'

The decree of banishment was proclaimed on 23 October 1649.

1649

DONERAILE CONSPIRACY

Twenty-one persons from Doneraile were charged with conspiracy to murder, among others, Admiral Evans, Bond Lowe and Michael Creagh. Daniel O'Connell was engaged to defend, but was not present in the courthouse (now known as the Queen's Old Castle) when four of the defendants, Leary, Shine, Roche and Magrath, were arraigned. The trial proceeded, and the members of the all-Protestant jury retired for approximately five minutes before returning a guilty verdict.

A messenger was immediately dispatched to summon O'Connell from Derrynane on arrival in Cork, O'Connell managed to get a mixed jury (Catholic and Protestant) selected for the trial of another four defendants, Connor, Lynch, Barrett and Wallis. The judges were Messrs Torrens and Pennyfather. The jury retired at 2.00 pm and, when they returned the following day, Barrett was acquitted, but they could not reach a verdict on the others. The next day two further defendants were acquitted and, on 30 October, the Solicitor General decided not to proceed with further prosecutions. The trial of the three on whom a verdict had not been given was held at the April Assizes, and while two were acquitted, Lynch was found guilty. The four originally found guilty in Daniel O'Connell's absence were sentenced to death, but the penalty was commuted and they were deported to Australia.

Daniel O'Connell rode from Derrynane to Cork to participate in the Doneraile Conspiracy Trials on 24 October 1829.

1829

TURNER'S CROSS CHURCH

Dr Coughlan, Bishop of Cork, presided at the solemn blessing of Christ the King Church, Turner's Cross, in the presence of a host of religious and civic dignitaries, including the Lord Mayor, Cllr F.J. Daly, Messrs Egan and Anthony, Teachtaí Dála, Senator T. Linehan, Mr Boyd-Barrett, architect, and Mr John Buckley, builder.

The Church of Christ the King is exceptional in that it was constructed of reinforced concrete, the first such building in the city. It is unusual in that it is wider than it is long and has no internal pillars. It is also unusual in that it was designed by an American architect, Barry Byrne of Chicago. There is some controversy as to how it came to be commissioned, but it is possible that the parish priest at the time saw an illustration of the design in a magazine and commissioned the architect.

The great statue of Christ the King at the church gate was designed by the American sculptor, John Storrs, but was cut from local limestone in the workshops of John Maguire at Mulgrave Road. Mr O'Connell of the 'Jewel Casket' supplied the gold key that was presented to the Bishop; William Egan and Co. made the solid brass sanctuary lamp and the monstrance. The marble terrazzo flooring was executed by Messrs J.J. O'Hara of Dublin, and it was the first occasion on which that process was used in Ireland. The total cost of the church amounted to £27,000.

The Church of Christ the King, Turner's Cross, was consecrated on 25 October 1931.

1931

JAMES J. MURPHY

James J. Murphy, together with his three brothers, William, Jerome and Francis, established the Lady's Well Porter Brewery in 1854. It was located in Leitrim Street, in buildings formerly used as a Foundling Hospital.

In 1884, the concern became a private limited liability company, and in 1889, the premises were remodelled and the most modern plant installed. In 1901, Sir John Arnott's Brewery in St Marie's of the Isle was acquired; the large number of public houses owned by that brewery provided guaranteed market outlets for Murphy's. The Riverstown Ale Brewery and Malt House was also acquired.

James J. Murphy was prominent in the public life of Cork. When, in the 1880s, the Munster Bank came under threat and the savings of many small investors were threatened, Murphy came to the rescue, and while the bank went into liquidation, his efforts ensured the safety of the investments. He was also responsible for the foundation of the Munster and Leinster Bank at that time, and remained a director during his lifetime. Unusually for that period, he was one of the few prominent businessmen to support the emerging Gaelic Athletic Association. On his death the Cork County Board of the GAA adjourned as a mark of respect.

James J. Murphy died on 26 October 1897.

1897

JOE MURPHY

Joe Murphy was born in America of Cork parents, but returned to Ireland with his family at the age of five to live in Pouladuff. During 'The Troubles' he joined the IRA. He was arrested on 15 July 1920, and lodged in Cork Gaol. It was alleged that he was in possession of a bomb, but he was never charged.

On 10 August, the prisoners, led by Terence MacSwiney, delivered an ultimatum to the Governor, stating that if charges were not laid against them they would go on hunger strike. The following day they refused food.

The hunger strike generated much sympathy for the men, but there was controversy about the morality of placing one's life in danger. Many efforts were made to persuade the prisoners to give up the strike. The authorities released some prisoners and deported others, so that only eleven prisoners were left in Cork Gaol.

Michael Fitzgerald died on 17 October. On the evening of 25 October, Joe Murphy died. A huge crowd gathered outside the gates of the gaol to witness the removal of the remains to the Lough Church. On the following day British Authorities limited the numbers permitted to walk in the cortège to 100. But thousands of people, by walking along the footpaths, followed the funeral to St Finbarr's Cemetery. British Forces did not enter the cemetery. Later in the day, after the crowds had dispersed, a party of Volunteers fired a volley of shots over the grave.

Joe Murphy was buried on 27 October 1920.

1920

THE CUSTOM HOUSE

The foundation stone of the custom-house on Lapp's island, was this day laid by Robert Aldridge, esq. the collector of customs, who was attended by the officers of the several departments. A brass plate, with a suitable engraving, was placed under the stone, and Mr Hargrave, jun. in the absence of his brother, the architect, presented a silver trowel to Mr Aldridge, with an address. When the ceremony was concluded, Mr Aldridge gave some bank notes to be expended by the labourers in drinking the king's health.

Tuckey, in his *Remembrancer*, records the foundation stone of the Custom House being laid on 28 October 1814.

1814

JOHN F. MAGUIRE

John Francis Maguire, publisher of the *Cork Examiner* and Member of Parliament for the city, was most influential in organising the Cork Industrial Exhibition of 1852. Maguire and his fellow promoters were inspired by the great Crystal Palace Exhibition, which had been held in London the previous year.

The Cork Exhibition, held on a site in Anglesea Street, was an outstanding success. Originally intended as a local show, it attracted so many exhibitors from all parts of the country that it became a national event. Visitors were astonished at the range and quality of the products, all of native manufacture.

Maguire, determined to perpetuate the memory of the occasion, published *The Industrial Movement of Ireland as illustrated by the National Exhibition of 1852*. It is an outstanding work of reference, detailing not only the numerous industries obtaining in the country at the time, but identifying also owners and crafts people. He provides a comprehensive list of the artists, painters and sculptors of the period. His book describes the various halls which were constructed to house the exhibition and identifies the contractors employed to erect them.

John Francis Maguire published this important book on 29 October 1853.

1853

JEROME COLLINS

Jerome Collins was born in South Main Street in October 1840. He was a Fenian and, as clerk of works, had supervised the rebuilding of the North Gate Bridge. Collins emigrated to America in 1864. Intensely interested in meteorology, he became the first weather forecaster to be employed on a newspaper, and his articles were widely syndicated.

Collins' employer, Gordon Bennett, publisher of the *New York Herald*, who had financed Stanley's expedition to find Livingstone, agreed to support an expedition to the North Pole by way of the Bering Straits. An American Naval officer, Lieutenant de Long, was placed in command, and Jerome Collins was appointed scientific officer. A steam yacht, the *Pandora*, was purchased, re-equipped and re-named the *Jeannette*.

The expedition was a disaster. The *Jeannette* proved to be unsuitable for the icy conditions, and de Long was not a competent leader. The *Jeannette* became icebound and drifted, locked in the pack-ice, from October 1879 until June 1881, when the crew abandoned ship. De Long divided the party into three groups, each taking a different route to safety. Collins travelled with de Long's party but they ran out of food and eventually succumbed.

A rescue party found the bodies and buried them in Siberia. The remains were later exhumed by a United States Naval party, brought to Hamburg and shipped to America, arriving in New York on 22 February 1884. Collins' body was sent back to Ireland and reached Cork on 8 March. He was buried in Curraghkippane Graveyard.

In his diary, de Long noted that Jerome Collins, Cork's Arctic explorer, spent his last day alive on 30 October 1881.

1881

TERENCE MACSWINEY

The body of Terence MacSwiney, Lord Mayor of Cork, who had died on hunger strike in Brixton Prison, London, lay in state in the City Hall. Thousands of citizens, unmindful of the inclement weather, filed past to pay their respects. Some time during the night a mourning wreath was torn from the door of the City Hall.

At eleven o'clock in the morning the body, accompanied by huge crowds, was removed to St Mary's Cathedral where mass was celebrated by the Bishop, Dr Coughlan, assisted by the Archbishops of Cashel, Perth (Australia) and Hobart (Tasmania). The Bishops of Ballarat, Cloyne, Killaloe and Kerry were also in attendance.

The coffin was borne along the route to the cemetery by relays of Volunteers, some carrying wreaths. Relatives of the deceased, the Lord Mayor, members of Dáil Éireann and Cork public bodies, members of the University, representatives of Sinn Féin and of Trade and Labour organisations followed the coffin. Bands, placed at strategic places along the route, played solemn music. The general public were precluded by the authorities from joining the cortège, but they lined the entire route. A military aeroplane, a rare sight in 1920, flew over the city.

At St Finbarr's Cemetery, a final absolution was given by the Bishop of Cork, Arthur Griffith delivered a short address, and a salvo of shots, fired over the grave, was the last tribute to the dead patriot.

Terence MacSwiney was buried on 31 October 1920.

1920

1 November

CATHOLIC MAYOR

Huge crowds gathered at the City courthouse to witness the election of the mayor of Cork. For the first time since the Reformation a Catholic was contesting the election, a situation brought about by the Emancipation Act of 1829 and the Municipal Reform Act of 1840.

'The City Courthouse', the *Cork Examiner* reported, 'presented a most strikingly imposing spectacle, as numberless thousands crowded the galleries and body of the spacious building. The crush was terrific beyond all powers of description. All classes, from the most influential gentry, merchants and citizens down to the humblest, were present on this most auspicious occasion.'

The outgoing mayor, Julius Besnard, presided, and the privilege of nominating the Catholic candidate fell to Alderman Fagan. There were 50 votes in favour of Thomas Lyons, with one dissenting voice, that of Councillor Vincent. He was a member of the notorious and discredited Friendly Club, which for generations had controlled the election of all officerships of the Council. Mr Lyons' election was greeted, the *Cork Examiner* reported, with 'shouts, clapping of hands and every conceivable form of demonstration'.

The outgoing mayor presented the chain of office to Thomas Lyons. The new mayor of Cork was carried shoulder high from the courthouse and, the *Cork Examiner* commented, 'was then chaired through the city, thousands and tens of thousands forming the joyous procession'.

The first post Reformation Catholic Mayor of Cork was elected on 1 November 1841.

1841

SHEARES BROTHERS

Henry Sheares was a prominent banker in Cork in the latter years of the eighteenth century. Originally from Shipool, near Bandon, he had a 'country villa' at Glasheen, now known as Sheares Villa. His city residence was on Fenn's Quay, later called Nile Street, before being finally renamed Sheares Street in honour of the family.

Henry Sheares was one of the most philanthropic men of the age and instilled in his sons, Henry and John, a deep sense of social responsibility and a great love of liberty. Both young men visited Paris in 1789, ostensibly to visit Henry's children then in Paris but, in fact, to observe the French Revolutiion. They were present at the storming of the Bastille, and in October witnessed the return of King Louis XVI into Paris.

They returned to Paris in 1792, where they attended a meeting of Irish, English and Americans residents, and voted in favour of a motion expressing support for the Revolution and the National Assembly. They remained in Paris until 1793 and actually witnessed the execution of the French king.

Henry and John Sheares attended that meeting of foreigners in Paris on 2 November 1792.

1792

3 November

AGRICULTURAL MUSEUM

In the 1840s Lloyd's Hotel stood on the site in Oliver Plunkett Street now known as Conway's Yard. Sir Thomas Deane selected it as the venue for a meeting that he had called, the purpose of which was to enlist support for a project he was promoting, namely, the establishment of an agricultural museum in Cork.

Sir Thomas was the foremost architect/builder in Cork. He had travelled widely and was impressed by a similar museum which he had recently visited in London. Lord Bernard, MP for Cork, had, at Deane's request, agreed to preside at the meeting. Deane outlined his ideas to a large attendance, pointing out that Ireland was a bountiful country and the land was capable of producing much more than what was being produced. He advocated land drainage, and suggested that different drainage techniques be displayed at the proposed museum to enable farmers to decide on the most effective system for their particular purpose.

Mr Beamish, speaking from the floor, pointed out that a regular supply of reliable seed was essential for good husbandry. He argued that new machinery available in England could be purchased and fabricated at Cork foundries. He also suggested that the curriculum of study in the museum include practical subjects in addition to classical languages.

A Mr Kelleher expressed his disappointment at the poor attendance of farming people at the meeting and concluded that the impetus was coming from the urban classes. After considerable debate it was agreed to form an organising committee.

The meeting to discuss the establishment of an agricultural museum in Cork was held in Lloyd's Hotel on 3 November 1842.

1842

GEORGE BOOLE

George Boole, a native of Lincoln, England, showed a marked aptitude for mathematics while still a young man and began his career as an assistant in a school. Shortly after he opened his own educational establishment in Lincoln, which met with considerable success.

In 1844, Boole was awarded a gold medal by the Royal Society. He developed a new branch of mathematics which, much later, enabled Einstein to arrrive at his theory of relativity.

Boole began to offer papers to the *Cambridge and Dublin Mathematical Journal* and shortly after he published *The Mathematical Analysis of Logic*. Boole's system, now called Boolean algebra, led to the development of computer science. Although he did not hold a primary university degree he was appointed Professor of Mathematics at Queen's College, Cork (now University College).

His first publication after his appointment in 1854 was *Investigations of the Laws of Thought, on which are founded the Mathematical Theories of Logic and Probabilities*. He was elected a Fellow of the Royal Society. Two other works followed: *On the Theory of Probabilities* and *Differential Equations*. The latter was used as the textbook in Cambridge University.

George Boole married Miss M. Everest, a consummate mathematician in her own right. She was the niece of Colonel Everest, surveyer of the Himalayas mountain range, after whom Mount Everest was named. Professor Boole's daughter, Ethel Voynich, became a celebrated novelist.

Professor George Boole, mathematician, who died in Blackrock, Cork, on 8 December 1864, was born on 4 November 1815.

1815

A CATHOLIC BISHOP

The arrival of the Reformation in Ireland was the source of much disquiet and confusion in the Irish Church. Bishops were being appointed to sees by both the Papacy and the King of England.

John Benet was the last unquestioned bishop of Cork. On his death, the English Crown appointed Dominic Tirrey to the vacant see of Cork and Cloyne. Tirrey was regarded by some as a supporter of the Reformation and by Rome as a schismatic. Rome named John O'Heyne to the vacant diocese of Cork and Cloyne.

Bishop O'Heyne was, however, transferred to Elphin when Rome realised that he could not take up his appointment in Cork because of the presence of the schismatic Tirrey.

Bishop John O'Heyne was appointed to the see of Cork and Cloyne on 5 November 1540.

1540

NORTH GATE BRIDGE

It is impossible to state, at this point in time, when first a bridge was erected on the site of the present Griffith Bridge – previously, and still, colloquially, known as the North Gate Bridge.

In 1637 a wooden bridge was carried away in a storm and in 1678 Lord Shannon, the Governor of Cork, had a drawbridge built. In 1713 Coltsman, a builder and stonemason, built the first stone bridge. This remained the only bridge over the north channel of the river until 1789, when the first St Patrick's Bridge was erected.

In 1831, the then North Gate Bridge was renovated and two iron footpaths were added. Sir John Benson was commissioned to construct a new bridge in 1859. The engineering work was supervised by Jerome Collins, who was to gain fame – but lose his life – while participating in an expedition to the North Pole. This bridge, which was opened to traffic in 1863, was deemed unsafe in 1954. The Corporation commissioned a new bridge, named Griffith Bridge, in commemoration of Arthur Griffith, founder of Sinn Féin. It is 62 feet in width, whereas the older bridge was only 40 feet.

Mr Anthony Barry, Lord Mayor of Cork, performed the official opening of Griffith Bridge on 6 November 1961.

1961

COUNTY FINAL

The Blackrock hurlers must have considered the year 1926 as their *annus mirabilis*. Theirs was, arguably, the greatest club team of all time. Players such as Seán Óg Murphy, 'Balty' and 'Gah' Aherne, 'Marie' Connell, Paddy Delea, Jim Hurley and Eudie Coughlan were the finest hurlers of their day.

On 24 October, Cork, led by their captain Seán Óg Murphy, had won the All-Ireland Hurling Final. As the ballad puts it,

> There were ten from Blackrock and Joe Kearney,
> One Finbarr to bring back the tale.

Two weeks later Blackrock and St Finbarrs contested the Cork County Hurling Final, with Blackrock installed as the firmest of favourites. The Finbarrs could not be compared with Blackrock, although they did include in their team the veteran captain Danny Coughlan, as well as 'Batna' Cronin, Mick Murphy, Tom Lee and 'Dannix' Ring.

Before a huge attendance, the 'Barrs' scored the first goal and threw down the gauntlet to the mighty 'Rockies'. Blackrock, however, soon imposed their supremacy and led at half-time. Ten minutes before the final whistle, they had extended their lead to a comfortable, seemingly unbeatable, three goals and two points. But the Finbarrs, to the astonishment of all, including many of their own disillusioned supporters who had left the Athletic Grounds early, scored four goals in those final minutes and snatched an improbable victory.

St Finbarrs defeated Blackrock and thereby won one of the most famous of all County Hurling Finals on 7 November 1926.

1926

8 November

HYDROPATHY IN CORK

In 1848, the year of the Great Famine, responsible Cork citizens were concerned, not only about the effects of the Famine, but at the spectre of the reappearance of cholera. The memory of the 1832 epidemic was still fresh in their minds.

Dr Richard Barter argued that, as the medical establishment had no cure for cholera, alternative methods should be tried. He advocated the application of hydropathy, a practice based on the curative power of water. He outlined the history of hydropathy, from its origins in Germany, and gave examples of many cures effected by the application of hydropathic techniques.

Dr Barter, who also extolled the benefits of hot air and Turkish baths, established a hydropathic clinic at The Hydro, St Anne's, Blarney. At a public lecture in the Imperial Hotel, reported in the *Cork Examiner* of 8 November 1848, Dr Richard Barter advocated the use of hydropathic medicine.

1848

DOCKERS' STRIKE

The dispute between the dockers and the Cork Steam Packet Company Limited in 1909 had been brewing for some time. The dockers sought parity in pay with their counterparts in the Clyde Shipping Company. At the time their wages ranged from five and a half pence to eight pence (old coinage) per hour.

The dockers walked off the *Inniscarra* and were supported by many other workers in their action. However, some who had remained on board were joined by the company clerks, and continued the unloading of the vessel. The striking dockers were infuriated and began to intimidate those working on the ship.

The Royal Irish Constabulary were summoned to protect the strike breakers. When the dockers moved in the direction of the company offices on Penrose Quay the police, wielding their batons indiscriminately, attacked dockers and onlookers alike. Many people were injured and were treated, initially in private houses in Alfred and King Streets, before being eventually removed to the North Infirmary.

Later in the evening of 9 November 1909, the dockers, accompanied by a huge crowd and led by a pipe band, marched to the railway station to welcome a trade union official who had been dispatched from Dublin to organise the strike.

1909

ST PATRICK'S BRIDGE

Members of the Cork, Queenstown, Fermoy, Youghal, Bandon and Kinsale Districts of the Masonic Order assembled at their headquarters in Tuckey Street. They were joined by the band of the Lancashire Artillery Militia and the assembly marched in procession to Lavitt's Quay.

The Lord Lieutenant had arrived in Cork in order to lay the foundation stone of St Patrick's Bridge. The Mayor, Mr John Arnott, presented him with specimens of all the coins of the realm and a document, which he placed in the foundation stone. The document was dated 5859, in accordance with the Masonic Calendar.

Even more eccentric was the ceremony that followed. The Provincial Grand Master of Munster, having recited the masonic prayer, sprinkled grains of corn, wine and oil over the foundation stone. Only then was it placed into position.

The Lord Lieutenant conferred the honour of knighthood on Mayor John Arnott on the occasion of the laying of the foundation stone of St Patrick's bridge on 10 November 1859.

1859

ROBERT J. LECKY

Robert John Lecky was born in Cork on 25 March 1809. He was a partner in the shipbuilding company of Lecky and Beale, located on Penrose Quay. The company later became Messrs R. J. Lecky and Co., Shipbuilders and Engineers.

The nineteenth century produced a new era in shipbuilding. Sail was giving way to steam, timber to iron, and Lecky's yard was in the forefront of the revolution. The first iron-hulled vessel built in Cork, the little cutter yacht *Chase*, was built on Penrose Quay – as was the first screw-driven steamer, *Blarney*, for the Cork Steamship Company.

Lecky paid considerable attention to rigging and sails – one of his products, the *Rattler*, a-two masted schooner of 209 tons gross with a 50 horse power engine, actually crossed the Atlantic under sail. The Penrose Quay yard produced the first large and effective dredger, the *Lee*, for the Cork Harbour Commissioners. Engineering commissions were also undertaken; it is thought that the iron railings fronting the Savings Bank on Lapp's Quay were constructed by the company.

Robert Lecky was, from boyhood, interested in astronomy and had an observatory, which enabled him to keep exceedingly accurate time. He was a member of the Cork Historical and Archaeological Society and contributed papers to its journal. He was related to Hartpole Lecky, the historian.

Robert John Lecky died in London on 11 November 1897.

1897

MARIE ANTOINETTE

The French Revolution of 1789 sent shivers of fear not only through the royal houses of Europe, but also through the churches. The revolution was perceived as a direct threat to religion, and the hostility of French expatriate prelates towards the new regime influenced the attitude of the Irish hierarchy.

Irish clerical students, studying on the Continent, were especially antipathetic to the Revolution. One of them was Florence McCarthy, a native of Macroom. He studied in Rome and was destined for the Papal diplomatic service until recalled to Cork by the bishop, Dr Moylan. In 1790, Florence McCarthy became administrator in the parish of Ss Peter and Paul. He was promoted to parish priest of Kinsale in 1792 but, most unusually, he exchanged positions with the parish priest of Passage West.

Fr Florence McCarthy was a regular visitor to his old parish in the centre of Cork. On 12 November 1793, he returned to Ss Peter and Paul's church in Carey's Lane to preach at a solemn requiem mass for the executed Queen Marie Antoinette of France.

1793

13 November

AFFRAY IN BRIDGE STREET

There were about twenty people enjoying their drinks in Mr O'Regan's pub, 4 Bridge Street, on a winter's evening in 1870. Suddenly a body of some 40 soldiers burst in upon them. Wielding sticks and swinging their belts, they proceeded to set upon the startled and disconcerted clientele. It took some time for the drinkers to gather their wits, but when they did, they launched a counter attack and gave a lot more than they received. They wrestled the sticks and belts from the soldiers and literally beat them off the premises.

A large band of citizens had gathered outside the hostelry on receiving news of the affray. They joined forces with the bar clientele, driving the soldiers up St Patrick's Hill towards the military barracks. The RIC intervened in an attempt to rescue the soldiers.

Later in the evening a large band of soldiers went marauding in King Street (now MacCurtain Street), attacking passers-by and doing damage to buildings. The RIC succeeded in preventing them from getting into Bridge Street, where a huge crowd of irate citizens was waiting to do battle, once again, with the military.

No reason for the attack on the pub was ever adduced. The regiment involved in the affray was the Highland Light Infantry, the HLIs, as they were known in Cork, and whose name has, since their ignonimous conduct on 13 November 1870, been synonymous with cowardice.

1870

THOMAS ADDIS EMMET

Thomas Addis Emmet was born in a house at the junction of Grattan Street and Sheares Street on 24 April 1764. His father was appointed to the position of State Physician in 1770 and removed his family to Dublin, where a younger son, Robert, was born. Thomas won a scholarship to Trinity College and graduated in medicine in 1783.

He subsequently took a further degree in Edinburgh Medical School, and then travelled extensively on the Continent. Following the death of his older brother, Temple, he abandoned medicine and returned to Trinity to study law.

Thomas, who had been deeply influenced by his father's nationalist politics, took the oath of the United Irishmen in 1795 and was elected secretary of the organisation. He opposed the insurrection of 1798, arguing that it should not be attempted until French help had arrived. Nevertheless, he was arrested with the other members of the Directory and imprisoned for two years after the Rising.

On his release he travelled to Holland and thence to France, where he received news of his brother Robert's abortive rebellion in 1803. He helped with the raising of an Irish Brigade in the French Army, but then emigrated to America and settled in New York, where he joined the bar and became a highly successful lawyer. A supporter of Catholic Emancipation in Ireland, he defended the rights of black slaves to remain in New York.

Thomas Addis Emmet died suddenly in New York on 14 November 1827.

1827

15 November

PUBLICANS PROTEST

In 1836, vintners in Cork felt that they had good reason to be perturbed. They perceived the recently established Total Abstinence Association as a serious threat to their livelihood, 'a heresy imported from abroad, unnatural in itself, and repugnant to the best traditions of Irish hospitality'. A further cause of concern was the lately enacted legislation that forbade the selling of spirits between the hours of nine o'clock on Sunday night and seven o'clock on Monday morning.

The publicans summoned a meeting at a hall in King Street (now MacCurtain Street), to protest at the legislation which empowered the police to inspect the public houses in order to ensure that the law was observed. The legislation was, one speaker asserted, a charter for informants, placing the publican at the mercy of every disgruntled customer. Another publican claimed that a stigma had been placed on every retailer, 'a brand more reproachful than the brand put upon Cain'. Yet another speaker claimed that a publican, taking the air at the open door of his establishment, could be deemed to be touting for business, and accordingly subject to the full rigour of the law.

This protest meeting of publicans took place on 15 November 1836.

1836

NORTH MONASTERY

The Cork Charitable Committee was established as a result of the enactment into law of the Relief Act of 1793, which made limited provision for the education of destitute children. The committee was under the aegis of the Catholic bishop and its membership list included the names of wealthy merchants, such as Mahony, Daly, Moylan, MacCarthy, Murphy, Hennessy and Sugrue.

By 1799 the Committee had provided schools for the education of 1,000 poor children, and had had them apprenticed to various trades. However, the major difficulty encountered was the lack of competent teachers. The Committee introduced the Lancasterian system of education to the schools, but this was not a success.

In the meantime, the Catholic Bishop, Dr Moylan, had sent two young Corkmen, Jerome O'Connor and John B. Leonard, to Waterford to be trained by Ignatius Rice in accordance with the principles of the newly-established Christian Brothers Order. On their return the Cork Charitable Committee presented them with a premises at Chapel Lane in the north-side of the city.

The first Christian Brothers School in Cork, later known as the North Monastery, was opened on 16 November 1811.

1811

DANIEL F. O'LEARY

Daniel Florence O'Leary lived in a house now numbered 89/90 Barrack Street. Having had a good liberal education he joined a group called the 'Patriots', founded to support Simon Bolivar, the South-American patriot. When the British Government organised a regiment to assist Bolivar's rebellion against Spain, O'Leary was awarded a commission, possibly through the help of his cousin, Fr Arthur O'Leary.

In South America he attracted the attention of Simon Bolivar, who appointed him his private secretary. O'Leary distinguished himself in the Peruvian campaign of 1829, was promoted to colonel and eventually made a full general. He joined the diplomatic service and Bolivar entrusted him with the difficult, untimately unsuccessful, commission to create a united federal state of Peru, Colombia and Bolivia.

Having retired from active service O'Leary was appointed British Consul and subsequently British Minister Plenipotentiary to New Grenada. He returned to Cork in 1834 to visit his widowed mother, then living in Cook Street, and made a presentation of a valuable collection of South-American gems, minerals, plants and birds, which are now in University College, Cork.

O'Leary died on 24 January 1854, and the anniversary of his death in 1954 was celebrated with great pomp in Venezuela and a biography was published.

The news of Daniel Florence O'Leary's marriage to Lolita Soublette, a niece of Simon Bolivar, was received in Cork on 17 November 1829.

1829

18 November

BAKERS' COMBINATIONS

Sir,

Having seen in the report of the proceedings at the Police Office this day, that Timothy Connell swore informations against four persons, three of them Bakers, for an assault arising out of combinations against night work, and as such a proceeding is calculated to cast a stain on the society to which I belong, permit me on the part of the Operative Bakers of this City, to most solemnly deny any part, participation of knowledge of said act, and to denounce and condemn generally all such proceedings.

I do further declare that in the present struggle against Night baking we never contemplated any other way of redress, but by the powerful and efficacious influence of public opinion and public sympathy, or by the interference of Parliament in our favour. Yes, Sir, the Bakers of Cork are disciples of the moral force school; they are opposed, on principle, to violence and coercion. Would to God that the Masters opposed to it would try the question at issue by the same just ordeal. If they did short indeed would be the decision between us. The public have already most unequivocally decided on whose side are justice and humanity, and although those few would-be tyrants endeavour to make a handle of this petty drunken broil for their own selfish purposes, still we are confident that a discerning Public will easily conceive the motive of injuring a holy and just cause by coupling it with such a proceeding.

In conclusion, Sir, permit me to add that the most vindictive of those night workers know full well, that no illegal combination exists among the Operative Bakers; they know that we are pursuing the course that will ultimately render our cause successful, and which has gained for us the good will and support of our benevolent fellow citizens.

I remain, Sir, on the part of the Operative Bakers, Your most obedient Servant, John Manly, Sec.

The above letter appeared in the *Cork Examiner* on 18 November 1842.

1842

JOHN V. THOMPSON

John Vaughan Thompson, having studied medicine and surgery at Berwick-on-Tweed, became a surgeon in the British army and served in Gibraltar and the West Indies in 1803. While stationed in Madasgar and Mauritius for four years, 1812 to 1815, he studied the birdlife of the islands, including the now extinct dodo.

A keen biologist from youth, he published a catalogue of the plants indigenous to Berwick-on-Tweed. In 1816, he was posted to Cobh as district medical inspector and dedicated himself to the study of the marine biology of Cork Harbour. Thompson was, apparently, the first person to use a tow net to collect plankton, five years before Charles Darwin did so. He made three original contributions to zoology: the discovery of polyzoa, the nature and life history of the barnacle, and the nature and life history of the feather-star. His work on the feather-star, entitled, *A Memoir on Pentacrinus Europaeus, a recent species discovered in the Cove of Cork*, was published in Cork on 1 July 1823.

Between 1828 and 1834 he published, also in Cork, six numbers of *Zoological Researches and Illustrations*. The first number contained a history of the shore crab, in which he corrected the theories of Cuvier. His identification of the Polyzoa, confirmed in later years by other zoologists, led to its classification as a phylum, one of the major divisions in biological classification.

In 1835 he was transferred to Sydney, Australia, as supervisor of the convict medical department, and died there on 21 January 1847.

John Vaughan Thompson was born on 19 November 1779.

1779

THE CORPORATION IN 1745

The Corporation meeting of November 1745 was typical of the meetings of that time. The Huguenot mayor, William Lavite, and Messrs Ford and Bruce, the Sheriffs, were in attendance, as well as Councillors Alden, Atkins, Millerd, Austin, Croker, Owgan, Winthrop, and Messrs Travers, Dring and Newenham, CS.

The most pressing item of business was the provision of finance, and the Corporation approved the borrowing of various sums of money: from Mr John Baily, curate of Christ Church, the sum of £100 at 5 per cent p.a.; £180 then in the hands of the lord Bishop of Cork for charitable purposes at 5 per cent p.a.; £140 belonging to the poor of St Peter's at 5 per cent p.a..

The members were considerate of the difficulties of past employees, and voted the sum of £10 to the widow and children of Ralph Vize, who had maintained the city fire engines, on consideration that she hand over the materials belonging to the said engines. Margaret, widow of James Crooker, Burgess, was allowed an annual pension of £15.

The Corporation also sanctioned payments in respect of expenses incurred in the training of the militia, and finally ordered that

66 halberts, 44 drums, 2 Grenadiers' Caps, and 2 pair of colours for the foot militia; 2 standards, 2 trumpets with tassels, and one pair of kettledrums with banners for the horse militia of this city, be forthwith provided on such reasonable terms as Mr Mayor, Alderman Atkins, Major Persy, Mr Tho. Browne and the CS can arrange for same.

That meeting of the Corporation was held on 20 November 1745.

1745

JAMES HODNETT

A meeting, opposing the payment of tithes, had been arranged for Whitechurch in July 1832. Major General Sir George Bingham, supported by a large body of military including the Lancers from Ballincollig, sought to prevent the proposed meeting and occupied the site. James Hodnett of Riverstown, a paper manufacturer, was arrested, taken to Carraig na bhFear, and detained.

Hodnett issued a summons against Bingham, claiming wrongful arrest and detention, and briefed Daniel O'Connell to represent him.

O'Connell stated in Court that his client had gone to the district to visit Fr Begley and to inspect the noted round tower at Whitechurch. A little short of their destination they met with Bingham, who became very excited and shouted to the Lancers, 'there is the head of the rebels! Cut him down! Ride him down!' Fortunately, the Lancers ignored the command but directed Hodnett to ride before them to a house in Carraig na bhFear.

Both Fr Begley and Sir Anthony Perrier testified to having heard the order given by Bingham. The jury found against Bingham, but the justice frustrated the process by awarding the derisory sum of sixpence in damages, and a similar amount in costs. A few days later the Corporation of Cork, in a sycophantic gesture, presented Bingham with an address.

The civil action taken by James Hodnett against General Bingham was initiated on 21 November 1832.

1832

WILLIAM KELLEHER

The leading citizens of Cork gathered to pay tribute to William Kelleher, librarian to the Cork Library in Pembroke Street, founder member of the Mechanics' Institute and the Scientific Institution and, in the words of Major Beamish, the *fons et origo* of a great many organisations in Cork during the first half of the nineteenth century.

Sir Thomas Deane declared that without William Kelleher's zeal and enthusiasm the British Association would never have come to Cork, and it was unlikely that the Queen's University would have been established in the city. A great slight had been done William Kelleher when he was passed over by the Board of Nominations at the establishment of the university, but the presence at the meeting of such dignitaries as the Mayor, William Fagan MP, Abraham Abell, Nicholas Murphy and Denny Lane, among others, was testimony to the esteem in which he was held.

The meeting passed three motions: firstly expressing admiration for the work done by William Kelleher; secondly expressing the view that the populace in general should have an opportunity to show appreciation; and thirdly that a subscription be opened to demonstrate their appreciation of his life's work. A committee was elected to promote these objectives.

Meanwhile William Kelleher had been grievously ill, and died a week after the meeting, on 22 November 1849.

1849

QUAY WALLS

Over the centuries three outstanding feats of engineering have been performed in Cork: the reclamation of the river channels and their conversion into streets, the excavation of the railway tunnel and the construction of the quay walls.

The names still associated with sections of the quay walls, Lavitt, Penrose, Pope, Kyrl, etc., indicate that various portions of the river banks were reclaimed over the years by individual merchants for their own business purposes. These primitive quay walls were invariably of rubble construction with timber facings. There was a shallow depth at their frontage so that only small ships were able to dock alongside. Furthermore, the river was continually silting up, restricting passage to the smallest vessels. The combination of these two factors was not conducive to the expansion of trade. Successive Acts of Parliament had been passed to alleviate the problem, but it was not until responsibility for the port was conferred on the Harbour Commissioners in 1814 that decisive steps were taken to deal with the condition of the quay walls.

The Harbour Commissioners drew up a comprehensive development plan, incorporating the dredging of the river channels, the provision of railway sidings along the quaysides, the construction of wet and graving docks and the realignment and refacing of all the old quay walls.

The Harbour Commissioners announced their plans to the public, by way of advertisement in the *Cork Examiner*, on 23 November 1849.

1849

CHARLES SMITH

Charles Smith was born about 1715, apparently in Waterford. He practised as an apothecary but he appears to have abandoned that calling. In 1744, in association with Walter Harris, he published a history of County Down. This publication was a milestone in Irish historiography, being the first major history of an Irish county. It appears to have been the intention of the authors to publish a series of county histories. With this in mind, Smith founded The Physico-Historical Society in Dublin in 1744, the function of the society being the accumulation of topographical information.

The society flourished for some years and it was under its imprimatur that histories of Cork and Waterford were published. Smith produced a history of Kerry in 1756. He was considered to be a reliable, accurate, conservative chronicler of history, although predisposed at times to accentuate the part played by families whose hospitality he had enjoyed.

In 1756, Smith was a founder member and first secretary of the Medico Philosophical Society. He died in Bristol, England in 1762.

Charles Smith is best remembered in Cork for his work, *The Ancient and Present State of the County and City of Cork*, published on 24 November 1750.

1750

ART EXHIBITION

The critic of the *Cork Examiner* was lavish in his praise of the art exhibition arranged by the Cork Art Union in 1841.

The quality of the exhibits astonished him, particularly the work of the artists, Messrs Mahony, Skillin, Huston, Brenan, Noblett, Atkinson and Hayes. He gave a detailed description of their works and, by design or otherwise, has provided us with potentially invaluable contemporary descriptions of places and people. Mr Mahony presented a painting 'Interior of Pope's Quay'. Another work by the same artist, 'The Procession of the Consecration', accurately portrayed the Catholic bishop, Dr Murphy.

The *Examiner* critic much admired the work of George Atkinson, who painted series of views of Cork Harbour, showing beautifully drawn brigs, schooners, cutters and steamers. He also enjoyed George Hayes' 'Wreck of the Killarney Steamer'. He singled out the work of the young artist, L. Connell, and noted a portrait of Richard Dowden (Richard) by an anonymous young lady.

The pièce de résistance, however, was W. Morgan's 'Landscape Storm', 'a gem of gems, charming beyond all powers of description'.

The exhibition of the Cork Art Union was held in Marsh's Rooms on 25 November 1841.

1841

FRITZ KREISLER

Fritz Kreisler, the Austrian violinist and composer, was born on 2 February 1875. Having studied music at the Vienna Conservatory, where he won a gold medal, he later studied with Delibes and Massart at the Paris Conservatoire. He toured America, but returned to Vienna to study medicine.

In 1898, he resumed his musical career and became one of the greatest virtuosos of his time, famous for an intensive vibrato and economy of bowing. His publication, *Classical Manuscripts*, purported to be arrangements of pieces by Vivaldi, Porpora, Pugnani and others. However, he admitted in 1935 that these were his own original compositions.

Kreisler toured extensively. His repertoire included Elgar's violin concerto, the first performance of which he gave in 1910. He performed in Cork, playing the Elgar concerto in addition to works by Handel, Martini, Couperin, Dittersdorf, Paganini, Tartini, Dvorak, Chaminade and Brahms.

The admission charges to Fritz Kreisler's concert were 7/6, 5/-, 2/6 and 1/6. He performed to a capacity house, that included 'every professional musician in Cork anxious to sit at the Master's feet', at the Assembly Rooms, South Mall, on 26 November 1910.

1910

POLICE VIOLENCE

The local elections of November 1889 were held in a welter of excitement, as the Nationalist Party challenged the Establishment Tories. To add to the excitement, the elections clashed with the commemoration of the Manchester Martyrs. The police were determined that the occasion would not be used by the Nationalists to rally support at the ballot box.

The success of the Nationalist Party in the election was greeted with great enthusiasm and the Butter Exchange Band and Carpenters' Band paraded to give a festive flavour to the occasion. Crowds called at the homes of the successful candidates to demonstrate their support. They were followed by a force of about 100 police.

Late in the evening the Carpenters' Band, followed by a squad of police, returned to their clubroom. A stone was thrown in the direction of the police and, without further provocation, the 100 strong force of the Royal Irish Constabulary launched an assault on the band members. They tried to storm the premises but were beaten back by the bandsmen.

'There was a display of wanton, mischievous malice, and a desire to find some objects for assault, which shows that the police have entered into the business of coercion and oppression with a zest which is not alone unnatural but unreasonable', was how the *Cork Examiner*, on the morning of 27 November 1889, described the violence perpetrated by the RIC.

DR 'GLORY' MURPHY

Dr Patrick Murphy inherited a nickname, and a public house, from his father. Mr Murphy senior owned a hostelry, known as 'The Sunburst of Erin', in Blackpool. Underneath the sign he had added the words, 'The Glory of the World'. He was duly christened 'Glory', a soubriquet passed on, in traditional fashion, to his son.

For many years before his death Dr 'Glory' Murphy, who lived alone in Old Great George's Street (now Lower Oliver Plunkett Street), had retired from the practice of medicine. The only person calling to the house on a regular basis was the bread man who, noticing one morning that the bread deposited on the doorstep had not been taken into the house, alerted the authorities. On gaining entry, Dr Murphy's body was discovered. He had been dead for several days.

An inquest was held in the Crown Hotel by Coroner Galwey. Evidence given by Dr Wycherley indicated that Dr Murphy had died from exhaustion produced by mortification in the legs.

Dr 'Glory' Murphy left the bulk of his estate, amounting to £16,000, to the Sisters of Charity, on condition that it be spent on the construction of a cancer hospital. St Patrick's home for the Incurable was built from the proceeds of the will of Dr Patrick 'Glory' Murphy, who died on 28 November 1867.

1867

DENNY LANE

Denny Lane, the son of the proprietor of Riverstown Distillery, was born in 1818. He was educated in a famous Cork school, Hamblin and Porter's in Queen Street (now Fr Mathew Street), and subsequently at Trinity College, where he took a BA degree. Having obtained a BL degree in London, he returned to Dublin to practise law. He was a friend of Thomas Davis and a member of the Young Irelanders. Although advising caution in their plans for insurrection, he was interned in Cork Gaol for four months because of his involvement with Young Ireland.

Having succeeded his father in the family business, he was instrumental in persuading the other Cork distillers to amalgamate and establish the Cork Distilleries Company. Very active in the business life of the city, he became the first Secretary and resident engineer of the Cork Gas Company, a director of Belvelly Brickworks and Springfields Starch Works, Chairman of Macroom Railway Co., and a director of the Cork, Blackrock and Passage Railway Company.

Lane was intensely interested in the arts, a founder member and Vice-President of the Cork Historical and Archaeological Society and Chairman of the School of Science. He wrote many songs, the best remembered being the ballads, 'Rose of Araglen' and 'Carrigdhoun'.

Denny Lane died on 29 November 1895.

1895

ST FINNBARR'S CATHEDRAL

In the middle of the nineteenth century, Bishop John Gregg suggested the replacement of the old cathedral built in 1735. Accordingly, an architectural competition was organised and 68 entries were exhibited in the Athenaeum (old Opera House). The winning design, in French early pointed Gothic, was by William Burgess, a strange, even eccentric individual, who lived for a time in Blackrock Castle.

The foundation stone was laid on 12 January 1865. Robert Walker was appointed builder, but was replaced by Gilbert Cockburne and Sons, Dublin, who completed the work. The exterior is constructed of local limestone while the interior arches and columns are of Cork red marble and Bath stone. The great piers are of Stourton stone.

The main structure was completed in 1870. In 1876, Mr Delaney was awarded the contract to erect the great spires, which were completed on 6 April 1878. Two prominent citizens, the distiller, Mr Francis Wise, and the brewer Mr W.H. Crawford, donated almost £40,000 between them towards the cost of the building, much of which was spent on the stone carving on the west front.

The Cathedral of St Finnbarr's was consecrated by Bishop John Gregg on 30 November 1870.

1870

MARINA RECLAIMED

In 1763, as part of a plan to make the River Lee more navigable, work began on the construction of the Navigation or New Wall, now known as the Marina. The completion of the wall led to a large tract of land, stretching from the Marina north to Victoria Road, being left in a semi-flooded condition. Mr Edward Russell CE was commissioned to present plans for the reclamation of this land, some 230 acres of what he described as 'the most valuable land in the vicinity of the city'. He envisaged the reclaimed land being used as either a public park or as agricultural land.

Russell's plan proposed the extension and widening of the Navigation Wall, to exclude tidal waters entering the land. He proposed the construction of a reservoir (the present Atlantic Pond), and the erection of sluice gates to facilitate the drainage and exclusion of water. Russell pointed out that the natural fall of land, south from Victoria Road, would facilitate the work.

Mr Edward Russell's plans were presented to the public in the pages of the *Cork Examiner* of 1 December 1843.

1843

2 December

MARIE'S OF THE ISLE

The Convent of the Mercy Order of St Marie's of the Isle is built on the site of the original Dominican settlement in Cork. The stone from the ruins of the Dominican Abbey was, it is said, removed and used in the construction of the present Dominican Church on Pope's Quay.

Mr William Atkins was commissioned by the Mercy Order to design a convent, the existing buildings in Rutland Street being inadequate for the Order's needs. The original plans provided for the erection of a lofty steeple on the southern end of the building and a tower at the northern end, but both projects had to be abandoned because of the marshy condition of the soil. The convent, of Gothic design, was built in local stone, red sandstone with limestone coignes, mullions and dressings. Mr Atkins' plans also provided for the construction of a House of Mercy, a National School and an orphanage, but commencement was deferred until funds became available.

Work commenced on the convent chapel but was abandoned for a time due to lack of finance. Through the generosity of many benefactors, especially the Murphy family of Clifton, the building was completed in 1870.

Bishop William Delaney laid the foundation stone of the Convent of St Marie's of the Isle on 2 December 1850.

1850

3 December

His Royal Highness, the Prince William, paid an extended visit to Cork in 1787. The *Pegasus* delivered him safely to Cobh and the following day he journeyed to the city by barge, disembarking at the Grand Parade.

He dined with a select group in the Bush Tavern on the Parade, and stood at the window, allowing himself to be seen by the populace, for whom he provided plenty of porter. He drank the health of Ireland and prosperity to Cork trade. In the evening he attended a soirée and danced with several of the ladies. The Corporation presented him with the freedom of the city and a gold casket.

In the days that followed he received the Protestant clergy, and was presented with addresses from the merchants and the Quakers. Later the Dissenters were presented. He visited Castlemartyr, Drumanagh, Curraghmore and Waterford, and on his return to the city was entertained by the High Sheriff, the Earl of Shannon, Lord Kinsale, Sir James Fitz-Gerald, Sir Nicholas Colthurst, Bart., Sir James Cotter, Bart., and a great number of the respectable gentlemen. He reviewed the garrison regiments before departing for Plymouth.

Prince William Henry landed in Cork on 3 December 1787.

1787

STEPHEN MOYLAN

Stephen Moylan was born into a comparatively wealthy Cork family who lived on Kyrl's Quay. The family had interests in shipping and Stephen was sent to Lisbon to be educated, the Penal Laws making it impossible for him to be educated at home.

He represented the family interests in Lisbon, and went to Philadelphia in 1768 to continue his business career. He prospered and, in partnership with several other Cork emigrées, owned several ships. He fitted easily into American society and through his friendship with John Dickinson, he met and became friendly with George Washington.

Moylan was an advocate of absolute separation from England. 'Shall we never leave off debating and boldly declare for independence?' he asked. At the outbreak of the American War of Independence he joined Washington's army and was promoted a colonel and made Commissary General of Musters.

He appreciated the importance of America becoming a naval power in order to challenge Britain's supremacy on the seas. He converted a captured British merchantman and presented it, now named the *Lexington*, the first American warship to fly the country's flag, to John Barry of Wexford, regarded as the founder of the American navy.

The *Lexington* was handed over on 4 December 1775.

1775

5 December

JOHN DILLON CROKER

John Dillon Croker perceived, at an early date, the horrors that were to befall the country as a result of the failure of the potato in 1845. In a series of letters to the newspapers, and in lectures, he spelled out the consequences to the people and the country. At a lecture, the *Cork Examiner* informed its readers, he appalled 'his hearers by the vividness of his descriptions of the ruin of the crop and the certainty of famine'. He called the impending famine 'a curse of the country'.

He advised the authorities that 'the disease in the potatoes is most rapidly increasing. I maintain it is most fearfully extending itself and unless the most expeditious means are taken to check it famine and death are staring us in the face'. He spoke these words in November, and yet in early December John Dillon Croker performed an extraordinary *volte face* when, in a letter to the *Evening Packet*, he stated that the panic then developing was ill-founded, that there were, after all, sufficient potatoes in the country to feed the needy, and that the tubers rotting in the fields would, in some unexplained fashion, revive themselves.

The editor of the *Cork Examiner* questioned this latest outburst and in a savage editorial, he excoriated John Dillon Croker for the fatuous comments and the unexplained change of attitude.

That attack on Croker was made in the *Cork Examiner* on 5 December 1845.

1845

6 December

POVERTY IN CORK

'We deeply regret', the *Cork Examiner* told its readers in 1841, 'that it becomes our imperative duty to announce the fact that fever has alarmingly increased among the poorer clases of our people, and that there does not exist anything like an adequate remedial provision for their relief.'

The reports coming in from all parts of the city were frightening. Thousands and thousands in the northern and southern districts were actually starving to death. They had no means of purchasing food. Accounts from the Catholic clergy show a people destitute of food, drink and clothing, and with the prospect of having but one meagre meal every two or three days.

'Their only clothes is a single garment retained more from a sense of decency than anything else. Their beds are no more than piles of wet straw, not fitting for the kennel of a dog. The middle classes, the tradesmen and small room keeper, a class normally comparatively free from the ravages of hunger and poverty are also affected.'

'The cause of this desolation,' the *Examiner* asserted, 'cannot be traced to the idle, depraved, or drunken habits of the poorer classes. They are willing to work; they are virtuous and sober but they are destitute of all means of earning even a crust of bread by the hard labour of their hands. And rather than make their sorrows known to the world they hide them in some wretched garret, or some gloomy cellar, where sitting down with their only companions, Starvation and Death, they die without a murmur on their lips.'

The cause, the *Examiner* concluded, is 'Want of Employment'.

This account of poverty in Cork appeared in the *Cork Examiner* of 6 December 1841.

1841

LABOUR DELEGATION

In 1920, a delegation from the British Labour Party arrived in Cork to make an independent assessment of the situation in the country. The delegation was accompanied by Tom Johnson, Secretary of the Irish Labour Party and Trades Union Congress. They were met on arrival at the railway station by Mr G. Nason, the Chairman, and other members of the Cork and District Trades and Labour Council. They were provided with office accommodation in the City Hall, and proceeded to gather information on the conduct of the British Forces.

The presence of the delegation did not intimidate the military who continued to harass the public, conducting spot searches and firing their guns at random targets. The members of the delegation were escorted around the city to view for themselves the damage caused by the military. They inspected shops and houses burnt to the ground by the soldiery. Some of the members went to Bandon to view the considerable damage perpetrated there by the British forces within the immediate past.

The members of the Commission included Mr G. Cameron, Chairman of the National Executive of the British Labour Party; Messrs Lunn and Lawson, MPs.; and Brigadier C.B. Thompson, Military Adviser.

They were in Cork on 7 December 1920.

8 December

SICK POOR SOCIETY

During the famine year, 'Black '48', a number of Catholic businessmen came together to try and help alleviate the terrible distress being suffered by the poor. They agreed to undertake the work of burying the destitute dead, and visiting the sick and the dying. An organisation called the Sick Poor Society of St Finbarr's was formed. Bishop Delaney approved of the Society and arranged that it be formally dedicated to the Immaculate Conception. The first president was Mr Patrick J. Scannell.

In 1865, Fr Timothy O'Mahony went to Rome and obtained from Pope Pius IX many spiritual endowments for the new society. The work continues today, the members providing financial and moral support to the needy.

The Sick Poor Society of St Finbarr's was formally dedicated on 8 December 1853.

1853

IMPEACHMENT OF CORK MP

When Mr Daniel Callaghan was summoned to appear before a committee of the House of Commons to answer a charge that he was illegally elected, it was a case of history repeating itself. The previous year, 1829, his brother, Gerard, had been similarly charged. On that occasion Gerard Callaghan had been disqualified from holding his seat as Member of Parliament for Cork city, a decision that had brought about the election of Daniel Callaghan.

The charge put against Daniel Callaghan by the government, in the name of Herbert Baldwin, was that he was, at the time of the election, a contractor to the British Government and, accordingly, ineligible for election. During the course of the investigation, it was alleged that Daniel Callaghan had arranged with a Thomas Kelly to act as contractor, but that the terms of the contract, the supply of 13,000 tierces of beef, would in effect be fulfilled by Callaghan. It was further stated that the allegations had been brought to the attention of the electorate during the conduct of the election campaign.

Daniel Callaghan denied the imputations, and when evidence was produced that he was not, in fact, the contractor, the counsel for the petitioner asked to be released from the case, stating that Daniel Callaghan could not be found guilty on the evidence produced to the enquiry.

The petition to unseat Daniel Callaghan, MP for Cork city, was held on 9 December 1830.

1830

A LOCAL RAILWAY

The band of the 67th Regiment played 'God Save the Queen' as Lady Deane turned the first sod on the Cork/Blackrock/Passage Railway on 15 June 1847. Sir John MacNeill was the chief engineer and the contractor was Messrs Moore of Dublin.

The service was inaugurated on 8 June 1850, and the city terminus was on Albert Road, in premises occupied for many years by Metal Products. The line ran down the Marina, through Blackrock, and then over the Lee by way of the Douglas Viaduct to Passage. The railway line was extended to Crosshaven in 1904.

On 8 August 1922, Republican forces defending the city against the Free State Army advancing from Passage had blown up a section of the Douglas Viaduct. However, repairs were effected in 1923. The line is notable for the many fine stone bridges, particularly those spanning the cutting from Dundanion to Blackrock.

Competition from road transport and spiralling costs forced the closure of the Cork/Blackrock/Passage Railway on 10 December 1932.

1932

11 December

LOUGH CHURCH BLESSED

By the 1880s the suburbs of Cork were spreading rapidly in all directions, but especially in the south side of the city. It was imperative that a new church, to cater for the parishioners of the Glasheen, Magazine and College Road district, be provided. Dean Neville of the South Parish undertook the task of raising the necessary finance.

Mr G.C. Ashlin was commissioned to design the church, and construction work was undertaken by the Cork builder, Barry McMullen. The Church of the Immaculate Conception, the Lough, is Romanesque in style and constructed of red brick with limestone facings. The altar rail consists of 60 red marble columns and has a Sicilian marble top. Massive Kilkenny black marble monolith columns separate the side aisles from the nave. The church was originally 100 feet long and 50 feet wide. The bell was cast by Messrs Murphy of Dublin.

In 1890, the church was elevated to the position of a parish church and called St Finnbarr's West. The continued growth of the parish demanded an extension to the church and accordingly James McMullen was commissioned to undertake the work. He opted to continue with the basic format originally adopted by Ashlin, but he changed the axis of the church so that it now faced north-south instead of east-west. The builder was John Sisk.

The Church of the Immaculate Conception was consecrated for Divine Worship by Bishop Delaney on 11 December 1881.

1881

CORK BURNED

Cork city was in chaos in mid-December 1920. The Irish Republican Forces ambushed a lorry load of Auxiliaries near Dillon's Cross. Within hours, the British Forces went on a rampage, and the most serious disaster to befall the city for some hundreds of years occurred. Soldiers set out to burn down Cork city.

Reprisals began in the vicinity of the ambush and several houses were set on fire. Soon after, the soldiers attacked the centre of the city and Grant's Shop in Patrick's Street was ablaze within a short time. The Munster Arcade, Cash's and Roches Stores were also ablaze. The conflagration was so intense it was feared that the whole city would be set alight. Later in the night the City Hall and the Carnegie Free Library were put to the torch. Several people were killed, including young Joseph Delaney of Blackpool, and many were injured by gunshot.

Curfew was imposed, and a pamphlet was found scattered throughout the city advising people to stay off the streets. It purported to come from the 'Secretary of Death or Victory league, God save the King!'

The Lord Mayor requested help from other cities, and the fire brigade was dispatched from Dublin on a special train. Firemen also came from Limerick. The Cork Gas Company turned off the supply of gas. Trams were burned and the company suspended the running of the system. Looting was rife.

Cork was burned down during the early hours of 12 December 1920.

1920

BISHOP RESIGNS

John Butler, third son of Lord Dunboyne, was born in Fethard, County Tipperary in 1731. In 1750 he began to study for the priesthood, travelling in Spain and Italy, where he attended the Irish College in Rome. He was ordained to the priesthood in 1758.

John Butler was appointed parish priest of Dualla and Boherlann, and was shortly after named as Secretary to the Archbishop of Cashel, who was his cousin. The bishopric of Cork became vacant in 1762, and the influence of the Butler family ensured his appointment as Bishop of Cork.

In 1786, an event took place which was to change the whole course of his life. Lord Dunboyne died and John Butler succeeded to the title. He petitioned Rome to be relieved of his clerical functions and be allowed to marry. 'It is no pleasure for me,' he wrote to the Pope 'after a life of celibacy, to share my bed and board.'

The Pope did not accede to the request. Bishop John Butler resigned the bishopric of Cork, inherited the title of Lord Dunboyne and married a cousin, Mary Butler. The news of his decision was greeted with scorn and hatred, and a scribe, writing in Irish, advised him:

Nuair a bheas tú in Ifrionn go fóill,
Agus do deora ag silleadh leat.
Sin an áit a bhfuagh tú na scéala,
Cia is fearr sagairt no ministéar.

John Butler, later Lord Dunboyne, renounced his position as Bishop of Cork on 13 December 1786.

1786

VOLUNTEERS IN CORK

The notice on the back of the admission ticket read simply 'this movement is strictly non political'. The purpose of the meeting was to establish a local unit of the Irish Volunteers in Cork. The organising committee consisted of J.J. Walsh, Liam de Róiste, J.L. Fawsitt and Maurice O'Connor.

Cork was a city riven in two between the adherents of William Redmond and William O'Brien, and partiality shown towards one faction would inevitably have antagonised the other.

Eamonn O'Neill, an O'Brienite, and John J. Horgan, a Redmonite, were invited to take their places on the platform and propose motions, but they declined. The invitation was extended to Roger Casement who happened to be in Cork. Eoin MacNeill was also present.

The meeting was held in the City Hall and was attended by a capacity crowd. An injudicious remark by Eoin MacNeill was misconstrued by a large section of the crowd and almost led to a riot. When he called for three cheers for Sir Edward Carson and his Ulster Volunteers he was met with cheers from the Redmonites and boohs and cries of 'Shut up!' from the O'Brienites. Crowds invaded the platform and were it not for the presence of mind of one individual who started to sing 'A Nation once again', in which all joined, serious injury would have been done.

The Cork Branch of the Irish Volunteers was formed at a meeting in the City Hall on 14 December 1913.

WILLIAM THOMPSON

Thompson was born in Cork in 1775 into a wealthy Protestant family. His father was an Alderman, Speaker and Mayor of the city and left his son a substantial estate estimated at about £2,000 a year. The estate included a house in Patrick's Street and land near Glandore.

Thompson, known to his contemporaries as 'Philosopher', is now recognised as one of the most original of political thinkers. Anton Menger considered him 'the most eminent founder of scientific socialism from whom Marx had directly or indirectly drawn his opinions and that the whole theory of surplus value, its name and the estimates of its amount are borrowed in all essentials from Thompson's writing'.

Thompson was an advocate of Catholic Emancipation and a firm believer in the equality of the sexes. One of his books is titled *An Appeal of one half of the Human Race, Women, against the Pretensions of the other Half, Men, to retain them in Political, and Thence in Civil and Domestic Slavery*. He was a firm believer in the Co-operative movement and from his own resources established a Co-operative in Carhoogarrive, near Skibbereen.

William Thomson's great work, *An Enquiry into the Principles of the Distribution of Wealth most conducive to Human Happiness*, applied to the newly proposed system of Voluntary Equality of Wealth, was published on 15 December 1824.

1824

'HONEST DICK' MILLIKIN

Richard Alfred Millikin was born in Castlemartyr in 1767. He was educated in Midleton and became an attorney. He was, in turn, musician, actor, painter and man of letters, and is credited with being responsible for the organisation of art education in Cork.

With his sister he edited, *The Casket or Hesperian Magazine*. He was a member of the Apollo Society of Amateur Actors, a philanthropic organisation with headquarters in the Appollo Theatre in Patrick's Street – the premises since occupied by the *Cork Examiner* newspaper. 'Honest Dick', as he was known, was involved in acquiring the Canova Casts, now in the Crawford College of Art, and was also responsible for the foundation of the Cork Society for the Promotion of the Fine Arts. As a mark of their regard for Millikin, 22 of his pictures were shown at their exhibition in 1816.

His greatest literary success was undoubterdly, 'The Groves of Blarney', but he was also responsible for 'The Riverside; a poem in three cantos'; 'Macha', 'Darby in Arms', a dramatic piece, The Geraldine', 'Dungourney in Egypt', etc.

Richard Alfred Millikin died on 16 December 1815.

1815

THE FENIANS PARDONED

'There happily appears', Mr Gladstone wrote to Sir William Carroll, 'to be a concurrence of circumstances favourable to such exercise of the Royal prerogative to mercy. Ireland is at present remarkably prosperous and generally free from turbulence or disorder. Its quiet condition allows a most marked improvement to that which prevailed a year ago.'

His statement continues:

> The measures taken by Parliament in reference to Ireland since that time have swelled the number and strengthened the hands of that great body of all parties and creeds representing the prosperity, intelligence and religion of Ireland which there is on the side of order and loyalty, while they have weakened the powers of disaffection and revolution. The earnest desire of her Majesty's ministers is to further the advance of this healing process, and it is because they believe the release of the prisoners will assist in this, that they have come to their present decision.

Mr Gladstone announced the exercise of the Royal clemency in respect of the Fenian prisoners on 17 December 1870.

1870

GAMES IN CORK

'This morning a tormented beast was beaten through the Main Street, Castle Street, quays, etc., for a considerable time, to the terror of the inhabitants; a man was thrown by the bull against a car, and narrowly escaped being killed. If some stop is not speedily put to this barbarous practice, the country people will be deterred from bringing their bulls to market, as they are generally forced from them, contrary to justice by those wicked miscreants.'

We are indebted to Tuckey's *Remembrancer* for providing us with a rare account of the pastimes of the ordinary people of the city. Cork being a city of narrow laneways, bull running was, of course, a very dangerous pursuit, especially for the residents of the city. Shopkeepers were compelled, on many occasions, to close their shops and suspend business.

'Throwing at Cocks', or cock fighting, was another popular, if no less barbarous sport. It was, however, more acceptable to the upper classes of the community, and it is remembered in the name of one of our streets, Cock Pit Lane. Hurling was another sport played in the confined areas of the city streets and, in 1631, the Corporation passed a by-law outlawing this 'very barbarous and uncivil kind of sport'.

Francis Tuckey recorded the sport of bull running in the streets of Cork on 18 December 1770.

1770

JACK THE RIPPER

The mystery of the so-called 'Jack the Ripper' murders in London in the 1880s gripped the imagination of a generation of Victorians.

In Cork, Thomas Farrelly Osborne was arraigned before the Magistrates, Messrs J.C. Gardiner, RM and Sir George Penrose, on the charge of having assaulted Mr Thomas Barry of 7, East View Terrace, Quaker Road.

Mr Osborne, having initially implied that he was not the defendant, then elected to defend himself. Mr Barry in evidence said that he had been attracted to a disturbance outside his own house. On going to the door to investigate, he was brutally assaulted by the defendant who struck him on the head with a large stick. The defendant was shouting that 'there is as good a man in Cork as Jack the Ripper'.

Thomas Farrelly Osborne proceeded to cross examine in a most eccentric manner. He posed a series of questions to Mr Barry insinuating that he was indeed the attacker, but in the next breath stating that the questions were hypothetical. When a witness claimed to be able to identify Osborne by his voice, the defendant declaimed aloud, 'the voice was the voice of Jacob but the hands were the hands of Esau'. The Magistrates convicted Osborne of assault and fined him ten shillings.

The trial of Cork's self-styled 'Jack the Ripper' took place on 19 December 1888.

1888

SAVINGS BANK

An Act of Parliament (57, George III), was signed into law on 11 July 1817, regulating the operations of Saving Banks. Savings Banks had been functioning before then, but the new legislation provided for the money saved to be deposited with the government, thus ensuring security. Previously, it had been customary to lodge the savings to the credit of a wealthy landowner who paid interest thereon.

Shortly after the passing of the Act, a meeting was called in the Commercial Buildings, now the Imperial Hotel, to discuss the establishment of a Savings Bank. The meeting was chaired by the Church of Ireland Bishop of Cork and Ross, and the Catholic Bishop, Dr Murphy, proposed the formation of the Bank. Several people were sceptical of placing the funds on deposit with the government, fearing that a system of income tax might be introduced and levied on the deposits.

The Cork Savings Bank initially opened in a room of the Cork Institution, business being conducted initially on Saturdays only. All labour was voluntary and done on rotation; if a volunteer did not attend he was fined five shillings!

The Cork Savings Bank opened for business on 20 December 1817.

1817

FIRST IRISH NEWSPAPER

Peter de Pienne, a printer and a Royalist, was forced to abandon Cork when Oliver Cromwell's forces captured the city in 1649. De Pienne had intended to publish a newspaper, tentatively titled, *Mercuricus Hibernicus*, but this plan was abandoned when he fled before Cromwell's forces.

Cromwell landed in Dublin on 14 August 1649, and terrorised the country before coming to Cork in mid-December to establish winter quarters. He was in the city on 19 December, and determined to publish a newspaper to record the events of his peregrinations around the country.

Cromwell produced a newspaper, the *Irish Monthly Mercury*. It was probably printed by William Smith and its name reflected the fashion in England of calling the early newspapers 'Me rcuries', in memory of the fabled winged messenger.

The *Irish Monthly Mercury* heaped praise on Cromwell and bemoaned the fact that he was returning to England before clearing the land of Teigs and Cavaliers. A copy of this paper is in the Library of the British Museum.

The *Irish Monthly Mercury*, the first newspaper to be published in Ireland, was printed in Cork on 21 December 1649.

1649

TRAMS IN CORK

Horse-drawn trams were introduced to Cork on 12 September 1872. However, a limited route structure and opposition from the Corporation caused the early demise of the venture, and the trams disappeared from the streets in 1876. The tracks were removed over the following couple of years.

In 1896, the Cork Electric Lighting and Tramways Company Limited, in agreement with the Corporation, undertook to provide a tramway system for Cork city and suburbs. There were three routes: Blackpool/Douglas; Summerhill/Sunday'sWell and Tivoli/Blackrock.

The principal contractors were British Thompson-Houston, and they appointed subcontractors, one of whom, William Martin Murphy of Berehaven – later to become proprietor of the *Sunday Independent* and architect of the 1913 lock-out in Dublin – built the permanent way (street track and brick paving). He was later to become Chairman of the company. Sir Edward Fitzgerald, later Lord Mayor of Cork, was the contractor for the power house, situated on Monarea Marshes (now known as Albert Road). The depot was also on Albert Road in premises occupied, in later years, by the Metal Products Group.

Cork was the eleventh city in Britain and Ireland to have trams. Thirty-five tram cars, commissioned from Brush Electrical and Engineering, Loughborough, England, operated on a two-foot, eleven and a half-inch wide track. This unusual gauge was adopted to permit an interchange between the trams and the light railways then operating from the city.

The trams began operating in Cork on 22 December 1896.

1896

SIDNEY IN CORK

Sir Henry Sidney, born in Penhurst, England, in 1554, whose godfather was King Philip II of Spain, was educated in Shrewsbury and Oxford. He was a celebrated poet, author of 'Arcadia' and 'Apologie for Poetrie'. He was Lord Deputy of Ireland.

In his triumphal tour through Munster he gathered around him the Gaelic aristocracy. McCarthy Mór, Earl of Clancarthy, had his countess, infant children and fourteen lords of counties of his own family in attendance. The Lords of Muskerry and Carbery (McCarthy Reagh) were present. McCarthy Reagh had, in his entourage, his two sons, as well as the O'Mahony of Ivagh, O'Driscoll Mór, the O'Donovans, O'Dalys and O'Crowleys.

'Many of the ruined relics of the ancient English inhabitants of this province, Arundels, Rochforts, Barretts, Flemings, Lombards, Tirries ... now all in misery,' came to Shandon Castle to pay their respects to Sir Henry Sidney.

Meanwhile, his troops were billeted amongst the ordinary citizens of Cork for six weeks. Half the soldiers' wages was paid to the townsmen to provide board, fire and lodging, an agreement with which the citizens were 'well satisfied, and the soldiers in like manner well contented to give it'.

Sir Henry Sidney approved of 'the good estate and flourishing of that city' when he entered Cork on 23 December 1575.

1575

24 December

COAL QUAY SONG

Chant of the Quay called Coal
(vernacularly versed) by 'Phineas O'Gander'

Were I sublimer than the Grecian
    rhymer,
Than Prisistratus or bold Bonaparte,
Could I when lyrical, like Moore, that
miracle,
Endue my dialect with tuneful arte –
I'd pen a ditty of this beauteous city,
So wise and witty 'twould beget
    renown,
And with thrush or curlew, I'd extol
    that purlieu,
The Coal Quay Market of my native
    town.

It's there good liquor can be had on
    tick, or
If you'd like it quicker for the ready
    shot,
With high gentility to breed civility,
In every company of this famed spot;
No disputation upon sect or nation,
In this location will be ever found,
Where you'll see proud Normans and
both Jews and Mormons,
With the Flynns and Gormons
    drinking on one round.
Did I Versailles see, or the Shams de
    Lazy,
Or Tsarkoe Selo, I would tell them
    true,

Their Boulevarding and their Mobile Garden
Is all blackguarding, the mere foreign crew;
Let god and goddess, without vest or bodice,
Display proportions in each leafy seat,
But, for sublimity of dainty dimity,
There's no extremity like Market Street.

You'll see the cook shops, with their store
    surprising,
Most appetising both to sight and scent,
Each swain emerging with his favourite vir-
gin,
Those bowers resorting for nutriment;
Oh that's the sporting with those couples
    courting,
Their crubeens picking between every kiss,
With the hostess smiling at their ways
    beguiling,
While adding cabbage to their feast of bliss.

I've seen Killarney, I have been to Blarney,
The Tower of Babel, and Sweet Convamore,
But for all wonders of convivial grandeurs,
There is no galaxy like this bright shore;
When at that ferry whence black Charon's
    wherry,
Shall bear me, merry, o'er the river Styx,
Could I when parting choose the point of
    starting,
My lovely Coal Quay is the place I'd fix!

The 'Chant of the Quay called Coal', of which the above are selected verses, appeared on the *Cork Examiner* of 24 December 1870.

1870

THE 'WILD GEESE' LEAVE

The Treaty of Limerick was signed on 3 October 1691, Patrick Sarsfield signing for the Irish, and General Ginkle for the Williamite forces.

'On October 6 1691, our whole forces, perhaps 16,000 strong, marched out of Limerick under arms, and with their standards flying. Hundreds of the soldiers were in rags and unshod, but all bore themselves well and had a dauntless spirit.' Gerald O'Connor, later a general in the French Army, has left a contemporary account of one of the saddest moments in Ireland's history. About 11,000 soldiers opted to take service in France.

The Irish force marched to Cork, the point of embarkation for the continent. They had been promised that their families could accompany them, but there were not sufficient transports, and the wives, parents and children were left on the quaysides. 'Loud cries and lamentations broke from the wives and children who had been left behind,' O'Connor continued. 'Some dashed into the stream and perished in their depths; some clung to the boats that were making off from the shore; many of the men, husbands and fathers, plunged into the waters; not a few lost their lives in their efforts to reach dry land.'

Patrick Sarsfield sailed on 19 December 1691. Six days later, on a Christmas Day of bitter memory, a contingent of 'Wild Geese' sailed from Cork for France.

1691

EMMANUEL MORTIMER

In 1380, Emmanuel Mortimer, Earl of March, Lord Lieutenant of Ireland, arrived in Cork accompanied by John Cotton, Dean of St Patrick's Dublin, and Chancellor of Ireland.

The Prelates, Peers and Commoners of Ireland; the bishops of Cork and Ossory, Cloyne, Lismore and Waterford; James de Bottiler, Earl of Ormond; Ger Fitzmaurice, Earl of Desmond; the Mayor of Cork; John Pomfeide and Thomas Lawely, Citizens returned for the City; Daniel Fitzthomas Roche and Milo Staunton, Knights returned for the County of Cork; Roger and Adam Lenfant, Knights for the County of Limerick and many other nobles and commoners were summoned to attend in St Peter's Church, North Main Street, on the Thursday after the Feast of the Epiphany to constitute a Parliament.

The function of this sitting of the Irish Parliament was to elect a successor to Emmanuel Mortimer, Lord Lieutenant, who had died in the House of the Friars Preachers (Dominicans) in St Marie's of the Isle on 26 December 1380.

1380

CIRCUS IN CORK

One of the regular groups of entertainers to visit Cork in the middle years of the nineteenth century was a troupe known as Batty's Circus or, as it dramatically styled itself, 'Batty's Equestrian Evening Dreams of Wonder'. It performed at the Circus Royal in Mary Street, and the admission fees ranged from three shillings for the dress boxes to six pence for the gallery. The management made it quite clear that smoking was not permitted during performances.

Batty's Circus exhibited the smallest living horse in the world, and featured the exploits of Mr Paddington, a Corkman who, festooned with fireworks, gave a brilliant display on the the flying rope. Another performer, introduced with great acclaim, and hailed as the 'Equestrian Heroine Wonder of the World', was a Mrs Hughes whose husband was the riding master and manager of the circus. In a publicity stunt, he undertook to drive fifteen horses through the city streets.

Mr Hughes proposed to donate the receipts of one performance to the Cork Dispensary Fund, a most laudable gesture. 'Batty's Equestrian Evening Dreams of Wonder' Circus performed in Cork on 27 December 1841.

1841

28 December

THE LAST SEANACHAÍ

One of the last of the *seanachaithe*, or storytellers, of Ireland died in Carrignavar in 1933. He was Dónal Ó Ceallaigh or Daniel Kelly or, as he was affectionately called locally, 'Doanies'.

Daniel Kelly was, for many years, the All-Ireland champion in story-telling and won several prizes at the Oireachtas competitions. 'His powers of memory were extraordinary,' Éamonn Ó Donnchú commented, and recalled 'spending a week of long nights by a blazing fire listening to him recite a single story in Irish of a Fianna Chief or a Red Branch Champion'.

There were many other notable Gaelic scholars from the district around Carrignavar, including Seán na Raithíneach, who was head of the Bardic School in Blarney, Father Eoghan Ó Caoimh, and Fr Conchubhair MacCartain.

Daniel Kelly's father-in-law was Daniel Dorgan. He died in 1916, when he was over 100 years of age, and was the author of one of the great-est laments in the Gaelic language. Dr Douglas Hyde considered 'Dónal Óg' to be one of the best and sweetest poems in the Modern Irish. It has been translated by many authors but the most well known is the translation by another Corkman, Frank O'Connor.

Dónal Ó Ceallaigh, Seanachaí, was buried in Dunbulloge cemetery on 28 December 1933.

1933

CORK ELECTION

Before the introduction of the universal franchise, the right to vote was based on ownership of property. This limited suffrage did not ensure either decorum or acceptable behaviour, and elections in the nineteenth century were remarkable for their being conducted with an intense, even deadly, rivalry.

In 1826, a vacancy arose in the Cork city constituency and was contested by Gerard Callaghan and John Hely-Hutchinson. There was, for all practical purposes, little in substance between the candidates, but Hely-Hutchinson attracted the support of the more liberal elements of the electorate for his espousal of Catholic Emancipation.

The voting began on 16 December. A daily tally recorded the state of the election, the results being sent by stage coach each evening to Dublin. On the afternoon of 24 December, supporters of the candidates, among them William Hayes, a cousin of Callaghan, and John Bric, a supporter of Hely-Hutchinson, awaited the arrival of the coach. An argument developed, and Bric challenged Hayes to a duel.

The participants met at a site near the Royal Canal in Glasnevin and, after an exchange of shots, Bric fell, mortally wounded. While warrants were issued for the arrest of Hayes and his seconds, they were apparently not executed. Bric was buried with elaborate ceremony in St Andrew's Churchyard.

The election concluded in Cork on 29 December 1826, John Hely-Hutchinson being successful.

1826

'FREEDOM OF THE CITY'

On Christmas Day 1796, Bishop Francis Moylan of Cork addressed a pastoral to the people of the diocese following on the news of the arrival of the French in Bantry Bay:

> At a moment of such general alarm and consternation, it is the duty I owe you, my beloved flock, to recall in your minds the sacred principles of loyalty, allegiance and good order, that must direct your conduct on such an awful occasion .... Loyalty to the sovereign and respect for the constituted authorities, have been always the prominent features in the Christian character; and by patriotism and obedience to the established form of government have our ancestors been distinguished at all times ... For blessed be God, we are no longer strangers in our native land ... To our gracious Sovereign we are bound by the concurring principles of gratitude and duty ...
>
> Under these circumstances, it is obvious what line of conduct you are to adopt if the invaders ... should make good their landing and attempt to penetrate into our country ... they will not fail to make specious professions that their only object is to emancipate you from the pretended tyranny under which you groan ...
>
> Be not deceived by the lure of equalizing property which they will hold out to you ... for the poor, instead of getting any part of the spoil of the rich, were robbed of their own little pittance.
>
> Obey the laws that protect you in your persons and properties. Reverence the magistrate entrusted with their execution, and display your readiness to give him every assistance in your power ...
>
> ... if the sway of our impious invaders were here established, you would not, my beloved people, enjoy the comfort of celebrating this AUSPICIOUS DAY with gladness and thanksgiving ...

On 30 December 1796 the Corporation of Cork conferred the Freedom of the City on Bishop Moylan because 'of his pious exertions on promoting the peace and good order at the moment of menaced invasion'.

1796

FR PROUT

Francis Sylvester Mahony was born into a wealthy family of woollen merchants in Blarney. He aspired to become a member of the Jesuit Order but settled for ordination as a secular priest. He was of an irascible nature, but a celebrated linguist, mastering and writing in many modern European languages as well as Latin and Greek.

In 1832, having worked throughout the cholera epidemic in Cork, he had a dispute with the Bishop and left for London. Although he affected a religious garb for the rest of his life, he apparently did not practise his priestly functions, engrossing himself instead in the literary life of London. He was associated with *Fraser's Magazine*, worked with Dickens on *Bentley's Magazine* and was Roman correspondent of the *Daily News*.

Fr Prout, the pen name adopted by Francis Mahony, took issue with such personalities as Tom Moore, charging that Moore had plagiarised many of his melodies from other countries. Fr Prout produced translations, written by himself, to discredit Moore. He savaged Dr Kenealy who had dared to attack Thomas Davis, asking 'is Repeal become such a common urinal that any blackguard can make a convenience thereof?'

Prout turned his satire against Daniel O'Connell, 'the bog trotter of Derrynane', incensed that, during the Famine, O'Connell had accepted a sum of £20,000, donated by the poor:

Hark, hark, to the begging box shaking,
For whom is this alms money making?
For Dan who is cramming his wallet while famine
Sets the heart of the peasant a-quaking.

Francis Sylvester Mahony, alias Fr Prout, author of 'The Bells of Shandon', was born on 31 December 1804.

1804

Other Titles of Cork Interest

Forgotten Cork

Photographs from the Day Collection

COLIN RYNNE AND BILLY WIGHAM

From the second half of the nineteenth century to the closing decades of the twentieth, three generations of the Day family created a unique and unsurpassed photographic record of Cork city and its environs. The Day collection is published here for the first time. History leaps from these pictures in rich detail, with historic events like the visit of Edward VII to Cork in 1903 and the last recorded photograph of the departure of the *Titanic* from Cobh in 1912.

HB   ISBN: 1-903464-56-0   €30.00

Cork Silver and Gold

Four Centuries of Craftsmanship

JOHN R. BOWEN AND CONOR O'BRIEN

Published to coincide with an exhibition in the Crawford Gallery Cork, this book is the first to chronicle the little-known work of Cork silversmiths and goldsmiths. Research into public and private collections now makes available the outstanding output of these craftsmen. The items described range from early ecclesiastical pieces dating from the late 1500s to a profusion of secular items, coffee pots, salvers, freedom boxes, maces and flatware.

HB   ISBN: 1-903464-95-1   €60.00
PB   ISBN: 1-903464-96-X   €35.00

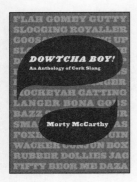

Dowtcha Boy!

An Anthology of Cork Slang

MORTY McCARTHY

Becoming familiar with Cork lingo isn't easy but *Dowtcha Boy!* will make the reader 'crabbit' (cute, wise to) with little effort. Morty collected over 400 words and phrases voiced by Corkonians. Memories will be jogged and the humorous illustrations by Fergus Keane will surely make it worth a sconce.

PB   ISBN: 1-903464-68-4   €7.99

A Dictionary of Cork Slang

SEÁN BEECHER

This is a collection of those words not usually found in dictionaries but which give colour, vigour and individuality to a language. Each word is explained, examples of usage are given, and their derivations are traced.

PB   ISBN: 0-951603-61-2   €12.95

A Doctor's War

AIDAN MACCARTHY

Introduction by Pete McCarthy

Researching *McCarthy's Bar* Pete McCarthy entered MacCarthy's Bar in Castletownbere, west Cork. While there Adrienne MacCarthy gave him a copy of her father's wartime memoir. Pete found it 'unputdownable'. An RAF medical officer, Aidan served in France, survived Dunkirk and was plunged into adventures in the Far East. Finally interned on the Japanese mainland, his life was saved by the dropping of the atomic bomb.

PB   ISBN: 1-903464-70-6 €12.95

Stone Mad

SEAMUS MURPHY

This account of time spent as an apprentice stone carver is an acclaimed Irish classic. The young Seamus Murphy took the unusual step of apprenticing himself to a master stone carver to learn the ancient craft of the mason. *Stone Mad* tells the story of his seven years of growing knowledge, of the challenges and joys of stone – and of the men who worked it. The result is a book of unsurpassing beauty, full of warmth, humour and profound perception.

PB   ISBN: 1-903464-81-1 €12.95

Cork: A Pocket Guide

PAUL CUSSEN

To conicide with the designation of Cork as
European City of Culture 2005 this comprehensive
guide is a must for tourists, visitors and residents
alike. Packed with information to suit all ages, budg-
ets and tastes, from pubs and clubs to tourist trails,
day trips and shopping to children's activities, this is
an up-to-date guide on where to stay, where to eat
and drink and what to see and do in Cork city.

PB   ISBN: 1-903464-53-6 €8.99

A Taste of West Cork

FOREWORD BY REGINA SEXTON

This book presents recipes that will both delight the
senses and guide the user to the natural qualities and
flavours innate to west Cork. A modern twist and
style is brought to all dishes. Traditional recipes like
brown soda bread and stuffed pigs' trotters sit com-
fortably with the more adventurous, allowing both
the novice and the cordon bleu-inspired reader to be
stimulated.

PB   ISBN: 1-903464-67-6 €12.95

The Life of Other Days

A Memoir of Cork

TIM CRAMER

Tim Cramer describes himself as 'an unrepentant Corkman' with an abiding love of the city, its hinterland and its people. This is a delightful memoir of an Ireland that is no more. It describes a gentle place where serenity and the hardship of the daily grind rubbed shoulders. A story of a city in transition and of what it has lost.

PB   ISBN: 1-903464-65-X €15.00

Seán Ó Riada

His Life and Work

TOMÁS Ó CANAINN

Seán Ó Riada is one of the most fascinating and significant characters in twentieth-century Irish artistic life. In this wide-ranging account of his life and work his friend and colleague reveals the complex personality of a unique individual. From schooldays in Clare to student days in Cork city and then working in Dublin and Cork, the author paints a vivid picture of an ambivalent talent.

PB   ISBN: 1-903464-40-4 €17.95